FINLAND

HELSINGFORS
SVEABORG
(Fortress)

HANGO

O

KOTKI

BIORKO
KRONSTADT
PETROGRAD
KRASNYA GORKA
(fortress)

Ininim fortress
(Finnish)

GATCHINA
Furthest point of advance
of White Russian Army
under YUDENITCH

NOVGOROD

REVEL
(Tallin)

NARVA

ESTONIA

DAGO

SEL

PERNAU

DORPAT
(Tartu)

VALK

PSKOV

U. S. S. R.

GULF OF
RIGA

LATVIA

RIGA

JELGAVA
MITAU

R. Dvina
(Dungava)

DVINSK

VITEBSK

SHAVLI

LITHUANIA

KOVNO

MINSK

POLAND

0 20 40 60 80 100
Miles

BALTIC EPISODE

BALTIC EPISODE

A Classic of Secret Service in Russian Waters

by Captain Augustus Agar V.C., D.S.O.

NAVAL INSTITUTE PRESS

I dedicate this book
to the memory of
Admiral Sir Walter Cowan, Bart.,
and those officers and men
of the Royal Navy and Air Force
who served with him
in the Baltic Operations 1919–20

THE EGG-SHELL

The wind took off with the sunset—
The fog came up with the tide,
When the Witch of the North took an Egg-shell
  with a little Blue Devil inside.
'Sink,' she said, 'or swim,' she said,
'It's all you will get from me,
And that is the finish of him!' she said,
And the Egg-shell went to sea.

The wind fell dead with the midnight—
The fog shut down like a sheet,
When the Witch of the North heard the Egg-shell
Feeling by hand for a fleet.
'Get!' she said, 'or you're gone,' she said,
But the little Blue Devil said 'No!'
'The sights are just coming on,' he said,
And he let the warhead go.

The wind got up with the morning—
And the fog blew off with the rain,
When the Witch of the North saw the Egg-shell
And the little Blue Devil again.
'Did you swim?' she said. 'Did you sink?' she said,
And the little Blue Devil replied:
'For myself I swam, but I think,' he said,
'There's somebody sinking outside!'

Rudyard Kipling

FOREWORD

A large part of this book was written between 1928 and 1935 when I was preparing lectures for the War and Staff Colleges of Greenwich, the Staff College of Camberley, the Tactical School at Portsmouth, and the Royal United Service Institution. Most of the material was collected from my own sources, but to ensure as much as possible the accuracy of operational details, the Admiralty very kindly gave me permission to make use of papers and documents relating to the Baltic in 1919 and 1920. In addition, I was allowed by the late Admiral Sir Walter Cowan, Bart., G.C.B., D.S.O. and Bar, etc. full access to all his correspondence and private papers. But to make sure of a true record, my close friend and colleague Sir Paul Dukes gave me his full collaboration when writing his book *The Story of S.T.25* published by Messrs. Cassell in 1938.

Between us we relived those hazardous journeys and were able to piece together the exact routes we took by land and sea, illustrated by the map on page 165 wherein is shown our boat tracks from Terrioki through the chain of forts to Petrograd with our two agents Peter and Gefter. For the latter's account of his journeys in our boats, I have followed his own version as published in a German pamphlet shortly afterwards, but of which trace has since been lost.

After putting all my material together in 1935 with helpful advice from Mr. E. Wynne Thomas and enthusiasm from the late Mr. Percy Hodder-Williams of Hodder and Stoughton, the Admiralty with regret refused permission for me to publish the result in a book, on the grounds that I was still a serving officer in the Navy. To quote Their Lordships' own words " . . . until such time as Captain Agar passes to the Retired List when the book may be re-submitted for permission to publish . . . " The manuscript was therefore pigeon-holed to the great disappointment of both publisher and author.

The subject matter, however, emerged in an abridged form in my book, *Footprints in the Sea*, published by Messrs. Evans in 1959 when their Lordships very kindly gave the original manuscript a full clearance. The complete story is now rewritten entirely in this book with added material taken from my journal after I returned to the Baltic to join the Staff of Admiral Sir Walter Cowan.

I wish to place on record my thanks to their Lordships and also to Messrs. Evans Brothers for allowing me to quote certain passages from *Footprints in the Sea*. I wish also to express a deep sense of obligation to Messrs. Hodder and Stoughton for their patience in waiting so long for my Baltic Story to see the light of day. In particular to Mr. Leonard Cutts and Mr. Haydn Stead for arranging and editing the new manuscript, and their valuable help with illustrations and diagrams. Also to Mr. Spark for his skill and patience when doing the cartography and Mr. D. Hall for his artistic book cover.

As for place names, I hope I will be forgiven for errors of spelling. In Russia and Finland, the changes were so frequent and rapid that it was difficult to follow them, and the same can be said for countries on the South Baltic littoral. As a compromise I have adopted the spelling of place names to that used at the time (1919-20), and so far as we could ascertain to those most commonly used by the inhabitants.

For reasons which the reader will obviously understand, I considered it unwise to disclose in this book the names of my couriers and other agents both English and Russian. The identities of ST's 30, 31, and others besides Peter and Gefter must therefore remain unknown and in due course no doubt will become legendary, but I can truthfully declare that their unselfishness, loyalty and courage left a memory our small party in Terrioki could never forget.

With ST25 as our lodestar, there was never at any

time any thought or sign of anyone turning back from our Mission once we had set out from Helsingfors for Terrioki, despite differences in age, nationality and professions of the various members of our party; until, with his safe arrival in England our task was accomplished, and the name of Paul Dukes disclosed to the public who acclaimed him as a brave civilian hero.

I would also like to bring the readers' attention to the generosity of the late Sir John Thornycroft, K.B.E., and the present Commander John Thornycroft, C.B.E., in giving C.M.B. No. 4 a safe resting berth on the banks of the Thames at Hampton where she was built.' One day perhaps the boat may be honoured with a place in the National Maritime Museum, Greenwich.

Finally we come to 'C', the Masterman and master mind. In due course posterity will know more about him, his life and his work. He has passed long since to his own Valhalla reserved for those who have given unselfishly the highest form of service for their country without thought of acknowledgement or reward.

March, 1963   Augustus Agar,
                                 Hartley Mauditt,
                                 Alton, Hants.

CONTENTS

LIST OF ILLUSTRATIONS

MAPS AND DIAGRAMS

INTRODUCTION

OSEA ISLAND lies on the Blackwater River in Essex, five miles south and east of the town of Maldon. The island is bounded on one side by a wide tidal river and on the other by a stretch of mudflats over half a mile in width, which is completely covered by the sea except at one and a half hours before and after low water. Across these forbidding-looking flats the late Mr. John Charrington, more recently of Tower Hamlets fame, who owned the island at the beginning of this century, built a rough causeway known locally as The Hard across which communication was held with the island by farm carts only at certain stages of the tide, and woe betide anyone who ventured to cross over after the flood stream had commenced to flow. Failing this, the only other means of approach to the island was a long journey by boat from either Heybridge or Maldon the nearest town.

It was because of this isolated position that the Admiralty during the First World War decided to exercise its powers under DORA (Defence Of the Realm Act) and take over the island lock, stock and barrel for the purpose of converting it into a base for motor boats. These were of a special type known as Coastal Motor Boats, or C.M.B.s, which our sailors called 'Skimmers' because they skimmed across the water.

At this remote little island, tucked away amongst the Essex flats and marshes and less than seventy miles from London, war preparations and training could be carried out with only the seagulls, wild fowl and crews of the oyster boats as witnesses. Secrecy was thus ensured.

The island contained a Manor House which had been used as a rescue home before the war, but was now empty, and a small farm of perhaps a couple of hundred acres which sent its produce across The Hard to Chelmsford market once a week. Beyond this there was no contact with the outside world.

It was on this bleak, deserted, out of the way spot that in the summer of 1917 a small army of workmen, bricklayers, engineers and officials from the Admiralty Works Department descended, much to the astonishment of farmer Bunting and his few farm labourers who were then the only inhabitants on the island.

Within a few months a rapid transformation was made. Wooden huts, first to house the workmen and later the personnel, sprang up everywhere like mushrooms; a pier was run out into the river with concrete slipways constructed to accommodate as many as fifty motor boats; moorings were laid and workshops erected on shore for assembling the engines; more workshops were added for testing and assembling torpedoes, mines, depth charges, Lewis guns, etc., in fact everything required by a naval base. The island was to be run as a ship completely independent of the mainland.

Early in 1918 the first special motor boats began to arrive and their number was added to throughout the summer months as fast as the builders could produce them. They were no ordinary motor boats these, such as motor launches or ships tenders, but a war invention of three young naval officers serving in destroyers at Harwich. They had a hydroplane-type hull which skimmed the water when driven at high speed (over forty knots) by powerful petrol-driven engines developing up to 500 horse-power. They were built in various parts of the country by small boat-building firms specially selected for the high quality of their craftsmanship by Sir John Thornycroft, K.B.E., head of the famous firm of naval ship- and boat-builders which today still bears his name.

Quite a number were built on the Thames at the Thornycroft works at Hampton, others at Portsmouth, the Isle of Wight and Lowestoft. The best craftsmen only were engaged in the work as the hulls had to be light to get the high speed required, at the same time strong enough to stand the strain of vibration and pounding set up when running in a rough sea with a full load on board.

For armament, a clever arrangement was invented by which they could fire one or two torpedoes, depending on the size of the boat, while they carried in addition, Lewis guns, depth charges and, if required, mines instead of torpedoes.

Two different types of boat were built. A small boat forty feet long known as a 'forty footer', and a larger one, fifty-five feet long, known as a 'fifty-five footer'. Both types were used with great success in minor operations on the Belgian coast and by Admiral Sir Roger Keyes in his famous attack on Zeebrugge and Ostend, when he fitted them with an apparatus for laying smoke screens. Close by at Harwich, Admiral Sir Reginald Tyrwhitt's force of light cruisers and destroyers towed or carried the small type to the scenes of their operations where, like greyhounds, they were released to skim over the minefields and attack enemy patrol craft near Heligoland beyond the reach of our own ships.

Profiting by the experience gained in these operations, the Admiralty decided to widen the scope of future activity for these boats and planned to attack the larger ships of the German fleet in their anchorages. So the Osea Island base came into being, but to the disappointment of the eager young officers who formed the boats' crews, the Armistice of November 1918 was signed before the scheme could be put into operation and fresh fields had to be found for their activities.

The personnel of this service, later to be known as the C.M.B. Service, was made up for the most part of young officers in the Royal Naval Reserve, with a sprinkling of officers from the Royal Navy. The whole being under the command of Captain Wilfred French, R.N. The service was voluntary and there was no lack of volunteers, especially amongst those who had been serving for years in big ships in the North Sea waiting for something to happen, or on dull routine jobs on shore. For these, C.M.B. life opened up a new outlet for their energies; it meant speed, action and, most important of all, a chance at last to use their initiative and prove their worth.

To young officers who had spent three years at Scapa Flow without having seen anything of the war the prospect of commanding one of these high speed motor boats was certainly thrilling. Handling them without lights at night and manoeuvring at high speed in formation was not only exciting, but an art worth learning at a time when our fastest destroyers could barely do thirty knots.

There were long waiting lists of volunteers from regular R.N. lieutenants and sub-lieutenants serving in the battle-ships of the Grand Fleet whose captains could spare them for the few vacancies available, and there was much dis-appointment in the gunrooms and wardrooms when applica-tions were turned down, simply because captains fought shy of losing their best young watch-keepers. An under-standable but selfish reason prevalent in the Navy of those days, and a survival of an old custom that whenever volunteer crews were required (for fireships perhaps, or armed parties on shore), they were chosen by the sailing master from those seamen he could best spare and were unlikely to be the best sailors.

For myself I could not complain of monotony during the war, as I was lucky enough to have seen service in the North Sea, White Sea, Dardanelles and Belgian coast before Captain French selected me for the C.M.B. Service as torpedo and mining officer largely because a specialist could not be spared from the fleet. My leg was well pulled by brother C.M.B. officers when working in the boats on their torpedoes and mines: I was referred to as that torpedo conscript!

We were a wonderfully happy community at Osea Island. All minds were concentrated on our jobs and the attack on the German fleet which was to be staged later in the year. Our work was entirely in the open air running torpedoes set to shallow depth in the river, fitting out the boats, practising high speed manoeuvres in groups of boats on the large stretch of water (ideal for the purpose) enclosed between Brightlingsea, Mersea and Osea Island, or an occasional war operation or exercise with the Harwich Force under Commodore (T). Working hours were unlimited, but in spite of this we found time to bathe and sail in the river and, thanks to the kindness of our neighbour Sir Claude de Crespigny, who had an estate near Maldon, we were given shooting in the neighbourhood and hunting with the Essex farmers' hounds.

Wilfred French,* our captain, was beloved by all in this community of sailors and civilians. He was the brain and mainspring of every activity whether it was planning in the Admiralty, persuading the civilian contractors to greater efforts, or firmly holding down C.M.B. crews to naval discipline and the efficiency which runs with it. To us, like Paul Jones, he was prophet, priest and king.

The female element too was not overlooked, for we had a small detachment of Wrens to look after our domestic arrangments instead of the usual stewards and cooks and were in consequence extremely comfortable. Two of them under the Surgeon Commander took over the Manor House garden which supplied us with fresh fruit, flowers and vegetables. A little farming was added to my technical duties, when I was given charge of the piggeries, and with the help of a dear old sailor pensioner who was dug out from his farm in Norfolk we raised several litters of pigs to supplement our own and the mechanics' rations. In short, like the castaways on Pitcairn Island we were a completely self-contained community of some five hundred souls.

When the Armistice was signed in November 1918 all thoughts of the BIG ATTACK had of course to be abandoned, but there were still other trouble spots where British Forces were engaged in active hostilities, and orders were

* Afterwards Admiral Sir Wilfred French, K.C.M.G.

received to keep the organization going on the island in case calls for our special boats were made. They were not long in forthcoming.

The first came from the Caspian Sea where C.M.B.s were required for operations against the Bolshevik gunboats at the mouth of the Volga and Enzeli. A flotilla of forty footers was sent to Baku in December 1918.

Next came a call from North Russia where a British Relief Force under General Ironside was fighting the Bolsheviks at Archangel. A flotilla was required for operations in the northern River Dvina. The larger fifty-five footers were despatched early the following year to cover the rearguard of the British Force during its evacuation of Archangel in August 1919.

Another call came from the British Army of occupation in Germany to assist in patrolling the Allied bridgeheads on the Rhine. This was followed shortly afterwards with an urgent call for two boats for special service in the Baltic, which is where my own personal story begins, but first I must take the reader back to the Russian Revolution of 1917 which I first witnessed at Murmansk in North Russia from the decks of H.M.S. *Iphigenia* when I watched the horrible spectacle of sailors of the Russian cruiser *Askold* in open revolt against their officers.

I should mention in passing that the *Askold* was no new acquaintance. She had been for a time our 'chummy ship' when I was serving in H.M.S. *Hibernia* at Gallipoli, and because she had no less than five thin narrow funnels was nicknamed by the sailors 'packet of Woodbines'. The Tsar sent her to the Dardanelles anticipating a British success, but like the rest of the Allied Fleet she was withdrawn when we evacuated the peninsula. We came across her later in Devonport dockyard and renewed our fraternizing, and when I found myself in the *Iphigenia* at anchor only a few cables' length from her in Murmansk I was looking forward to seeing my friends again in the old 'packet of fags' when mutiny broke out.

The transformation in that ship within a week was incredible. Our wireless operator had chatty pieces of conversation with theirs on a small buzzer circuit running rather like this: —

On the first day "The captain was taken on shore for trial by the Soviet Council and shot."

Next day, "Several officers placed under arrest and taken on shore" (presumably also to be tried and shot).

Next day, "The officers have now been turned out of their cabins and the wardroom. The sailors' committee is now in charge . . . " and so the story went on. The crew did no work at all but spent their time on the upper deck and forecastle while one after another mounted the capstan, which served the purpose of a rostrum, and harangued his 'comrades'. We never saw any of our Russian officer friends again.

The ship deserted by her crew after the last of the food, drink, stores, coal, cordage, etc., was expended was left swinging round her anchors completely derelict with only the sea birds in charge and rust accumulating on her funnels, deck and superstructure. Such was the Revolution.

In England our people were told this was a fine thing because a new Russia would arise and continue the war with increasing vigour. So we passed into North Russia more stores, guns, ammunition and equipment only for them to be left lying idle and rusty on the quays of Archangel and Murmansk until the autumn of 1918 when Britain was disillusioned. In the place of more stores we despatched instead a military expedition to Archangel under General Ironside to retrieve what was left. Meanwhile, the Admiralty decided my ship was expendable, so the dear old *Iphigenia* returned home to be gutted, filled with cement and sunk as a blockship off Zeebrugge harbour in Sir Roger Keyes' brilliant operation on St. George's Day, 23rd April, 1918.

Meanwhile I had joined Captain Wilfred French and his C.M.B.s just in time to be present for the operation when with Eric Wellman and Jumbo Annesley we laid smoke

screens outside Zeebrugge mole to cover the escape of the
crews of the blockships. How lucky I was to have had this
varied service in the Navy during the war while many of my
contemporaries were eating their hearts out in Scapa Flow.

During the summer of 1918 I gravitated between the
C.M.B. bases at Dunkirk, Dover, and the gun-wharf at
Portsmouth where I was given a short course at the mining
school before joining Captain French at Osea Island. The
Dover base was commanded by Eric Wellman a young
lieutenant and double D.S.O. chosen by Roger Keyes for
his initiative and fearlessness. He was not only an expert
in C.M.B.s and taught us how to handle them, but a
splendid personality. Normally the base should have been
commanded by a naval post captain but Eric, despite his
youth took it all in his stride and soon had all of us devoted
to him.

There was never a dull moment. If we were not out on the
Belgian coast at night sinking small craft and making
things generally unpleasant for the Germans, we were
slipping in and out of our sub-base at Dunkirk commanded
by Charles Harrison, who like Wellman was also a double
D.S.O., and from there up to the batteries at La Panne
manned by Royal Marine artillerymen. We crossed the
Channel in our fast skimmers whenever we pleased, doing
the trip in under an hour without passports or Customs
difficulties and taking what we liked with us.

Summer came and with it hard work at Osea Island
getting the C.M.B. flotillas ready for the "big show" which
never happened because the Armistice in November 1918
arrived as an anti-climax to all our efforts and put paid to
our hopes of digging out the High Sea Fleet from its
anchorages in the Terschilling roadstead to give battle to
the Grand Fleet. The disappointment in the Navy was
intense, especially on Osea Island, but Froggie (our friendly
nickname for Captain French) gave out he had orders from
the Admiralty to keep the base going during the winter
as there would be other things for the boats to do. So we

worked hard that cold winter in the biting easterly winds of the Essex marshes and mudflats, keeping our boats and base up to concert pitch. Not an easy job when many of the 'hostilities only' (H.O.s) young seamen and mechanics were longing to be demobilized and sent back to their homes; but they had faith in the Captain and the calls came soon after the new year.

Amongst them was one for the Baltic which is where Osea Island ends and my own story begins.

CHAPTER I

SECRET SERVICE

EARLY in February 1919 I was staying at the Waldorf Hotel having spent the previous evening with Sandy Proctor exchanging yarns about Russia and Archangel where we had spent the winter, he in his business on shore and myself in H.M.S. *Iphigenia*.

Early next morning I had a telephone call from my chief, Captain Wilfred French, at Osea Island.

"Hallo, you there Agar? Well, I've got a proposition for you and want you back at once." No more, just that and he hung up.

I hurried down by the next train and on the way kept speculating on what on earth it could be; that it was something out of the ordinary and quite unusual I felt certain, as otherwise French would have told me more on the telephone. Several possibilities occurred to my mind. Was I to return to Archangel where we had a flotilla of boats operating at the mouth of the River Dvina? Or would it be the Black Sea, where we had another small flotilla en route from Baku to the Caspian? Or perhaps it might be the Rhine, where the army, I knew, were asking for naval assistance in the occupation of their bridgeheads at Cologne and Koblenz. Indeed, there were many possibilities. On the other hand I might have been recalled to deal with some quite ordinary routine matter. I felt, however, something out of the ordinary was in the air.

Like many other young officers in the Navy with no responsibilities, I was still keen to see and take part in more of our war activities, especially in C.M.B.s where we were given more scope in an independent life and the possibility of adventure. As naval officers who had spent the war in big ships with many comforts, including regular meals and a canteen, warm bunks, hot baths, and dry clothes, we lived in strange contrast to the soldiers on shore and were often in complete ignorance of the war's real horrors. We had, as yet, no experience of the physical sufferings of a soldier and the constant strain of trench life, where every moment may be one's last. To us any fresh movement or activity, such as the White Sea, Black Sea, Baltic or Rhine, meant excitement, adventure and something out of the ordinary dull routine life in Scapa Flow and therefore to be welcomed. Little did I imagine that the experiences in store for me were such as it was the lot of few men, even in the vortex of the Great War, to experience.

I reported, as ordered, to the captain's office upon returning to the Island. The captain was studying intently a chart on the table before him and from his manner I realized immediately that the matter in hand was no ordinary one, for he called to his secretary working in a small annexe to go outside and leave him alone, after which he shut the door.

"Well Agar," he said, "would you like to go on Special Service?"

I replied that I certainly would. Continuing, he said it was top priority SECRET which was why he had sent the secretary out.

"No one must know where you are going until you are under way, not even your crew. This special mission is a highly dangerous one to the Baltic Sea and the Gulf of Finland. The work will involve use of two C.M.B.s because great speed at sea will be an essential. You alone will be in charge, and you will have no one but yourself to rely on. It is of the utmost importance that not a soul, either here in England, on the journey out, or even when you arrive in those waters, shall have any suspicion of your activities. I need hardly add that your mission is of great political importance, and for this reason SECRECY IS VITAL. For the rest, report tomorrow at the Admiralty and ask for Commander Goff of the Naval Intelligence Division."

A feeling of pride and gratitude filled me as I looked straight into the eyes of this man, my Chief and my friend, who suggested me for so unique a task. Well though we knew each other, I still was conscious that his clear blue eyes were searching me with unusual intensity. The habitual twinkle was absent. Grave and calm consideration took its place. But if any doubt did exist in his mind, it was dispelled at that moment.

"All right," he said, "that's all I am to tell you for the present. Above all—" (it was rare for him to reiterate) "NOT —ONE—WORD—TO A SOUL."

* * *

The next forty-eight hours appeared like one of those strange and vivid dreams where every detail stands out with startling and unforgettable clearness. It seemed to me as if I was living in a George Henty short story specially written for the *Boys' Own Paper* of my childhood days in the nineties, but in which I was to play a part.

I met Commander Goff at the Admiralty as arranged. After a short conversation about my work at Osea Island we left that building with its maze of corridors, constant patter of feet, the busy civilian clerks hastening to and fro, in contrast to the rather sombre military tread of the Admiralty messengers carrying their important-looking despatch boxes, and arrived in the Horse Guards. I was taken to another building, through more corridors, up many flights of stairs, through a small passage and yet into a third building. I felt as lost as in the maze at Hampton Court. Finally, when we reached the top of this last building, Goff stopped in front of a room on the highest floor. A young woman came out and spoke to him. Turning round to me and pointing to the door he said, "knock, and go in there."

At first I felt incredibly nervous, then curiosity got the

better of me and I looked around the room I had entered. Seated at a large desk with his back to the window, and apparently absorbed in reading a document was the most remarkable man I have ever met in my life. The thing that struck me most about him was the shape of his large, intelligent head, which I saw in profile against the light. Without paying the slightest attention to me as I stood by the door, he went on reading, occasionally making a note on the papers before him. Then with startling suddenness he put his papers aside and banging the desk hard with his hand said, "Sit down, my boy, I think you will do."

I knew then that something really eventful had come into my life. This was my first introduction to 'C'—the name by which this man was known to all who came in official contact with him. He had, of course, other names and one quite well-known in London society, but to us, or rather to those who served under him, he was always known and referred to by this single letter of the alphabet.

'C' was the Head of the British Secret Service.

* * *

I was in that room, I suppose, for an hour. My first sensation of nervousness quickly subsided. By his personality and charm of manner he soon put me at my ease. He questioned me for a time, and then suddenly plunged into the subject in hand. It was Russia. For some time, he told me, all communication with Russia had ceased. It was many months since our various missions and consulates had left, and over a year since the Embassy in Moscow had been shut down. Russia was now a closed book and hostile country with which we were virtually at war.

Communication, however, had still been maintained, by means into which he did not go. But it was not the past that mattered, it was the future. Those communications had broken down and it was essential to restore them. He said there was a certain Englishman—unnamed, and with regard to whom no details were given—who had remained in Russia to conduct Intelligence, whose work was regarded as of vital importance, and with whom it was essential to keep in touch. It was necessary to help him to get out alive, as he was the only man who had first-hand reliable information on certain things which was required urgently by our Government. There had been, 'C' explained, a kind of secret link or courier service between this man via Finland and Estonia, but latterly the couriers had been captured and nothing now came through. The proposal was that I should go out with two C.M.B.s and endeavour with their speed to land fresh couriers on the coast whence they could reach Petrograd, deliver messages to this man, and bring back his reports.

It was with regard to such a plan that Captain French had been approached and French had suggested me as just the man for this undertaking. I should cease to belong to the Admiralty. I would be transferred to the Secret Service and adopt a civilian occupation. Officially, the British Government would know nothing whatever about me. I should choose a picked band of young men for my crew who would also to all appearances be private individuals. Our destination would be Finland. We would travel, via Sweden, in the guise of yachtsmen or representatives of a boat-building firm with the ostensible object of interesting those countries in buying British motor boats. That was the general plan, but details I must work out myself. 'C', like French, laid the utmost stress upon the need for SECRECY. Not even my men were to be told our destination in advance, and as for relatives, they might be given to think we had gone on a special enterprise. No more.

He paused a moment, and looking at me straight in the face said, "Well, my boy, what do you think of it?" And without giving me time to reply went on, "I won't ask you to take it on, for I know you will."

He questioned me about my family affairs and asked whether I was married, to which I replied, "No." "Or engaged?" to which I again replied, "No." He told me that in selecting my party, as he chose to call it, I should pick men all of whom must be young and without ties of any kind.

Time was all important.

"Now go back to Osea at once," he said. "Captain French will give you all the help you need in getting your boats and men together. Discuss with him and Goff every detail and come back to me with all arrangements made, if possible, within forty-eight hours."

The interview was at an end.

I left the room and was standing outside the door, not knowing quite which direction to take when a charming voice behind me said:

"You look rather bewildered, come in here and have a cigarette."

It was the pretty woman I had seen talking to Goff and (I concluded) one of the secretaries.

"Well," she said, "what are you going to do about it?"

"Of course I'm going," I replied. "Who wouldn't? I have no responsibilities; besides, as far as we chaps are concerned, the war is over and there is not much left for us to do. This is a chance, maybe a great chance."

A thoughtful smile hovered round her lips.

"Yes. I can see you haven't had enough. Some of us have, though. And yet, if I were a man, I think I would do the same. I believe I envy you." Mrs. G., for that is what we shall call her, was not the only woman who spent the war anxiously waiting for the safe return of a husband.

There followed a hectic week during which an incredible number of details had to be arranged with the utmost secrecy, from buying reach-me-down civvy clothes for my mechanics, to arranging small petrol dumps in out-of-the-way places in Finland. Mrs. G. was always there to help and act as guide, counsellor and friend, and when finally I left London by train for Hull, and, for obvious reasons, had no friends or relatives to see me off, to my surprise her figure appeared just before the train steamed out of the station with a parting present of books and papers.

* * *

It would be impossible to record in this book the amount of encouragement and help I received from our captain at Osea Island. He was full of enthusiasm for our venture. Years later, when he was directing in Malta during the Mediterranean crisis of 1934-5 an organization many times larger and more important than ours at Osea Island, we reminisced with delight upon the events of 1919 which launched me on my expedition.

Two forty foot C.M.B.s were selected and under his energetic enthusiasm brought forward for service within a few days. Engines were refitted, tested and tried out, a complete set of spare parts provided, trial runs carried out by both boats in the Blackwater river and a hundred and one details attended to. For the personnel of our party I selected three young officers, all under twenty-one years of age, from the Royal Naval Reserve. They were: Sub-Lieutenant J. Sindall; Midshipman (afterwards Sub-Lieut.) J. Hampsheir; and Midshipman (afterwards Sub-Lieut.) R. N. Marshall. In addition I took two mechanics, one for each boat; Beeley for C.M.B. No. 4, and Piper for C.M.B. No. 7.

Our party thus totalled six, were all volunteers and keen as mustard to go anywhere and do anything, and a happier, more loyal or braver set of comrades was never man's good fortune to work with.

On the Island it was given out that we were to reinforce either the Archangel or Black Sea C.M.B. flotillas, and consequently the sudden departure of two boats gave rise to no talk or speculation, and was regarded as an ordinary routine affair. There now remained the problem of transportation to Finland. We decided, in order to attract as little attention as possible, to split the party. The first lot, consisting of myself, Hampsheir and Marshall, was to go on

c

ahead in a small coasting steamer to Stockholm, from there to Helsingfors in Finland, and on arrival, to make our initial preparations. The second party, consisting of Sindall and the two mechanics was to travel in another coasting steamer with the boats direct from the Thames to Helsingfors. Meanwhile the C.M.B.s were painted white to give them the appearance of pleasure craft.

Commander Goff and the lady upstairs soon got busy with shipping companies engaged in coastal trade between Finland and England, and secured for us passages in a small coaster leaving from Hull and, for the C.M.B.s deck-cargo space in a coaster leaving the Thames from the West India docks. Neither of these movements were likely to cause any notice. They managed this part of the business in an astonishingly short time and by means best known to themselves. We could, of course, have obtained immediate charters through the Government, but it was essential that everything we did should be done by normal commercial procedure and have the appearance of an ordinary undertaking by young men anxious to do commercial business after the war. We even took out a few new gadgets for motor boats as samples, and Sir John Thornycroft was persuaded to lend us a special charging plant for compressed air with which we started the engines, and which later on proved to be a godsend to us in our difficulties.

As far as stores were concerned, we decided to take as few as possible so as not to encumber ourselves; principal items required were, of course, spare parts for the engines and a little clothing for ourselves. For the rest, supplies of the most important item of all, petrol and oil, were being arranged in Helsingfors and once there I would myself arrange and select small dumps for it. For food, apart from a few cases of tinned rations in the boats, we would have to live on the country as best we could.

* * *

Our preparations were now in full swing and my forty-eight hours already up when I again found myself in the top storey room in front of 'C'. He always gave me the same form of greeting, "Well, my boy, sit down." Followed by, "Tell me how you are getting on and what your plans are."

Spread out on a side table were charts of the Baltic, by now quite familiar to me, and a few military maps which were prepared daily at the War Office, showing the various sectors and frontiers of Germany, Poland, Russia and the Baltic States.

Bending over the charts, I outlined to the Chief the plan I proposed to adopt. I proposed after assembling the two boats at Helsingfors to work our way along the Finnish coast, indented with innumerable little inlets, one of which we should pick as our secret base. I suggested that we should run our couriers from this base at night across the Gulf to some spot on the opposite shores of Estonia, as near as possible to the Russian frontier. Thence the courier would have to find his way into Petrograd. To do this successfully without attracting any attention we would have to operate at night and in the good weather usual in the Baltic during June, July and part of August. The distance across the Gulf of Finland averaged only thirty to fifty miles, depending on the points selected, making at the most a hundred miles run. At our high speed (over thirty-six knots) we could cover it quite easily in under three hours.

Such then would seem to be our best plan, but details could only be settled when we had studied conditions on the spot. In particular it would be necessary to discover the sort of watch kept on the coast both by Estonians and Finns. Two things were essential for the moment. The first was to get out there as quickly as possible and as secretly as possible—we must keep the boats out of sight and attract no attention to ourselves. The second was to establish contact as soon as we could with 'C's' agents in Finland,

particularly along the route between Helsingfors and our
base, so as never to lose telegraphic touch with headquarters
in London. I told 'C' how much Captain French had been
helping us and how enthusiastic he was over the business,
and I went on to explain how we had selected our party and
proposed dividing it up by sending the boats as ordinary
cargo under tarpaulin covers on the deck of a small freighter,
and ourselves going as ordinary passengers from Hull.
'C' followed every detail with the trained knowledge of a
sailor.

Finally I said: "And of course, sir, we shall need some
money."

I thought this would give rise to at least a few questions,
but he merely said laconically: "How much?"

Now this was the one matter to which I had not given a
thought, expecting rather that it would be decided for me.
As an impecunious naval officer, I had never handled
money in my life, my knowledge of finance being strictly
limited to sums paid periodically into my private banking
account by trustees, plus my pay, on both of which I
often used to draw before they were due. It never occurred
to me to calculate what our expenses might be for living
and so on, so when I realized I was expected to say
something, I made a bold guess. "A thousand pounds,
sir."

I thought I should be called upon to justify this estimate,
and I could hardly believe my ears when the old man pressed
a button to call a secretary and I heard him say quite
simply "Make a cheque to bearer, pay cash, for one thousand
pounds." It was just like that.

'C' must have observed the expression on my face, for
while the cheque was being made out he said "You must
not think we often give money away as quickly as that, but
this is an exceptional case and we know who we are dealing
with. I don't want you to keep detailed accounts, you will
have other things to think about, but we shall require,
later on, a rough statement showing how you have spent it.

You will all, of course, receive your service pay, but not from the Admiralty.''

The Chief then proceeded to explain to me his system of contacts. These contacts represented men in his organization doing Secret Service work, and for my purposes it would be necessary for me to know who these men were in the particular part of the world where I was being sent, that is in Sweden, Finland, Russia and some of the Baltic States. Each contact had a number. I myself would be given one and would be known only by this number, with which I was to communicate with headquarters. As the head of the area in which I would be operating had his headquarters at Stockholm, I would henceforth be known as ST34. Similarly the unnamed Englishman in Petrograd with whom it was my immediate mission to establish contact was designated as ST25. 'C' assured me that I could rely implicitly on each and every one of these contacts, who would be instructed to help me to the limit of their powers in money and every other way. I was also to use them as links in my line of communication with him. He finally uttered a special warning. He told me that if we did anything likely to embarrass British good relations with neutral countries we would be withdrawn immediately, and further, and most important of all, as far as the Bolsheviks were concerned, if we were caught 'on the wrong side of the line' it would be our own funeral, for in the circumstances nothing officially could be done to save us.

"You must take your chance," he said, and paused. I saw a grave expression, rather a sad one, flicker over his face.

"No," he went on, "you must be given some sort of chance. So if you foresee the possibility of the worst coming to the worst, you may each keep one set of uniform in your boat. It may save you. I will risk that. But only use it in emergency."

What prompted the old man to make that concession I cannot guess to this day. We acted upon the suggestion, each taking a suit of uniform, which in the end turned out extremely useful, but not until later on when our Secret Service work was over and had led up to other events.

He went on to explain that a force of British cruisers and destroyers were already in the Baltic carrying out various operations, the primary object of which was to stabilize the whole situation of the Baltic States and Finland and to prevent a possible breakout of the Russian Soviet fleet which was now in Kronstadt harbour. But our activities were to be quite apart from this. We were to avoid communication *even with our own ships* until we had established ourselves in Finland, lest there should be a leakage of information, and I must, when I saw the opportunity, establish personal contact with the Admiral who would be told of my mission, *but no one else*.

The interview terminated at this point, and I was then taken to another room on the top floor where I was further instructed in the mysteries of the contacts, who they were, how to approach them, and how to communicate with them. Also as to the method in which I was to make out my reports and to whom they were to be entrusted. I was shown how to make use of a most ingenious rough and ready cipher code which could be transmitted to memory and changed from time to time by both sides so that there was no possible risk of compromise. Also methods of using invisible ink on various kinds of the thinnest of thin paper. There was at that time actually in course of preparation a kind which could be digested, but we never used it. No detail of this part of our future job was overlooked, even as to the method I was to adopt of cross-checking reports made to me by our own agents whom I had to employ.

Stockholm (ST29) was our chief transmission point along the line. Helsingfors (ST30 and ST31) was also an important centre. There were a number of others, such as Revel (now Tallin) in Estonia, Riga in Latvia, Viborg in Finland and so on, until the chain of links converged on the person of ST25 in Petrograd. Speculation about this man became an obsession. Who was he? What was he like? How came he to be there at all? Was he still alive? Would I be in time to get to him? I must hurry—hurry, the devil! What a ghastly tragedy if I arrived too late. I pictured this man in the midst of the Red Terror and surrounded by Red agents of the Cheka, without food or money and with nothing but his brain and courage to sustain him. It was not until months after that I learned who he was.

* * *

At last my initiation was complete and I was ready to leave. Maps, routes, plans, names and signs were noted or learnt by heart as were also my methods of communication using codes, invisible inks, thin tissue paper, etc. Messages were to be carried in boots, if possible between the soles.

The day before I left, 'C' took me to luncheon at one of his clubs. We drove there in his large Rolls Royce, himself at the wheel, and I remember the boyish delight he took in driving at terrific speed past the sentries and through the arch of the Horse Guards Parade. He was one of the five men in London specially privileged to do so, and in spite of a wooden leg, the result of a wound received when trying to save his own son's life, he was an expert driver. Driving high speed cars and sailing sluggish boats were his only hobbies. He was indeed a great man. During luncheon Russia was not mentioned. We talked about sailing boats. Nor was there afterwards any awkward or dramatic good-bye. He just gave me a pat on the back and said, "Well, my boy, good luck to you"—and was gone. I walked to my club and finished a few last-minute jobs and reduced my luggage to one small suitcase. Next morning, with my companions, Marshall and Hampsheir, I left Euston for Hull.

How awkward the three of us felt at first, wearing civilian clothes! But the feeling soon wore off. It was the first time I had worn any for nearly five years. I bought them ready made at Moss Bros. in Covent Garden. Arriving in

Hull we boarded the small Swedish coaster in which we were to do the sea passage. She was small and very dirty: the kind of ship which during the war was always wrongfully suspected of running contraband goods. We slept in bunks in the saloon, which we shared with the captain, a Swede of magnificent physique. The ship did not normally carry passengers. We were entertained by this amusing Swede all across the North Sea with anecdote after anecdote of his curious experiences during the war, both ashore and afloat. He spoke in broken English and we laughed a great deal. I gathered that he was a gay bird when on shore in Hull.

For some reason or other the steamer's agents at the last moment decided to cut out our call at Stockholm and the ship was bound instead direct for the port of Abo in Finland. I had, therefore, to abandon, for the time being anyway, all ideas of making my contact with ST29 at Stockholm and rely on my contacts in Helsingfors. I made these immediately on my arrival at Abo where, in fact, I found both ST30 and ST31 waiting to meet me. They were both Englishmen, one of them with a certain business standing in Finland, the other was well known in the Baltic States. Both spoke Russian and German fluently and had already been warned by Stockholm of my arrival, but of course, they had as yet no idea as to the details of our scheme, nor of our boats and their equipment.

From Abo we proceeded to Helsingfors where I made my headquarters in the Hotel Fennia with Hampsheir and Marshall. It was a funny little place and in spite of primitive plumbing and bathing, quite clean and comfortable. It was here that we held our meetings and made our plans like conspirators in a private sitting room.

Meanwhile Captain French had the two boats, with our stores and spare parts inside, towed secretly by night from Osea Island to the West India Docks where he embarked them as arranged on the deck of a small freighter with Sindall and two mechanics. They were due in about a week or ten days' time.

We now had to make our plans, and it was at this stage that ST30 and ST31 gave us the most invaluable help and assistance. Many factors had to be gone into extremely carefully before we decided how to proceed, as one false step might have ruined the whole show. Two things, however, were in our favour. In Estonia and Finland British prestige stood very high, and, as ST30 and ST31 had direct access to Finnish Government officials, many formalities which would have made things rather awkward for us, such as close scrutiny of our passports or examination of our commercial papers, were, at their request, set aside. In many ways, things were made easy for the arrival and unloading of our boats, it being important they should be seen by as few people as possible and not excite undue interest.

Our first decision must be the locality and place on the Finnish coast which we were going to use as our base of operations, and the point on the Estonian coast on the opposite side of the Gulf of Finland at which we could land our couriers.

In our sitting room in the hotel we spent hours studying maps and charts of the Russian frontier on both the Finnish and Estonian side, especially where the frontier runs down to the coast. A glance at the map will show that from our area of operations in the Baltic there were, in peace time and under normal conditions, three avenues of approach to the Russian northern capital; (a) over land from Finland; (b) by sea direct; and (c) over land from Estonia. A study of the conditions prevailing at the time showed that the second of these was impossible as being completely blocked by the Kronstadt fortresses. On the other hand the last-named way of approach, i.e., over land from Estonia, which I had contemplated in London, besides being a dangerous route, involved a long journey for the courier after landing him on the coast. There remained the Finnish frontier, where our couriers had recently disappeared. This frontier was now so closely guarded from the Russian side that it would have been folly to attempt to cross it again until things had quietened down. Moreover the Finns themselves were not particularly anxious to allow anyone either to go across or to return, and in any case a successful return from Soviet Russia into Finland entailed a close search and fortnight's arrest in a Finnish concentration camp, which would of itself have destroyed the value of any information our couriers brought back. We thus found ourselves faced with no choice except to land on the Estonian coast somewhere between Narva and Luga bays, a run of 100 miles there and back.

For hours I pondered alone trying to find a solution, when a sudden brainwave revealed to me, that what at first had been discarded as an impracticable line of approach, might, *because of its apparent improbability* offer the key to the problem.

When Peter the Great built the city of Petrograd on the marshes adjoining Krestovsky Island, he chose indeed an unrivalled strategic position for his capital. The only approach to it by sea is through the tail end of the Finnish Gulf, narrowing to a width of less than twenty miles, across which lies the island of Kronstadt, acting as a natural fortress guarding the capital. Not content with this, he connected this island to the northern shore by a chain of smaller fortresses and on the south side built several large forts guarding the main channel and entrance to the river Neva.

The forts on the north side were connected together by a sunken breakwater about three feet deep, while the south channel was protected by minefields. The idea of penetrating these defences in order to reach the mouth of the river near Krestovsky Island does at first seem madness. But, I reflected, why not examine the plan from another angle? It is obvious that any approach to the main channel on the south side would be quite impossible, as the Commander of a powerful fortress of this size would naturally order a most vigilant watch on the main channel, and I therefore discarded that idea. I next turned to the north side where the principal defences were the chain of forts and the submerged breakwater.

Now the point occurred to me that the sunken breakwater, which was supposed to render the northern passage impassable, was only three feet below the surface of the water—*but my C.M.B.s drew only two feet nine inches* or thereabouts. I believed they could skim over the sunken breakwater with an inch or two to spare! The chain of forts ran the length between the shore and the north-eastern point of the island with two larger fortresses to the westward placed as outposts. There were altogether ten of them.* Surely, I thought, we could find a passage at night creeping along at dead slow speed between these fortresses and, with our high speed (over forty miles an hour) it should be possible to reach Petrograd and return to the Finnish frontier in three hours, provided we could get through the chain of forts. What a marvellous chance! Could it be done? Did the passages exist! If so where were they?

There was still the question of the Russian minefields which we knew were laid within six feet of the surface. I calculated we could accept that risk as we would skim over them. Any likely to cause us damage would be those floating adrift. Lastly, there was the question of the vigilance of the forts, and here I thought if we crept in slowly at night to avoid the noise of our engines betraying our presence, our chances should be good. Finally, instead of taking a week to make our contact with Petrograd, as we would if obliged to use the Estonian coast plan, or ask the courier to accept the risk of crossing the Finnish frontier, the idea of going straight into the lion's den seemed to me to possess most chances of success. The couriers and ourselves would run exactly the same risks which was good for morale.

Once landed on shore they knew exactly where to go and

---

* See plan on page 165. The forts are numbered according to the old chart. Some were blocks of masonry about 20 feet high mounting light batteries only. the larger ones had searchlights and accommodation for men.

how to act. They were specially picked for the job and were fearless Russian patriots with an intimate knowledge of the city of Petrograd.

Thus I mused and thus I determined to have a try at this unrunnable gauntlet. I would bank first on our speed in covering those stretches of water in the shortest possible time; secondly, on cunning, by skimming over the mine-fields and slipping through that chain of forts at night unobserved; thirdly, on Russian psychology, since I had chosen the point where the Reds would be least on the lookout; and fourthly on my luck, for I am the thirteenth of a family. In war it is often the boldest course which succeeds and I regarded this venture of ours in exactly the same way.

The idea would, I knew, be hailed at first with many misgivings by my party and also by ST30 and 31, but I gradually talked them round and in the end convinced them it was worth at least a try.

The first essential was to procure a Russian chart of the defences. Like a magician, ST30 produced one on a Russian document. It was obviously an old one, and showed altogether eleven forts and batteries with two small boat passages in between. There was no indication on how wide or shallow these passages might be. They may now be blocked up or just for rowing boats. Anyway they indicated a possibility of getting from one side of the submerged breakwaters to the other.

My hopes began to rise. I also discovered there was, at a place called Terrioki on the Finnish coast, a tiny sheltered cove close to the Russian frontier ten to fifteen miles only from the chain of forts. It was used before the Revolution for sailing yachts, and if I could get my two C.M.B.'s there unnoticed it should be possible to slip through one of these boat passages. Once through, I could cover the distance, at high speed, between the forts and Krestovsky Island at the mouth of the river Neva. My hopes rose still further. ST30 at once set to work to find out more about Terrioki. It was most important to know who the Finnish Commandant was and what sort of reception we were likely to get. He also began at once to make secret arrangements for a store of petrol and oil to be taken there. How and in what manner, I don't know, but he did it.

Having convinced ST30 and 31 that my plan of running through the forts really did have some chance, and was not too mad, however much it might appear to be, they loyally accepted it and explained it to the Russian courier who was enthusiastic, as were also all my C.M.B. party who entered into the spirit of the adventure with the greatest enthusiasm and longed to get cracking.

The first courier, who was to be my passenger was ready and waiting. He was a Russian whom ST25 had sent out from Petrograd. He had some military training, and at one time was a student of law. We will call him Peter. He had superb physique and in addition was full of guts and courage, I took a liking to him immediately, and although I knew little Russian and he no English at all, we managed to understand each other and never had any differences. We became very close friends especially when our fortunes were linked together on many future occasions.

There were still more problems to solve before completing our preparations, the most difficult being how to get the boats from Abo on the extreme western point of Finland to Terrioki on the extreme eastern point, a distance of 150 miles, which was beyond a safe cruising radius. We could of course have coasted by short stages, calling on the way at pre-arranged inlets for petrol and oil, but this would have entailed running still further risks of detection and perhaps delays as well. I hit upon the idea of having the boats towed there. But here again, who was to tow them? Where could we get a suitable vessel and, how could we make certain of the discretion of the master and crew? The solution, however, came in an unexpected manner.

Walking along the water front, we watched a British

destroyer,. make fast alongside one of the quays, disembark a few officials and cast off again after loading bags of mail and fresh provisions for the Fleet. ST30 who was in close touch with our consulate, said she had come from Revel in Estonia and was one of the destroyers of the naval forces in the Baltic under the orders of Admiral Sir Walter Cowan. Mindful of what 'C' had said to me in London I thought to myself, here was our opportunity. All we had to do was to meet this destroyer at a rendezvous at sea not far from Abo, and be towed to the entrance of the Finnish Gulf. Somehow or other I must make contact with the Admiral and explain our predicament, yet I had to be most careful, our presence in the Baltic was not to be disclosed to anyone, including the Fleet.

I wrote a letter to the Admiral explaining who I was, and asked for an interview. In the letter I begged him to stress the need of strict secrecy. ST30 undertook to have this letter delivered as soon as possible, through the consular office which was done at once. The Admiral sent the same destroyer back with a reply that he would see me immediately at Revel. The destroyer that brought the reply was to take me there and in order to keep my identity secret, I was to come officially as a foreign office messenger with any name I chose to call myself. I boarded the destroyer as a supposed consular official where I was received as usual in the navy, in the most kind and hospitable way. The trip across took only a matter of a few hours and was done at high speed so as to return to Helsingfors the same day during the daylight hours. Like any other civilian, I was shown over the ship and into the engine room and purposely, of course, asked a few simple questions. So far, so good, and no one had the slightest idea that I was an officer in the naval Service, until I arrived on board the Admiral's flagship, H.M.S. *Cleopatra*, when who should I see standing on the top of the gangway but an officer very well known to me, Lieutenant James Rivett-Carnac.* There was only one thing to do,

* Vice-Admiral J. W. Rivett-Carnac, C.B., C.B.E., D.S.C.

feign complete ignorance, which I did, even after he came up to me, saying, "Surely you are Agar, are you not?" to which I was obliged to reply that I had a cousin who was often taken for me as we were so alike, and I must confess I got certain amount of amusement out of the incident which Carnac later shared with me. Captain Little* showed me into the Admiral's cabin.

As on my first meeting with 'C', I remember almost every detail of my first meeting with this fine sailor. He was short and stocky in stature, with a youthful face, a soft, gentle voice and the most charming smile. His breast on both sides of his uniform was a blaze of colour from the many decorations he had received for war services and also for saving life at sea. I think, excluding the late Lord Beatty, he was the most decorated sailor in the Navy, and without doubt one of the bravest. He had seen active service with Lord Beatty in many parts of the Empire during his life. Commencing with the old *Barossa* 1895–96 he took part in the Benin campaign (West Africa), from thence to the Nile gunboats 1898–99 in *H.M.S. Sultan* in time to fight the Dervishes at Ondurman and upper Nile, and from there to shore service in the South African War on the staff of Lord Roberts. In the Great War he was one of Beatty's captains and had taken part in every engagement in the North Sea. His reputation in the Navy stood extremely high as a fighter and leader of men, and he was yet to prove during this eventful year in the Baltic that he was, in addition, a man with much wisdom and power of command. To me he was always a wise counsellor and a wonderful friend. The sailors loved him and nicknamed him 'The Little Man' because of his short stature. I realized instinctively as soon as I saw him that this was a man to serve under, a man who would demand the most of his officers and men and who would in return give the most himself.

As with 'C' our introduction was brief. He came straight to the point. "Tell me what I can do for you, and exactly

* Admiral Sir Charles J. B. Little, G.C.B., G.B.E.

what you want." With a man like him there was never any beating about the bush, so I told him the whole story from beginning to end, keeping nothing back; it was the best way, and I could see he liked me the better for it. He said that actually he had been warned by the Admiralty that we should be arriving but that he did not expect us so soon. Officially, I was quite outside his control, so he could not accept any responsibility for anything I did nor could he give me orders what to do, but he would be grateful for any information I could pass on to him, especially anything to do with the Bolshevik fleet at Kronstadt, about which he was most anxious, since their ships were in strength superior to his own. He realized at once the many difficulties that we would have to contend with, particularly the difficulty of keeping our mission secret as long as possible, and he assured me that if he could help us in any way, he would.

I promptly asked him to give me the services of a destroyer to tow my boats from a rendezvous which I would arrange off the western part of the Finnish coast to Biorko Sound on the eastern side, from where I intended to go to Terrioki, a distance of only thirty miles. He said he intended to establish an advanced base for his ships at Biorko Sound, and that if I made use of Terrioki and my plans went well, I could always fall back on the Fleet and if I wanted any assistance or help from his destroyers all I had to do was to ask for it. I realised at once he was flat out to help me.

I then explained to him the details of my plan, and how I intended to run the gauntlet of the Kronstadt fortresses at night so as to reach Petrograd and land the agent to contact ST25. As I went on expounding it I could see his eyes light up with pleasure and enthusiasm. It was the sort of thing he liked. He summoned his flag captain and sent for the confidential charts of the Gulf of Finland and such plans as he had of the Kronstadt defences. The flag captain was at first sceptical about our chances. Those nasty looking three red lines on the chart connecting the chain of forts, drawn in heavy type and representing the underwater breakwaters about which I have already written, appeared to him the most serious obstacle, apart from the minefields.

"You know you are finished if you get stuck on those, don't you?" he said. "Besides, that area will be stiff with floating mines as we know from experience." The Fleet had already lost the cruiser *Cassandra*, and the cruiser *Curacoa* had been seriously damaged, both by mines. The Admiral listened to this, and other things besides, from the flag captain, who had to be both practical and cautious. He obviously was not keen on the idea largely because of the large risks, in what to him was a 'civilian affair' and should be undertaken by civilians and not naval officers in disguise. Such was his view. But the Admiral was different. To him this was an enterprise after his own heart and the kind of thing he would have liked to have done himself. He was full of optimism and obviously on my side.

"Nothing is ever worth while doing unless there's a risk in it," he said, "ALWAYS CHOOSE THE BOLDEST COURSE if you have any choice at all; it is always the boldest that stands the best chance of success." I remember his words so well, and I cannot describe with what relief and encouragement I heard them, as it dispelled any doubts I had about my plan and gave me confidence in myself. He then told the flag captain to send me back in the same destroyer that brought me to Revel, and also to arrange for another destroyer to meet my boats at a rendezvous of my own choosing near Abo and tow them to Biorko Sound.

Before leaving, I made one final request, which did not appear at first an important one, but was later, as things turned out, to have the most important bearing on our future. I asked to be provided with two torpedoes, one for each of my boats. I explained that although in London I had been told quite definitely that I was to avoid all operations which would involve us in a hostile act, as our boats were supposed to be civilian in character, yet these torpedoes might come in very useful in self-defence if we found ourselves up against Russian warships. I could see

D

the Admiral did not immediately take to the idea. The thought of men in civilian clothes using weapons (of which the torpedo was about the most dangerous) did not appeal to him.

I then went on to explain the concession which I had been given by 'C' that each of us were allowed to carry one set of uniform in our boats *for emergency purposes only*, and I promised him faithfully that if we used our torpedoes, we would wear our uniform and fly the White Ensign. This evidently removed any doubts he had in his mind, for he gave further orders for two spare torpedoes to be specially prepared by the senior officer* of our submarines and placed on board an oiler then at anchor in Biorko Sound, and then with a "Good luck to you, Agar", I left his cabin. Before leaving he arranged to pass all our future communications in cypher to the Admiralty and from them to 'C'. From that day on I knew I had in Walter Cowan a real friend, and one who would never fail us in our mission.

It was with a light heart that I returned to Helsingfors in the evening, as I felt that our plans were now assuming real shape and it would not be very long before we would be active. The destroyer made the passage at high speed, over 25 knots, so as to get through the Helsingfors channel and out again before dark. It was a lovely run in between the islands as the setting sun threw the pine woods and forests of birch, intersected here and there by the red roofs of the Finnish *datchas*, into a most beautiful picture. It was already the end of May, and I realized for the first time, that the 'white nights,' when the twilight extends into the night and early morning, would soon be upon us. This made it vitally important to get our courier through to Petrograd while there was still some darkness left. On the way up the channel we passed close to an island on which was a large hotel about to become the headquarters of the British Military Mission, shortly to arrive under the direction of General Sir Hubert Gough and as we steamed on near the

* Admiral Sir Martin Dunbar-Nasmith, V.C., K.C.B.

eastern side of the channel another conspicuous hotel flying the German flag. This housed the Staff of the German General von der Goltz who afterwards caused both the Admiral and our allied military missions so much trouble with his activities in the Baltic States in Lithuania and Latvia.

It was now 9 p.m. and still some twilight left when we pulled up alongside the market quay where I disembarked. I noted the hour carefully and the visibility to seaward which for us was vitally important. That night ST30 came to my room in the hotel with good news. It seemed to pour good news that day. He had just received information that the boats were due to arrive at Abo in two days time. The agent whom he had despatched to Terrioki had also returned with the most encouraging report, upon which he assured me I could rely.

The village, he said, had fallen into decay, some of the old Russian *datchas* were still inhabited by refugees, some were empty and a few commandeered by Finnish troops who made a concentration camp by enclosing them with barbed wire. The Commandant of the Finnish troops had established his headquarters in the village and was, so the agent reported, most kindly disposed towards the British. The small harbour at the end of the village, which had, in the old, pre-revolutionary days, been used as a sailing club by the aristocracy of St. Petersburg, was simply ideal for our purpose. There was sufficient room to moor two large motor boats, in complete shelter, screened from observation to seaward by a wall about ten feet high. Adjoining this harbour was the disused headquarters of the yacht club.

This whole report seemed too good to be true, since, from the agent's description, the place seemed to be just made for our particular purpose.

ST30 went on to tell me that the arrangements for making a petrol dump there were well under way. It had been a very tricky job which entailed transport partly by boat across a portion of the coast, then by train and finally by horse and cart, and he had, I fear, expended a large sum of money on it, but that was only a secondary consideration. We had also established a reliable contact at Viborg, some fifty miles from Terrioki and not far from Biorko Sound, so once I had established myself in my secret base, I should have a link of direct communication with Helsingfors and consequently with London. None the less, I foresaw that the position in Terrioki would be fraught with all sorts of difficulties, as it was close to the Russian frontier — too close I thought. Any new arrival there would create suspicion in the eyes of the Finnish soldiers, a thing we had to avoid at all costs. Moreover, between Biorko Sound and Terrioki lay the large Finnish fortress of Inonini (Ino) which we should have to pass on our way there by sea. And although I was prepared, when the time came, to let the Commandant of Terrioki into our secret (as I would be obliged to do in any case), I did not want to let the Commandant of Fort Ino into it, as that would have meant giving it away to too many people. However, there would be time to decide those points later, the main thing was to get the boats unloaded at Abo as quickly and as secretly as possible and then get off to our waiting destroyer.

It was arranged that ST30 and I would go down to meet them accompanied by Marshall and Hampsheir and that ST31 should remain in Helsingfors so as to relay messages with our contacts either at Revel or in Viborg. I also decided to take Peter with me in the boats to get him accustomed to our ways.

In two days time we were back at Abo and met Sindall with the boats and the mechanics. Everything had gone to plan. The boats were loaded in the West India Dock without causing any comment and were neatly stowed on the deck of the steamer, well covered up by tarpaulins. My party were in great fettle and eager to get away and get busy.

As was to be expected, there were some difficulties with the customs authorities and port officials when it came to unloading. ST30 again in some peculiar way managed to smooth them over, and the boats were eventually unloaded, placed in a secluded corner of the port where they would least attract attention, and again covered up by tarpaulins. ST30 gave out the explanation that we were bound for Hango, which is a well-known pleasure resort on the coast, frequented by many kinds of pleasure craft such as motor boats, motor yachts and sailing yachts, which explanation satisfied the port officials, and I don't think they gave us another thought.

Meanwhile, we rushed a message over to our contact at Revel to ask the Admiral to have a destroyer at our pre-arranged rendezvous on the following evening and, dividing ourselves up into three parties, we secured rooms for the night in the town.

Next evening, after filling up with petrol and oil, we set out for our rendezvous at sea where, true to his word, the Admiral had sent the destroyer, H.M.S. *Voyager** (Commander C. G. Stuart, D.S.C., D.S.O.). The weather was perfect. Even the name of the ship seemed to me a good omen. The tows were connected up, one on either side of the destroyer which Stuart worked up to twenty knots so as to get us into Biorko early the following morning. Everything so far pointed to success, but it was already 7th June, and only a fortnight was left before the commencement of the "white nights". Time was so precious. and the slightest hitch would delay all our hopes and plans. I tried hard to conceal my many thoughts and anxieties. Was the flag captain right after all? Were we embarking on a wild goose chase? Would it not have been better to have taken things a trifle more slowly before rushing on to Biorko and Terrioki? All such doubts and fears came and went through my mind during that first voyage in the destroyer. Then I thought of ST25 waiting for help and they disappeared.

* H.M.S. *Voyager* was specially earmarked by the Admiral for giving us tows and taking care of us generally when at Biorko to ensure as much secrecy as possible. He could not have chosen a better ship or commanding officer.

I had learned during my interview with the Admiral on board his flagship details of the naval situation at the time. He had under his command a mixed force of cruisers, destroyers and submarines. One cruiser had already been lost and another put out of action on minefields, but whether these minefields were German or Russian it was impossible to tell. The bulk of the Russian fleet had, early in the year, moved east and were now in Kronstadt harbour under the protection of their fortresses. Two destroyers, however, had been cut off at Revel and surrendered to the Estonians. These two destroyers, the *Lennuk* and *Yombola*, now formed the nucleus of the Estonian navy that was later on to render such valuable service under the redoubtable Estonian sailor, Admiral Pitka.

Early in May, certain units of the Bolshevik fleet, consisting of cruisers and destroyers and supported by their heavy ships, came out of Kronstadt, and steering west beyond the Finnish Gulf, made several sorties towards both the Finnish and Estonian coast. On coming within range, however, of the British ships, they invariably turned about due eastward and went back to their base.

This sort of situation, although satisfactory for the time, was not satisfactory for the future, and if the Admiral intended to keep a close watch on the exit to the Gulf, it was obvious that he must have a base further to the east, that is east of Revel, from which to work. Biorko Sound was the only suitable one, and thanks to our Minister in Helsingfors, Mr. H. M. Bell, who had great influence with General Mannerheim, the Finnish Regent, and the Finnish Government, the Admiral was granted permission to make use of this base. In addition Bell obtained from the Finnish Government a promise to do all they could to help in its defence—a promise which they faithfully kept for the remainder of the year.

During the short time I waited in Helsingfors for the boats to arrive, I learned something about the conditions and state of affairs in Finland. It is remarkable how the Finnish nation with its sturdy race of people, secured for themselves their independence in so short a time after the country had been impoverished by Tsarist Russia in the war against Germany. The Red revolution soon spread to Finland when Red Finnish Communists stripped the country bare and virtually held the people in bondage until with the help of German troops, they were liberated by their national hero General Mannerheim.

It was thrilling to hear at first hand from eye-witnesses their stories of Mannerheim, who with a handful of Finnish volunteers, and a few pieces of artillery borrowed from Sweden, boldly advanced against the combined forces of Red Finns and Russian Bolsheviks before help arrived from the German troops. These were sent over from Danzig on Easter Monday 1918 in eight transports, but while the German soldiers gave good service afterwards, it was Mannerheim and his volunteers who liberated the people from the Red Finns.

His example of resolution and courage against immensely superior numbers at the battle of Tammerfors in northern Finland, a bitter struggle in which 3,000 Reds and 600 Whites were killed, paved the way for his march south to the capital and the rest of Finland and the replacement of the red flag of the hammer and sickle by the Finnish white and blue ensign.

The White Russian general Yudenitch, with a staff of ex-Russian officers, held Court in the largest hotel in the town *Societenhusen*. A motley collection of speculators and hangers-on in his wake were all eager for posts and profit upon the fall of Petrograd, which it was hoped to accomplish by an army, then in process of formation in the strip of territory known as Ingermanland, wedged in between the frontier of Estonia and the frontier of Soviet Russia. This army had already received the blessing of the Allies, who had despatched a military mission to help it under General Sir Hubert Gough.

It was planned to obtain the consent of the Estonian Government for their army, commanded by General Laidoner, to co-operate with Yudenitch in an attack on Petrograd. The question on everyone's lips was would the Finns join in too; because if they did and the three attacks could be synchronized, i.e., the Finns, the White Russians and the Estonians, Petrograd City caught in a pair of pincers would inevitably fall. Few asked themselves the questions: "What would happen if it did?" "What would be the result?" "Who would gain? and how long could it be held against the Bolsheviks?"

The Finns, however, must have done so, and judged the situation from their point of view. They had no friendship for Russia whether red or white and had suffered enough from both. At the same time, they did not wish to offend the British Government from whom they were expecting full recognition of their national independence. It was a difficult position for General Gough the head of our military mission who had orders to support Yudenitch and even more difficult for our Admiral, who had naval forces in active opposition to the Bolsheviks. To add to his difficulties and responsibilities, he had an even worse situation to deal with in the Baltic States themselves, as will be explained in a later chapter, because the peace treaty with Germany had not yet been settled. The whole of the Baltic was in a state of uncertainty, the Finns antagonistic to the Russians because of their deep-rooted feuds and rivalries centuries old; the Estonians likewise mistrustful of White Russian leaders and although pledged to help them, were unwilling at heart to have White Russian troops on their soil. In Latvia, German and Lettish soldiers were at each other's throats while the devil himself seemed to be established in Moscow.

I had all this from my new-found friends ST30 and 31. Both had taken part in the Mannerheim liberation campaign, and having spent a part of their lives in the Baltic States before the war knew the political set-up as well as, and perhaps better than, the foreign Missions including our own. But in the meanwhile I was wholly pre-occupied with our own mission to contact ST25 somewhere in the heart of Petrograd city.

*   *   *

CHAPTER II

TERRIOKI

OUR C.M.B.s in tow of the *Voyager* stood the long journey from Abo very well. Stuart slipped the tows off Biorko entrance, when we started up our engines and proceeded up the Sound into the anchorage, where we brought the boats alongside a small British oiler which was sent there in advance by the Admiral as promised, and was anchored close by the village of Koivisto.

I had Peter with me to familiarize him with our C.M.B.s. He was amazed at first when we skimmed across the water at high speed with the engine all out, but soon became accustomed to it and no longer doubted my plan to get in and out of Petrograd by night provided we could get through those forts. He was as full of confidence as I was and enthusiastic about the boats.

I was determined to get on to Terrioki as soon as possible, where ST31 had already gone ahead by land to help us smooth away difficulties on shore. But before making the thirty mile journey there from Biorko, I resolved to take no risks and to give our engines a trial run at full speed in the shelter of Biorko Sound and under the wing of the oiler while we had the chance. It was while we were doing so that we had our first set-back. During the trial run, one of the boats developed a serious defect in her engine which put her out of action. It was cruel hard luck, after having got so far and overcome so many difficulties. Normally with a base close at hand, we would have hauled the boat up a slipway, taken out the engine and put another one in its place which would have been a simple matter. Here in Biorko this was out of the question, but our mechanics were not beaten. In technical terms the engine had run a big end. We had spare parts in the boat; but to replace it entailed stripping the top covering off the boat and hoisting the engine out, no easy affair with a 250 horse power engine weighing over half a ton and mounted on bearers in a small boat.

We set to work at once on the deck of the oiler, where with the help of the oiler's crew we rigged sheer legs and tackle, hoisted the engine out, and by working non-stop throughout that day and night and the following forenoon, had the boat ready again on the afternoon of the 10th June, when this time the trial run proved satisfactory. We set out that night just after twilight on the last lap of our adventure.

We had only our small-scale chart plus the Russian tracing and as there were no lights on the coast, it was a tricky business to know exactly when to make the turn inwards towards the land for the tiny village of Terrioki. Any mistake in our calculations would have meant over-running our mark and finding ourselves on the wrong side of the frontier. Terrioki was only three miles short of the heavily guarded posts separating Russia from Finland. To help us out of our difficulty ST31 arranged to hide in the woods near the yacht club each night until we arrived, and armed with a strong electric torch, carefully shaded from the land, flash a signal to seaward every five minutes between midnight and 3 a.m. which would give us a line on our turning mark and act as a guiding light.

The night was fine with an early setting moon, and we could see the coastline through our binoculars about two miles away. I was anxious to avoid Fort Ino on the Finnish side lest they might mistake us for smuggling boats which ran liquor into Finland from the Estonian coast. We made a short detour to seaward to remain out of their sight before turning in towards Terrioki. Throttling the engines well down I slowly approached the black line which was all we could see at first of the coast. Gradually the line began to take shape, and we could recognize the woods and trees of the forest as we came closer until at last there was a flash a little to the right of the point where we were aiming by our compass and then another one. It was ST31 giving his signal, so with great relief we headed straight for the spot. Within a few minutes the shape of a white building emerged near the waters' edge which was the yacht club. It was the first sight of what was to be our secret base for the next few months and a tremendous thrill.

I crept towards the shore at dead slow speed when things began to take shape which, as we came nearer, proved to be the arm of a small stone breakwater.

It was 2 a.m. and flat calm so I stopped the engine, and using our long light boat hooks as punt poles, rounded the breakwater and entered this tiny harbour not more than fifty yards long and less in breadth; with a long white club house directly in front. For our purposes, it was the most perfect small base which we could possibly have wished for. A small fishing boat lay inside, made fast to the only mooring in the harbour, and we brought both boats safely alongside this fishing boat, which was empty and which we used as our mooring. We were just unlashing our small rowing pram, which I had bought in Finland and carried on the deck of my boat, when I heard the tramp of feet on shore and voices hailing us not more than fifty yards away. These were anxious moments. Were we going to be arrested? That would indeed have been a bad beginning to our expedition! Was ST31 perhaps having difficulty?

I told Peter to reply, but not in Russian, as perhaps they might have already taken us for smugglers, in which case the sentries might open fire without any further warning. Another voice, however, called out, this time in English, and I knew we were safe. It was ST31 directing us where to land in the small pram boat and also warning me in English to keep Peter concealed in the C.M.B., as the Finns were most suspicious of any Russians landing in boats and it was best for the meantime for his presence not to be known.

On landing we were met by sentries and ST31, who explained to them in Finnish (which he spoke fluently as well as Russian) that we were a reconnoitring party from the Finnish Navy in Biorko sent to help them guard the frontier and with special permission from the Government to use the small harbour of Terrioki. He supported this argument by producing an official document in Finnish with the Government stamp, which satisfied the patrols. We were allowed to proceed to a *datcha* in which ST31 had arranged for us to live, on condition that we were not to leave it until we had seen the Commandant the next morning. Judicious offerings of cigarettes and a little rum settled any doubts they may have had about us, and, leaving one of our party in the boats to keep Peter company, we tramped along a narrow path through the woods and arrived at our *datcha* which had once been, I suppose, the summer home of a wealthy Russian nobleman. We had brought a little food with us from the boat, a few tins of bully beef, biscuits, Bovril, etc., but ST31 had already arranged a hot meal for us and as soon as we had it we were only too glad to get a few hours sleep while we had the chance.

Next morning ST31 and myself were taken before the Commandant, Colonel Sarin, an extremely courteous and charming man, who, at one time had been an officer in the Russian army and for that reason was not popular in some quarters. I had to explain who I was and what I had come for; more important I had to convince him that we had a genuine purpose in coming there, and wanted permission to use the small harbour and the yacht club building. Our unexpected arrival in the early hours of the morning I knew would tend to make him suspicious, but that part of it couldn't be helped. I decided it was best to tell the truth, but not the whole truth as it would be useless to produce a cock and bull yarn about enthusiastic yachtsmen cruising in these unhealthy parts, and we must at all costs get him on our side. ST31 acted as interpreter.

"The British Admiral," I began, "has, as you may know, permission to make use of Biorko Sound as a naval base."

He replied that he was aware of this, but that Biorko Sound did not come into his area, but lay within the area of the Commandant of Fort Ino, and that he was concerned primarily with the task of guarding the frontier, about which there were very strict regulations. I replied that the task of the British Admiral at Biorko was to watch the Russian exit from Petrograd Bay to the sea, which was the sea frontier of Finland, and therefore that the two tasks, both his and that of the Admiral, were a common interest and would he please treat our party and myself as friendly colleagues.

This allayed somewhat his suspicions and having got that distance I went on to explain that from Biorko it was necessary to run out further sea outposts to reconnoitre the Bolshevik coast and the Kronstadt channels and obtain for the Admiral as much information as possible. "You will appreciate, Commandant," I continued, "that the essence of such work, if it is to be successful, is SECRECY, and that therefore the fewer people who know about us the better chances we have of success, and I now wish to ask, not only your permission to use Terrioki harbour and its cover for my boats, but I also want your help."

The Commandant paused before replying. I think he was sizing me up.

"But why," he asked, "do you come at night? And why come here without first asking my colleague at Fort Ino?" This was the large Finnish fort guarding the northern entrance to the gulf.

ST31 had already primed me for this question, for he had discovered that there was a certain amount of professional rivalry between the two Commandants, so I replied that, for our purposes, Inonini had no sheltered harbour: it was therefore impossible for our boats to call there. Besides, if we had passed close by we had arranged no recognition signal and might have been mistaken by them at night for smuggling boats which would have been the end of us.

This explanation seemed to satisfy him but I could see he was still unconvinced and suspicious and replied that for the meantime, we must stay in the harbour until he had communicated with headquarters in Helsingfors. This was indeed awkward; his decision would mean at least several days delay and probably result in our plans miscarrying, as I knew Helsingfors was well served by Bolshevik spies. I begged him to reconsider this because of the delay which this would involve. I stressed that every day was of vital importance owing to the White Nights and that we could obtain intelligence only when our boats could not be seen from the shore. For return I promised him faithfully that if he gave me permission to use the harbour, I would give him personally a full report of any intelligence I obtained in my boats, which he could pass on to Helsingfors as his own.

This, I could see, rather appealed to him, for he then would be able to score a trick or two over his colleague at Ino and also increase his credit at headquarters.

He said he would consider the matter and would see me again that afternoon.

ST31 and I were almost desperate. What was to be done? Helsingfors officially knew nothing about us, so how could we possibly get official permission through Finnish headquarters to use the base within twenty-four hours? The document which ST31 possessed before leaving Helsingfors, it is true, was an order signed by a Finnish high official requesting those he came in contact with to give us any assistance they could; but this document was one we could only use in an emergency, such as on the previous evening, and not one which we could use with the Commandant. I thought of Bell, our acting Minister, who had immense influence at Helsingfors. It was through Bell that the Finns expected to receive *de jure* recognition of Independence from the Allies. To appeal to him would again entail delay. But it was worth trying, so, although I could not hope for a reply for at least forty-eight hours, I told ST31 to get an agent sent off to Viborg post haste, explaining our situation to our contact there, who would send a message through to the right people. Fate, however, came to our rescue in this dilemma in the most remarkable way.

* * *

On the 10th June there occurred an event of immense importance which determined the future course of events in the Petrograd region. The garrison of the fortress of Krasnaya Gorka, about which I have already written, which was situated opposite Fort Ino and guarded the Kronstadt entrance on the southern side, revolted against their Communist Commander and Commissars whom they put under arrest, and hoisted the white flag as a signal to the White and Allied forces to come to their rescue. The import of this premature rebellion against the Reds was lost upon nobody, and was regarded as the beginning of a general revolt inside Petrograd.

Its importance was also duly appreciated by our friend the Commandant, who sent an urgent summons for me to reappear in his office early that afternoon. I went there post haste alone as ST31 was busy arranging for an agent to go to Viborg. My Russian and German not being of conversation standard, we conversed through the medium of his wife, who spoke a little English. The Commandant informed me of this revolt and that in his opinion it would have the most serious consequences, for he was quite sure that the Bolsheviks in Kronstadt would plan an attack to recapture the fortress and in all probability would send their warships to bombard it from the rear. He was convinced that these warships would appear that day or the next morning, and that in these circumstances, he would

Captain Augustus Agar, V.C., D.S.O.

Beeley

Hampsheir

Marshall

Sindall

give me permission to make a reconnaissance that night off the western point of Kronstadt in the neighbourhood of Tolbuhin lighthouse, provided I returned immediately and made my report to him.

What more could I want? It was the very freedom of action that I had been praying for. I could run Peter into Petrograd and on my return make a reconnaissance in the early dawn off Tolbuhin lighthouse and report if anything had come out of Kronstadt harbour. I thanked the Commandant and added: "Now that we are working together as friends, will you please give orders that the strictest secrecy is to be preserved about our boats and post sentries to prevent anyone approaching the small yacht club harbour." Turning again to his wife, I asked if it would be possible through the Commandant's good influence to secure for me the services of a local pilot whom I would reward adequately, and that I would prefer, if possible, one of the fishermen smugglers of which I had been told there were a few in the neighbourhood.

I noticed a smile lurking round his lips. He said he would do what he could, but made no promises as he was not officially supposed to know of their existence, but as regards the boats, orders would be given to the sentries to forbid anyone to approach them except ourselves. I explained to him that we would be leaving late that night, and returned to our little *datcha* elated.

My plan was now complete in every detail except the pilot, who appeared mysteriously at our *datcha* late that evening. He was a weird looking ruffian, but he knew the coast and that was all that mattered. ST31, who had reappeared by this time, assured me that my money would buy his silence. I forget what I paid him, but it was at least ten pounds for each journey, which to him, of course, was a small fortune.

One more point, and an important one. Supposing we were delayed on the other side of the line of forts for any reason, such as engine trouble, and were overtaken by the

E

daylight on our way back, our position would have been, to say the least of it, an unpleasant one indeed. How could we reduce our chances of capture. I had thought of this when making out the plan in Helsingfors and hit upon the idea of turning our boat into a Commissar's motor launch cruising between Petrograd and Kronstadt and coming from the Petrograd direction, flying the special flag used by the Fleet Commissars. Fortunately, ST25 had given a description of this special flag when he sent out his report on the Kronstadt defences, so it was an easy matter to have a copy made and placed in the boat.

I calculated that in the event of our being spotted on the return journey, the look-out sentries of the fortresses, on seeing a motor launch coming *from* Petrograd towards Kronstadt flying the flag only Commissars were allowed to use, would naturally conclude that our boat was one of their own and would allow us a free passage through the forts. Our clothes would not betray us, as we would be wearing the same leather jackets and caps customary for every Commissar.

*   *   *

All was now set and the evening well advanced. Beeley, myself and the pilot made our way down the little path through the woods leading to the boats, where Peter was still patiently hiding since the day before. On no account must the Finnish Commandant know that we had a Russian in the boat and that that Russian was bound for Petrograd. I could not, of course, keep the secret from the Finnish smuggler who was to act as pilot, but when we got into the boat it turned out that Peter already knew the man. They had evidently done smuggling business together of the same sort over the ice during the previous winter and were in a sense 'comrades in crime', so again luck was with us. Smuggler he certainly was: but pilot—I hoped. He said he knew of three passages through the forts and was certain he could get us through. I had the chart spread out before us, and we three, Peter, the contrabandist and myself, studied it again and again tracing our route so as to make certain there could not possibly be any mistake. We also settled the exact point off Krestovsky island where Peter should land. I had checked our compass on the run down the day before and found it in good order. The little skiff or 'pram' which we carried and which I had bought in Abo, was already lashed to the deck; our emergency rations neatly stowed away under cover; our watches carefully synchronised and Lewis guns and revolvers placed handy in case of need.

In Helsingfors we had discussed the question whether we should take with us any tablets in case of capture, as all sorts of stories were current of the tortures inflicted on their prisoners by the Cheka, especially on counter-revolutionaries, as we would undoubtedly have been regarded if we fell into their hands. But we discarded the idea and decided to let things take their normal course and hope for the best.

Peter reviewed his equipment for the last time. His despatches were safely concealed in his boots, together with a note from me for ST25 in which I stated exactly the dates and time (with a corresponding Russian time) when I would return, as I could not trust this vital piece of information to his memory. The four of us sat in the boat and waited patiently for the twilight to disappear. How slow time seems to pass on these occasions! We were wearing our nondescript serge trousers, leather jacket and cap. In Petrograd we might easily have passed as ordinary people, and Peter undoubtedly as a young Red recruit, since all he had to do was to pin on his Red badges once we were on the wrong side of the line.

I looked at him and wondered what was running through his mind, he who was going to steal into the enemy's camp and risk his life more than any of us but he had obviously strong reasons. And the smuggler? To him it meant money, which was sufficient incentive, for he had evidently done this same thing in the winter across the ice when the Gulf was frozen. And my mechanic, the faithful Beeley? He thought of his engines only, I am sure, and how they would stand up to our trip there and back. And myself? I prayed for success for Peter. Would he find the nameless ST25? Would he be able to deliver his despatches and receive the answer? Would he perhaps bring him back in two nights' time when I had arranged to go in again to fetch them out?

The sun had already set over the silent pine forests that lined the Finnish shore. In the long twilight mysterious shapes appear, long shadows, spreading like tentacles in the curious mirage, gave birth to strange apparitions. The gloomy mass of Kronstadt slowly assumed an indistinct shape with the fortresses surrounding it hanging like heavy leaden weights upon the sea and growing broader than they really were as the twilight mirage increased. All was still and peaceful. Somewhere over there, across the water in that black mass, a great drama was being played, for that day, on two occasions, a white flag had definitely been seen, while farther beyond, in Krasnaya Gorka besieged men were awaiting relief. Farther still, in the vortex of that revolutionary city, was a man whom it was my mission to succour —a man whom I did not know except by a cryptic cipher letter, yet I knew must be incredibly brave and courageous. Where was he at that moment? What was he doing? Who was he? Why should it mean so much that I should be sent all the way from England on this, perhaps, foolhardy, perhaps fatal adventure?

I was leaving behind Sindall, Marshall, Hampsheir and the other mechanic, Piper, as I did not wish to risk any additional life on this, the first, journey and I left detailed instructions as to what they were to do in the event of our non-return.

I turned to Sindall: "It's ten o'clock, Cast off. We must start now. Remember, if we don't return, you are not to attempt the passage, but when ST30 finds another courier, take him across the Gulf and land him on the Estonian shore. All ready? Then start up. Goodbye."

We moved slowly and silently out of the tiny harbour with the engine throttled down to dead slow and the figures on the jetty fading into the gloom. Soon we were in the open sea and increased to twenty knots, our 250 h.p. Thornycroft engine, which never failed us, making at this moderate speed a purring hum instead of the deafening roar it made when travelling all out. My smuggler pilot directed me towards the gap between forts Nos. 6 and 7, which were closer to the Finnish shore. They loomed up nearer and nearer, ominously, silent masses of menacing masonry on either bow. I slowed down to eight knots, at which speed we made little noise, invisible in the dark waters. There was no moon and only light clouds overhead through which one could occasionally see the stars. It was an ideal night for our purposes. Was the smuggler pilot sure of himself? Upon him everything depended at this critical moment. Would we successfully pass over the sunken breakwaters? Or would we find ourselves suddenly brought up to a standstill by them or some other obstruction? Those sinister forts seemed to dive down upon us and not we towards them. Four pairs of eyes were glued on them as if hypnotized. Every nerve was tense, every muscle taut. Would there suddenly flash out the beam of a searchlight? I was ready at a second's notice to give the order "full speed ahead", yet meanwhile we were stealing forward noiselessly and invisible—could we thus creep through unobserved?

The strain was terrific. The forts were now on either hand a few hundred yards distant. Soon the black masses were retreating behind us. We had got through and were now on the 'wrong side of the line'. I could already see the shimmering lights of the port of Petrograd lying ahead of us and a little to the left. I should soon have to open up as we had still far to go and must return once more through that passage before the earliest glimmering of dawn. But I stayed my hand as long as possible, as I was anxious about the noise of the engine and waited until we had put at least three miles between the forts and ourselves, when we should be out of the range of their searchlights.

At last I gave the order, "Let her go, Beeley! Full speed!" The Thornycroft motor roared. The boat leapt forward with her nose well in the air and the stern into the trough of the wake, throwing up two large wings of water on either side. We were skimming along the surface at thirty-six knots.

In a quarter of an hour—no more—we found ourselves nearing the delta of the Neva. I reduced speed. Away to starboard were the lights of the city. I steered for the northern mouth of the river. Trees loomed up and I could soon see a low line of tall rushes fringing one of the islands on a point jutting out from the mainland where a few barges were moored in the river. I stopped the boat, we were a few hundred yards only from the shore.

No time was lost in unlashing the small pram and sliding it into the water. Peter immediately jumped in and took the oars. He was to hide the boat in the rushes and be at the same spot again in forty-eight hours. I pointed out the spot to him again to make quite sure of it and took some compass bearings.

'Do-svidanya—Godspeed! till the night after tomorrow!'

He rowed noiselessly away and disappeared into the darkness. It was already well past midnight and I could count on no more than another two hours' darkness, if that. I waited there for his signal—it came soon, three short flashes on his electric torch from the direction of the rushes. He had landed safely and now we must get back. We had the Commissars' flag ready in case we should need it and, putting on full speed again, rushed towards the entrance through which we had just come. We slowed down as we approached the forts, this time to about ten knots, which would be the speed of an ordinary

Bolshevik motor despatch boat. And again that awful feeling of tenseness. One felt one's collar too small for one's throat and had difficulty in swallowing. At last we were through and found ourselves leaving them behind. I had accomplished the first part of my task, and now for the second.

We headed towards the Tolbuhin so as to obtain what information we could about the Bolshevik ships and discover whether the Commandant's prophesy would prove to be right. As we got nearer to this end of Kronstadt, the first pale streaks of dawn appeared on the sky showing us that he was right, for I could see quite distinctly the shapes of two large ships at anchor on the far side of the lighthouse in front of two small fortresses at the entrance to the main channel. Half a mile away and surrounding them I could distinguish the shapes of smaller ships, probably destroyers, and from the position in which they were anchored it was obvious to me they could bombard Krasnaya Gorka at long range from the rear.

But what was really happening? Why had the forts allowed my boat to pass in and out? Was it perhaps that the story of the Kronstadt mutiny, coinciding as it did with the two appearances of the white flag, was true? Or was it because the watch kept by these fortresses on the northern side was less vigilant than that kept by the other fortresses, as I had hoped would be the case? The whole situation seemed to me obscure and mysterious.

Having thus got the information I wanted I turned my boat towards Terrioki. I felt it was enough for that morning and in any case I was in the middle of the Russian minefield and might at any moment strike a floating mine. It was vital that I should get back alive so as to send my news to headquarters in London, and also to let Sindall and the others know that the boat passage existed and could be relied upon. We landed safely at Terrioki about 3 a.m. The others were there to meet us and there was much rejoicing as we made our way back to the *datcha* where

Sindall had food already waiting for us, and we soon turned in and slept the sleep of the exhausted.

*　　*　　*

A few hours later I was back in the Commandant's office accompanied by ST30 who acted as interpreter. I gave the Commandant the information I had obtained of the Bolshevik battleships and destroyers, but not a word of course about the courier and our trip to Petrograd through the forts, and I indicated to him the position of the Russian ships on the Finnish charts which he had spread out before him. It was obvious from the position they had taken up that it was their intention to threaten Krasnaya Gorka from the rear. Moreover they themselves were well guarded by their own minefields and the guns of the Kronstadt fortresses. I asked him to provide me with a reliable Finnish courier to take this vital information immediately to Biorko where it would be passed on to the Admiral, emphasizing that time was important. The Commandant acceded to my request and promptly despatched a courier whom he said would deliver the information within a few hours.

Cordial relations were now established between us, and I could see that he was not only pleased but most impressed with this important piece of news that I had brought, and he went on to discuss the position further with me. He asked me if I thought the Admiral would attack these Bolshevik ships now that they had come out of Kronstadt harbour and were anchored in the open roadstead off the Tolbuhin lighthouse, but I pointed out to him that this was impossible without first sweeping up the intervening Russian minefield (quite apart from the risk of entering the minefield). I don't think he realized the difference between the British and Russian ships, until I explained that as ours were light cruisers without armour it would be foolish to match them against the Russian heavily armed and armoured battleships and cruisers.

At this point in my narrative I should make clear to the reader that others in Finland and Baltic countries, besides the Commandant of Terrioki were under the same illusion. It was a common idea amongst the White Russians that just because the British had a fleet in the Baltic, their ships were in equal strength to the Russian Fleet, and therefore should have attacked the Bolshevik ships bombarding Krasnaya Gorka immediately.

The White Russians claimed that had the British Admiral done so, Kronstadt would have surrendered to the Fleet and thus laid the way clear for their reoccupation of Petrograd and the end of the revolution. Such wishful thinking ignored completely the minefields and the fortresses. Nor had the White Russians any trained personnel to take over the fortresses, if the Bolshevik garrison, of which Trotsky himself took over personal control, had surrendered during those fateful days in June when Communist morale was at its lowest pitch. The accusations made later by White Russian organizations in London and Paris that the British failed them in the Baltic in their hour of need were utterly groundless.

The truth is that the White Russian leaders in Helsingfors were at loggerheads with each other, and their train of henchmen and hangers-on even more useless than the illiterate rabble who formed the Soviet sailors and soldiers' committees in Kronstadt and Petrograd. These however were being rapidly disciplined and organized for action by Trotsky in person.

* * *

Returning to my own immediate problem, I informed the Commandant that I could not make another reconnoitring trip for at least forty-eight hours. We required the time for making good a few minor defects in the boats and getting them ready for my next trip to bring back Peter. It was also possible that ST25 might be with him. Beeley and Piper set up a temporary workshop in the yacht club building, which the Commandant now assigned to us for our exclusive use. We proceeded to store our supplies of petrol and oil here, while we ourselves lived in the *datcha*.

Later that afternoon I received a further summons to the Commandant's Office. He told me he had just received news from Fort Ino that a boat was seen proceeding from one of the fortresses towards Ino flying a white flag, and that the boat had the appearance of a tug. He also said that he thought there was some activity amongst the Bolshevik ships, as a lot of smoke was seen to be coming from Kronstadt, and he invited me to accompany him to his private look-out station on the top of the high church steeple overlooking the little harbour of Terrioki.

We were met by an old Russian priest who guided us up the narrow, winding steps leading to a little platform at the top of the high steeple. From this superb vantage point well over five hundred feet above the harbour, we had an excellent view of Kronstadt and beyond to the opposite shore by Oranienbaum. On our left I could see through my glasses quite clearly many details of the forts through which we had passed that night. In front of us lay Kronstadt island, and, a little to the right, Tolbuhin lighthouse, with two Russian dreadnoughts and several destroyers and other smaller vessels at anchor in the vicinity. Smoke was coming from their funnels.

The Commandant gave me permission to use this magnificent look-out whenever I liked. All I had to do was to go to the little house adjoining, where lived the priest, and ask him to unlock the door leading to an inner staircase. I was indeed grateful and spent many hours there searching the island and fortresses with my glasses until they were well photographed in my mind. There was no further movement that day from the Red ships.

It was the 13th June. Later during the day ST30 and I had another long talk with the Commandant. He said he felt that anything might happen, but that situated where he was in Terrioki he was out of touch with the real position which could only be gauged at Helsingfors. He said that if it was true that Krasnaya Gorka was now in the possession of the Whites and could be relied upon to hold out, and that if a force of Estonians or White Russians, or a mixed force of both were to advance east from the Estonian frontier towards Petrograd, then it would be quite possible for a small Finnish force to advance from the north and catch the city in a pincer grip. Kronstadt would then be isolated and must inevitably surrender.

He said, however, that as far as the Finnish Government was concerned he did not think there was the slightest chance of them undertaking any such thing, as the Finnish White Volunteer Army were not anxious to extend their activities beyond the Finnish frontier. The Volunteer Army, he pointed out, was primarily concerned with what went on in Finland. He also told me that a reaction had already set in against General Mannerheim, a reaction not towards the Left but towards the Centre. All these factors, he added, definitely pointed to non-intervention on the part of Finland, so that from the military point of view, if mutiny of Krasnaya Gorka was to be exploited, military action must come from that side only. The trouble was, however, as far as he could see, the Yudenitch Army was not ready to move, and he doubted himself if it ever would.

The Commandant's summary of the situation proved to be correct. Early next morning the deep boom of heavy guns coming across the gulf could be heard. From the church tower I watched the Bolshevik battleships bombard the unfortunate Krasnaya Gorka at regular intervals. It was a terrible thing to see, knowing as I did that the fortress had no means of replying to a bombardment from the rear. There was nothing to be done. I was tempted at first to give up all idea of fetching Peter out from Petrograd that night and instead to attack those battleships with the torpedoes we carried in our boats. But I soon gave this up as our duty to ST25 must come first.

We spent the remainder of the day watching the bombardment and again making our final preparations for our dash through the forts. This took our minds off the tragedy that was being enacted before our eyes. The Commandant told me that Fort Ino had reported another tug coming out from Kronstadt with the white flag flying, but that it soon turned back. Towards the evening, bombardment ceased. There was a lot of smoke from Kronstadt which obviously indicated activity amongst the Russian Fleet. The Commandant said the British ships had arrived at Biorko less than forty miles away and kept on asking if they would attack.

About nine o'clock the smuggler pilot turned up at the *datcha* and once more we made our way along the narrow pathway through the woods to our boat and sat waiting for the twilight to turn into darkness. This time, in addition to Beeley, I took Hampsheir with me in case Peter was seen by the patrols rowing the 'pram' from the shore. I reckoned in that event we might have to make a fight for it and use our machine guns to give Peter some cover while he scrambled on board the C.M.B. Weather conditions were ideal, but we had an even shorter period of darkness in which to do the trip than on the first occasion. We adopted the plan that had proved so successful before, and luck was with us when we glided past the same two forts and then went all out to the rendezvous. Thus we saved time for the return journey and also allowed a longer interval to wait for Peter, should he be delayed. I had previously told him that at the most I could spare him half an hour.

We were soon at the mouth of the river opposite Krestovsky island. I ordered "slow", and shortly afterwards "stop". We could see the dark line of rushes which fringed the shore a quarter of a mile away, and waited anxiously for the pre-arranged signal of three short flashes. Nothing appeared, but after about five minutes I thought I saw ahead and rather farther off than I had expected, a flickering light, which might, at that distance, be the flash of an electric torch. We went ahead to close this light and, yes, there could be no doubt now, it was Peter's signal. I stopped and waited while I gave the reply signal, exactly in his direction. A few minutes later we heard the sound of oars, followed very shortly by a low hail. I heard my name called. I called out in reply, "Horosho"—'all right'— and Peter was alongside. We shook hands and lost no time in lifting the 'pram' on deck and lashing it down. Starting up the engine, I gave the order "In clutch", and away we went at full speed towards the forts on the return journey.

Peter was just about dead beat, as well he might be after the strain of his last forty-eight hours. We didn't speak at all. Hampsheir gave him some biscuits and rum and I think he went to sleep.

We were now approaching the forts, and slowed down. Hampsheir got out our Commissar's flag in case it was needed, but luck was with us again and we succeeded in getting through unobserved.

The first streaks of early dawn had already begun to make their appearance. It was now only 1.30 a.m., so I decided to make straight back for Terrioki and forego any further reconnaisance off Tolbuhin lighthouse as I did not want to betray the presence of our boats to the patrol vessels and destroyers who were guarding the Red battleships, and who, for all I knew, might be under way and following us. In any case, Peter and his precious despatches were the most important thing for the moment.

ST30 and Sindall were, as usual, waiting by the small yacht club for our return. I could see them as we slowly glided in to the little harbour, but I could see also that they were talking to the Finnish guards, and I motioned to Peter to hide below next to Beeley in the engine room. We were soon berthed alongside our other boat, and much rejoicing and shaking of hands took place when ST30 and Sindall rowed up to take us on shore. And indeed we had cause to rejoice, for we had at last established contact with ST25.

Peter immediately explained to us that for reasons of his own, ST25 had decided not to return yet but to stay in Petrograd one more month until the White Nights were over. He would then come out on one of the nights of either the 18th, 21st, or 25th July, which I had stipulated as alternatives in my message to him. The date chosen by ST25 would depend, Peter explained, upon circumstances prevailing at the time, such as the degree of vigilance on the part of the forts, or extra guards which the Bolsheviks might place for patrolling the river.

He then carefully extracted his despatches, whilst still in the boat and handed them to ST30. They were precious documents, the contents of which must be at once transmitted to London, while the despatches themselves followed later. The immediate problem before us, however, was Peter himself. To get him out of the boat and past the Finnish sentries into our *datcha* without being seen was no easy matter, but we hit upon the idea of putting him into Beeley's overall suit and taking him on shore as my mechanic, while Beeley remained in the boat. The ruse proved successful.

It might be argued here that I was double-crossing the Commandant, and so I was. But we had too much to risk by a full disclosure of all our plans, and after discussing the point with ST30, we felt justified for the present in acting as we did.

We sat up until well into the hours of the morning discussing with Peter the state of affairs in Petrograd, and I listened with horror as he recounted experience after experience during his last forty-eight hours and of his dramatic meeting with ST25 in broad daylight in a public park. But as this part of the story is fully recounted in ST25's own description of it, I will leave it at that.* It was arranged for him to leave Terrioki as soon as possible and

* See *The Story of ST25*.

wait at Helsingfors until the White Nights were over.
Our courier service by sea was temporarily closed. We had
done our job in contacting ST25 which was our main
task; the rest depended on further instructions from
London.

*   *   *

CHAPTER III

THE *OLEG*

FROM Peter's description of the state of Petrograd we learned that there were not only all sorts of rumours flying around amongst the populace, but that the Bolsheviks themselves were in daily fear of counter-revolution — hence their intensive house to house searches. Peter and ST25 left the open public parks and slept in cemeteries.

They were particularly apprehensive of another mutiny amongst the sailors at Kronstadt who were dissatisfied with their Commissars and local Soviet Committees. He said that ST25 had told him that there was brewing in Petrograd a counter-revolutionary plot, designed to synchronize with the mutiny started by the Ingelmanlanders at Krasnaya Gorka, but that unfortunately the Ingelmanlanders had made their first move before the time was ripe. All was not lost, however, if either the Kronstadt garrison mutinied or Krasnaya Gorka held out.

From our position at Terrioki, we could see that so long as the Red dreadnoughts were free to bombard Krasnaya Gorka from the rear, it would only be a matter of a few days before the fortress must capitulate, unless the Red ships were forced to retire. If this could be done it would perhaps give a lead to the Kronstadt garrison to surrender. Meanwhile, the energetic Trotsky had not been idle. Peter told me he was now at that moment rushing between Krasnaya Gorka and the outer defences of Petrograd instilling, by threats and cajolery, fresh heart into the Red Army soldiers and that if anything was to be done from our side, it must be done now. I thought immediately of our two C.M.B.s and the two torpedoes we carried. Surely they could provide, like a couple of hornets, the very

C.M.B. leaving Osea Island for the Baltic and the Kronstadt Raid

C.M.B. hoisted at davits of a cruiser to fit new propeller

The cockpit of C.M.B.4

C.M.B.s lying alongside H.M.S. *Vindictive* in Biorko during cold weather.
Note Gordon Steele's boat on left with a V.C. on the wind screen

C.M.B. 4 travelling at high speed

sting required to drive those Red bombarding ships away
and help the fortress to hold out.

I was now faced with the problem of taking a vital
decision. Should I or should I not, singlehanded and
without orders, set out to attack the bombarding battleships? I was comforted with the thought that, if I took
the matter into my own hands, our Admiral would, I felt
sure, approve of my action and back me to the hilt. What
would he do in my position, I asked myself? Surely he
would never hesitate. Yet my orders from London were
specific and confined me to intelligence work only. Could I
go counter to them? I immediately sent ST31 to our
consulate in Viborg with a cipher message to London
asking permission to attack, adding that I had already
fulfilled the primary task of effecting communication
with ST25 in Petrograd. Some hours must elapse
before the reply could be received, and these we spent
preparing the boats with torpedoes and snatching a few
hours sleep.

ST31 and I again appeared before the Commandant at
noon when I reported little change except a lot of smoke
and activity in the inner harbour and dockyards of Kronstadt. Nor was there any activity on the part of the Kronstadt
fortresses on our side between Kronstadt and Terrioki. The
Commandant told me that the Bolsheviks had reinforced
their guards on the Finnish frontier during the last twenty-
four hours, evidently expecting a move against them from
the Finnish Volunteer Army, but as far as he was concerned
his orders were definitely to stand on the defensive and take
no provocative action. He said the Commandant at Fort Ino
was anxious lest the Reds sent out from Kronstadt patrol
boats or destroyers close to the Finnish shore, in which event
the Ino Commandant would fire on them. Such action on his
part might be taken as provocative. Was I quite sure that
the presence of my two boats at Terrioki was still unknown
to the Bolsheviks? To which I replied that their only
source of information could be from Terrioki itself, and

F

therefore would he again take special measures with his guards to keep everyone away from the harbour.

We left the office together and ascended the church steeple. It was now eleven o'clock in the morning and so far all had been quiet. I was beginning to think that this lull was an indication that the Red ships had abandoned the bombardment, but no sooner had we reached our look-out post than the familiar boom of the guns reached us across the intervening sea. The bombardment had recommenced. We watched it for several hours. There was nothing to be done except wait for the reply from London which came through late in the evening by a message from Viborg to ST30 who was waiting for it in Terrioki. It simply stated "BOATS TO BE USED FOR INTELLIGENCE PURPOSES ONLY — STOP — TAKE NO ACTION UNLESS SPECIALLY DIRECTED BY S.N.O. BALTIC."

I discussed this with Sindall. The second sentence left us a loophole, but as there was no time now in which to go to Biorko and get a specific order from the Admiral, I must make the decision myself. Yet I was quite certain in my mind what his wishes would be and decided to attack the Red ships that very night.

The C.M.B.s were ready, torpedoes primed and final adjustments made, and I knew, as far as the personnel was concerned, that they were ready and eager for the action. There was to be no Secret Service about this business. Our uniforms were in the boat and would be worn on reaching the open sea, and we would fly in each boat a small white ensign.

Once the decision had been made I felt tremendously relieved in my mind. I knew we would be making our contribution in helping the Admiral and his ships to carry out their difficult task. There was yet time to save the fortress, and if successful, the result might have a profound effect on the future course of events. I immediately informed the Commandant that both boats would be going out on patrol that night and would return in the early hours of the

morning. Waiting is always the most difficult part of any
operation especially one like this with so many 'ifs' about
it, so we busied ourselves for the remainder of the evening
doing final odd jobs and getting ready. We were taking no
pilots, as I had now in my mind an exact picture of the
coast as far as Tolbuhin lighthouse. The rest depended on
ourselves and luck of which we needed plenty.

Sindall and I worked out our tactics and how to approach
and move after delivering our attack. We decided to
concentrate on one target, as I felt it would be better to
fire two torpedoes into one ship with a greater chance of
sinking her, than chancing one torpedo against separate
targets.

As for our plan we decided to attack just before early
dawn when there would be sufficient light from the
westward to show up our targets and yet insufficient light
to the eastward for our boats to be seen by the destroyers.
The short hours of darkness kept us at Terrioki until just
before midnight and I tried to get in some sleep, but it was
impossible, partly because of the daylight, partly because
of excitement and partly because the bombardment was
still going on at irregular intervals up till 10.30 p.m. when
I went to the church steeple for one last look. Eventually
it was time to go and when clear of the jetty we headed
for the open sea and Tolbuhin lighthouse, our ensigns
flying and our personnel dressed in our leather coats and
uniform caps.

All went well for the first half hour. Then I noticed
Sindall's boat dropping astern, so I turned round and
went back to see what was the matter. His boat had hit an
obstruction. In the darkness it was impossible to see what
this was, but it was probably a floating mine which luckily
had not gone off. The force of the impact had broken the
propeller shaft of his boat, so there was nothing left to do
but abandon the enterprise for the night and tow his boat
back to Terrioki. It was cruel, hard luck on Sindall and
his crew.

We reached Terrioki by daylight, very crestfallen and downhearted. Piper—Sindall's mechanic—immediately stripped and dived overboard to examine the extent of the damage and I knew by the look on his face when he came to the surface that there was no hope. The propeller shaft had been fractured clean through! So there we were deprived by one unlucky stroke, of the use of one of our boats and 50 per cent of our striking power.

"Well," said Sindall, "that's that." But I could see that he meant far more than those words implied. I knew there was a spare propeller and shaft on the way out from England, but it would be at Helsingfors and would take at least a fortnight before we could get it fitted.

Meanwhile, what was to be done? Could I risk my one remaining boat? If I lost it, what about ST25 and the arrangements made to fetch him out in July? I felt that the more important of the two problems at the immediate moment was the relief of Krasnya Gorka. Much could happen in the next three weeks between now and the middle of July. I decided to try again, this time in my own boat, alone. I had already sent a message informing the Admiral we were going to attack on the night of the 15th-16th June, and I now sent another, explaining that one boat was out of action with a broken propeller and I would attack again on the night of the 16th-17th. I argued to myself that if my attack failed and we were unable to return, there was yet time for Sindall to get his boat repaired and make the connection with ST25 in Petrograd in July as arranged.

There was no bombardment the next morning, but from our familiar look-out position we could see columns of smoke issuing from the Red ships near Tolbuhin lighthouse, indicating that they were on the move. Later in the afternoon the battleships had disappeared from view, so I concluded they had returned to the naval harbour in Kronstadt. They were replaced by a large armoured cruiser—the *Oleg*—and the same escort of destroyers and patrol vessels could be

seen quite clearly at anchor close by her forming a protective
screen.

The Commandant was inclined to think that the bombardment had either ceased for lack of ammunition in
which case the battleships would very shortly reappear,
or that it had been successful and that Krasnaya Gorka
was now back in the hands of the Reds. Nothing happened
until the afternoon, when the *Oleg* fired a few salvos in the
direction of Krasnaya Gorka, from which we concluded
that the fortress was still holding out.

The remainder of that afternoon and evening passed off
without any untoward incident, though I heard afterwards
that a small patrol vessel (the *Kitteboi*) had emerged from
the Russian shore in the neighbourhood of Krasnaya Gorka
and proceeded westwards towards Biorko with a white flag
flying. This vessel surrendered to the British and was
afterwards turned over to the Estonians. Her captain was
an ex-Russian naval officer.

By nine o'clock in the evening the weather changed and a
nasty southerly wind began to spring up which caused a
short, choppy sea to run in the Gulf, but not sufficient to
interfere seriously with the progress of our boats.

As on the previous evening, Hampsheir, Beeley and I
waited in our C.M.B. in the shelter of the harbour until
just before midnight, when, once more, we set out and
headed for the Tolbuhin lighthouse. This time we were
alone and the object of our attack was the cruiser *Oleg*.
Arriving off the lighthouse we could clearly see the destroyer
screen ahead of us. It was necessary to pass through it in
order to reach a position from which we could fire our
torpedo at the cruiser. I slowed down to minimize the
risk of noise and spray which, with a strong wind dead
ahead of us and a high speed, was being thrown up over
our heads. We were now creeping through the destroyers
in precisely the same way as we crept through the forts on
our way to Petrograd, and all seemed to be going well
when I suddenly felt the whole boat quiver and shake. I

thought we had hit something and stopped. Hampsheir appeared from below the hatch with an agonized look on his face.

"The charge has fired, sir," he said.

I must explain here that we had in the boat an ingenious device for firing the torpedo by ejecting it from the stern with a hydraulic rammer. The impulse by means of which this rammer was propelled was supplied by firing a small cordite cartridge in a cylinder which created a pressure against the head of the rammer. Somehow or other, in loading the cartridge, Hampsheir had accidentally fired it, and it was this that caused the shock we had felt. Fortunately, in addition to these mechanical arrangements there was also fitted in the boat two stout iron stops operated by a lever near the steering wheel which held the torpedo in the boat, irrespective of the rammer, *provided the stops were down*. Fortunately, I had placed this lever in the 'down' position so that when the cartridge prematurely fired, the only result was a severe concussion to the hull of the boat and a tremendous shock to Hampsheir who must have injured his hand.

I told him the torpedo was still safe in the boat. This good news reassured him, and I then ordered Beeley to help him extract the fired cartridge and put in another one—a difficult operation with the boat rolling in the sea. It was dark, and their hands were cold. I waited for what seemed an interminable time, though it must have been only ten or fifteen minutes. All through this time of intolerable suspense my eyes were on the destroyers on either side of us, now distant only two to three hundred yards. Ahead I could dimly see the silhouette of our target the cruiser *Oleg*, which I was about to attack.

We might at any moment be seen, as it was then just before one o'clock in the morning and the first streaks of early dawn were due to appear. Beeley remained wonderfully calm. There was nothing to be said. It was a time for deeds and not words. At last Hampsheir popped up from the hatch. "It's all right, sir, we have reloaded." With a sigh of relief, I slipped in the clutch. Throwing all caution to the winds, I put on full speed and headed straight for the *Oleg*, which was now clearly visible. In a few moments we were nearly on top of her. I fired my torpedo less than five hundred yards away, just as the first shot from her guns was fired at us in return. Then I quickly put the helm over, turning almost a complete circle, and, with the sea now following us, headed back westwards towards the same direction from which I had approached.

We looked back to see if our torpedo had hit, and saw a large flash abreast the cruiser's foremost funnel, followed almost immediately by a huge column of black smoke reaching up to the top of her mast. The torpedo had found its mark. We tried to give three cheers but could scarcely hear ourselves for the din of the engines. Yet we could hear the whistle of shells overhead, telling us that both forts and destroyers were firing at us. But in the uncertain light just before early dawn, speed made us a very difficult target to hit. We carried on in the direction of Biorko Sound as I wanted the forts to think that that was where we had come from instead of Terrioki, and we did not turn round to the northward until we were well out of sight of them.

Eventually we reached the yacht club towards three o'clock in the morning. Our comrades showered congratulations on our success. We were terribly cold and soaked to the skin, but willing hands helped to moor up and service the boat and gave us hot cocoa. Hampsheir was in a poor way, principally from shock, and I am sorry to say has never since recovered. The boat suffered no damage and was fit for service again almost immediately. Marshall told me that he was watching during the night from the church tower and with his glasses actually saw the flash and high column of black smoke from the *Oleg* as our torpedo struck home. It was broad daylight by the time we got to our *datcha*. One of our party took a photograph of us three, which I have to this day. And at last we slept the sleep of the exhausted.

But not for long, as I was again summoned before the Commandant early in the morning. It was a curious interview.

"The Commandant at Fort Ino saw the forts firing and the general commotion caused by the sinking of the *Oleg*," he said. "Can you explain to me what took place?"

I had to do some hard thinking because up to now I had kept the Commandant in ignorance of the fact that our boats carried torpedoes under tarpaulin covers. I decided once more to be frank and told him the whole story.

He was at first incredulous, for he could hardly believe that such fragile craft as ours could, single handed, attack and sink a large eight thousand ton armoured cruiser. I then explained that each boat carried a torpedo in a narrow trough which normally was covered by a canvas cover and it was with this torpedo we had sunk the cruiser. There was an awkward pause. I could see he was still perplexed. He pointed to my civilian clothes, saying: "How can you, in those clothes, commit an act of war? What is my position when it is known that by giving you harbourage and help I permitted you to do so? There are," he continued, "many Bolshevik spies near the frontier and, if this is known, perhaps the Kronstadt forts may retaliate by bombarding Terrioki, for the defence of which I am responsible."

I saw his dilemma and hastily explained to him how, although in Terrioki we had with his help to assume the guise of civilians for the purpose of getting information, once in the open sea we put on our uniforms, flew the White Ensign and transformed ourselves into a fighting unit from the British Navy. "But," I added, "our activities have not ceased and there may be other opportunities of repeating this venture. So will you please do everything in your power to help us to keep our secret." I explained that it was only in this way we can drive the Red ships back into

Kronstadt and so make certain of the defence of the Finnish coast, which was the concern of both of us.

I suppose I must have expressed myself rather forcibly, for when I had finished, he rose from his chair, put his hand on my shoulder and said something in either Finnish or Russian which I couldn't understand. ST30 who was with me during this interview told me afterwards that he had paid me a handsome compliment, repeating a well-known saying in Russian which meant that he felt himself in the presence of a brave man. He went on to say that he was concerned only with the defence of the Frontier and of the Finnish coast and that any act of mine which helped him in securing this defence was one which he would welcome and one which he felt sure the Finnish Government would appreciate. But he was now doubly concerned as to our safety and urged me to take both boats back to Biorko as soon as possible, pointing out that the Bolshevik aeroplane base at Oranienbaum was only a matter of thirty miles away, and it would be an easy task, if news of our whereabouts trickled through, for the Bolsheviks to bomb the harbour.

"That will suit me very well," I replied, "but may I stay two days longer to repair one boat which has been damaged?" I pointed out to him that it was imperative for me to get to Biorko for a personal interview with the Admiral and begged him to help me in this by giving me some form of transport over land. I also asked him to disclose our activities to the Commandant at Fort Ino and to stress to him the necessity of giving both boats a clear passage on our way past his fort.

He was most helpful. A Finnish car was placed at my disposal to take me part of the way to the village of Koivisto, after which it was arranged that I should complete the journey on horseback. He also told me he would call up the Commandant of the Finnish aeroplane station not far from Biorko Sound and ask him to give me any help he could in case I wanted to make a flight over the Gulf and verify the result of my attack on the *Oleg*. He proved indeed to be a good friend.

* * *

Leaving Sindall in charge of our party, I set out for Biorko arriving late that evening after a tiring ride through part of the forest. From Koivisto two cruisers and several destroyers could be seen in the Bay, and the oiler which was so familiar to me anchored at the tail end. I went down to the pier and asked the midshipman in charge of one of the naval boats if he would take me on board the oiler explaining that I had come from Viborg with an urgent message from our consul for the master.

The boat belonged to H.M.S. *Dragon* and although the young officer regarded me with suspicion, he gave me a passage at the same time telling me he would inform his captain. He said that they had just arrived in harbour and were leaving again in two hours' time adding that the flagship was due in the following day.

The master and crew of the oiler were very pleased to see me and welcomed me back. I was dead beat, badly in need of a shave and clean up and about to start on one when the *Dragon*'s boat reappeared alongside with a message from her captain that he wished to see me and know who I was, so back I had to go.

Captain F. A. Marten, C.M.G., or 'Figgy' as he was known to his intimates, was one of the most efficient captains in the Navy and a great friend of Captain French. Had I not convinced him of my identity, I might well have spent that night in one of the *Dragon*'s cells, but once convinced as to who I was and what I was doing, and (even more important to him) that I was working under the wing of his friend Captain 'Froggie' French (Figgy and Froggie were team mates in the *Britannia*) all was plain sailing and he was kindness itself. His ship had to rejoin the Admiral at sea so I was transferred back to the oiler where I spent the night, and resolved the following day to visit the Finnish aeroplane station and ask the commander to fly me over the Tolbuhin lighthouse. At least I would have one night's sleep, which I was badly in need of.

The master of the oiler gave me his cabin for the night while he slept in the charthouse. He said I looked a sorry sight and, indeed, I must have, for I hadn't taken off my clothes for five days and a patchy growth of hair had already made its appearance on my face. He was helpful and kind.

I left him early next morning and found my way, after a great deal of trouble, to the Finnish Aerodrome, where thanks to my friend the Commandant at Terrioki, I was at once made welcome. The Finnish Commandant, Captain Hjelt, afterwards Chargé d'Affaires at the Finnish Legation in London, spoke excellent English and very kindly gave up his seat in a Finnish aeroplane in my favour. He explained to me that this aeroplane was to make one of its normal flights over the Gulf that morning. They had strict orders to avoid flying over the Kronstadt defences, which were, of course, Russian territory, but he said with a wink that if the pilot made an error of a few miles so as to give me a view over the Tolbuhin area, he would ask no questions: it was the pilot's risk, for he knew that the anti-aircraft batteries mounted on the fortresses were in good order and most efficient. There was no mistaking where his sympathies lay nor those of the pilot Arthur Reichel, a brave and skilful Swedish aviator who volunteered to fly with Mannerheim's army. The machines were German and were of considerable use to the Fleet later in the year when the Admiral dropped leaflets from them over the Kronstadt garrison inviting their surrender.

In the meantime he flew me over the gulf making directly for the Tolbuhin lighthouse and within close range of the outer fortresses guarding the South Channel.

As we approached the spot where, just over twenty-four hours before I had fired my torpedo at the *Oleg*, I held my breath in excitement and anticipation. The machine descended to two thousand feet, and how shall I express my feelings when, in the exact position where I had attacked her, we could see quite clearly the hulk of the cruiser lying on her side like a large dead whale on the bottom of the sea. So my effort was a complete success. I had dealt a blow to the Red fleet. For a moment I experienced a feeling of horror at the thought that it was I who was responsible for the fate of this ship and probably the deaths of men inside her. But these feelings were soon dispelled after turning southwards when we flew over the large bastion of Krasnaya Gorka. Imagine our dismay when instead of a white flag which we expected to see flying there were at least two if not three RED ones instead. So after all our hopes the fortress was recaptured. My sinking of the *Oleg* then had not sufficed to drive the Red attackers away *in time*. My first reaction—of horror—at seeing the sunken ship gave way to feelings of disappointment and anger. I thought of the brave defenders of the fallen fortress, who had held out patiently waiting for help, but just not long enough, and completely unaware of the effort that had been made to relieve them.

It did not even occur to me that we had been flying well within the range of the Kronstadt anti-aircraft batteries, neither did I notice until after Reichel had landed me that the aeroplane was a German military one with two large black crosses painted on its wings. Captain Hjelt and his brother officers congratulated me when the pilot told them of the sunken ship. "Well," Hjelt said, "you will now find that will be the last you will see of them."

There have been and still are several conflicting accounts of the recapture of Krasnaya Gorka and the subsequent fate of Nedlukov and his white Ingelmanlanders. The story current at the time was that in spite of an honourable condition of surrender given to the Reds, they were murdered *en masse* in the same gunpits which they had for days so gallantly defended, having at first (so the Estonian Admiral, Pitka, later assured us) disposed of the locks of the guns. Another version was that the White Ingelmanlanders murdered their prisoners, of which they had between two and three hundred in the fortress, and then escaped over the frontier while Nedlukov surrendered and was subsequently shot by the Bolsheviks.

The truth probably lies midway between the two versions but the full force of this tragedy—for such it was—whereby the key to any advance by land on Petrograd was lost, was never quite realized by the White Russians until later in October. Nedlukov's men surrendered, not from lack of ammunition but from shortage of food and water and a low morale.

It was past midnight when H.M.S. *Delhi* accompanied by H.M.S. *Dragon* anchored in the bay, but in spite of the late hours I felt sure the Admiral would see me, and rowed myself across in a skiff. He had already turned in for the night but when the flag lieutenant told him I was there, he sent for me immediately. I well remember the scene in his sleeping cabin as he sat up in bed at that late hour and dragged from me every detail of the events of the last week and especially of the sinking of the *Oleg*. I could see how pleased he was. As he aptly put it, "This enables me to show them that I have a sting which I can always use if they ever show their noses out of Kronstadt." He told me he approved absolutely of everything I had done, and that if there was trouble with the Foreign Office about exceeding my instructions he would make my position quite clear and stand by me.

As for Krasnaya Gorka, it was a dreadful business, he said, but from his point of view another story altogether. He wondered how long the fortress would have remained in the hands of the White Russians, even supposing there had been no bombardment at all. For there was no White Russian army behind it and there was the ever-present difficulty of reconciling the White Russians, the Ingelman-landers and the Estonians, who were always quarrelling with each other. He advised me to return to Terrioki, pick up my two boats and bring them back to Biorko, where I could have them repaired by the artificers of his flagship or by some other ship which he would detail to look after us. I could wait there, he said, under his wing, until we were ready to recommence our activities next month when the white nights were over.

I came away from that rather strange interview (for it ended at 2 a.m. in the morning) with a feeling of exhilaration. I went in feeling depressed, apprehensive, and a little frightened—and I left in an exactly opposite mood. The reason for this, of course, was that this man, who was modesty and courage itself, had the marvellous gift of inspiring others. When in describing our attack on the *Oleg* I came to the point where we made our effort to give three cheers and told him laughingly how the cheers were drowned by the noise of the Thornycroft engines, he said simply: 'I'll see that put right.' I could not make out what he meant at the moment, but when two days later I brought both boats back to Biorko, one in tow of the other, and we passed through the lines of his ships, the whole fleet manned ship and cheered us. Such moments as these can never be forgotten.

*   *   *

Next day I was back in Terrioki. Thanks to Paul Hjelt and my Finnish friends, the journey was made much easier for me as I was given a car this time for the whole trip. Getting into it I was surprised to see two large and ominous looking axes strapped on either side. On asking what they were there for, I was told that we might need them on our way through the forest as the road often dwindles into a narrow track which occasionally had to be widened by cutting down here and there an old spruce or fir tree. In spite of this, it was a most delightful drive, for it was then the middle of summer and the country at its best. Everywhere there was forest or green fields which afforded wonderful pasture for the occasional herds of cattle. Berries and flowers grew in profusion.

Sindall had the boats ready and we arranged to leave next day for Biorko with my boat towing the damaged one.

I had one more interview with the Commandant who, as usual, was most kind and courteous. He told me that during the last three days a number of refugees had tried to escape across the Russian frontier into Finland, but with the exception of a few, had been either caught or shot on the wrong side of the frontier. The few that had succeeded were now in his concentration camp and he related the most harrowing tales of the new Red purges ordered by the Petrograd Soviet as the result of the mutiny in Krasnaya Gorka. Trotsky, it was said, was already reorganizing the Red army and instituting strict measures of discipline in the fleet. To make quite sure of good professional leadership, he had seized the families of ex-Russian naval officers as hostages and in this way forced the officers to take duty in the Red ships. In fact the only result of the Krasnaya Gorka incident was to stiffen up the Bolshevik defence and increase their morale. If the Yudenitch army was to move, it must move now, while there was still a chance before resistance would be too strong.

I had by now become quite attached to this man who had, in helping me, taken a chance. It was obvious that he was professionally a most capable soldier and had moreover a sound knowledge of the whole military situation prevailing in the Gulf of Finland. He gave me several messages for the Admiral. The first was a suggestion that a small party of British sailors should land and establish a look-out position at a point called Stirrs Point where there was a Finnish lighthouse with a small building adjoining it. There they could live and be in telephonic communication with Biorko. The second message was that there was a level piece of ground near Terrioki which, if necessary, could be transferred into a temporary landing ground should the Admiral wish to make use of it. And the third was that in my absence he would telephone any information of importance, such as the moves of Bolshevik ships, to either Stirrs Point to be passed on direct to the Admiral, or to the Finnish headquarters at Koivisto, whence this information could be transmitted through a Finnish Liaison Officer.

All this was to the good and I knew it would help us. I told him I would be returning in a month's time, when the White Nights were over, for more reconnaissance work, and that meanwhile I would be grateful if he would still keep the Finnish Guard on the old disused yacht club, where I was leaving a few stores. ST30 or ST31 would remain behind in the *datcha*.

I did not want my boats to be seen at sea during the daylight, so left that evening for Biorko with Sindall's boat in tow, arriving in the Sound early next morning. Whom should I find on guard outside but the same destroyer which had towed us from Biorko to Helsingfors H.M.S. *Voyager*. We passed quite close to her and I could see Stuart from the bridge summon all the sailors on deck to give us three cheers. We were very touched by the compliment, but there was more to follow as we entered the harbour and passed through the fleet. Cheer upon cheer came from each ship until finally we brought the boats alongside H.M.S. *Dragon*. It was a wonderful welcome and it is difficult to describe the kindness and attention we received from everybody.

I left Sindall with the boats in Biorko to have them refitted and went to Helsingfors where Peter had preceded me to get contact with ST27 in Stockholm and to make fresh plans.

*   *   *

We had now three to four weeks in which to complete the boats' refitting. My boat needed a new engine which had already been despatched from Osea Island, while Sindall's boat required a new propeller and shaft. Sindall and Marshall took over this part of the business and with our two mechanics, did it remarkably well. My boat, No. 4, was towed to Helsingfors and the new engine put in at the

Finnish Naval Arsenal where the authorities were only too anxious to help us in every way.

Hampsheir had to be sent into a Finnish Sanatorium to recover from shock. Luckily there was an English matron there who looked after him. I divided my time between Biorko and Helsingfors with one visit to Revel.

*   *   *

CHAPTER IV

BALTIC IMBROGLIO

GEOGRAPHICALLY, the littoral of the Baltic Sea was at this time about to be shared by no less than eight independent and sovereign States where, hitherto, it had been under the control of three, viz. Germany, Russia and Sweden. The new entries were Finland, Poland, and the three Baltic States of Estonia, Latvia and Lithuania.

Politically, the new set-up was due to President Wilson's principle of The Self-Determination of Nations, but in putting it into effect, the Allies drove a wedge of four buffer states between Russia and Germany which appeared at first sight to be an easy and satisfactory solution to the twin problems of stopping the spread of Russian revolutionary doctrines to the West, and halting German expansion to the East. There is no doubt that if left unchecked, German militarism would have found compensation in the Baltic States for what they had lost as a result of War One in Alsace-Lorraine and their colonies.

Of the four countries who were to form this wedge, only Poland was able to look after herself and resist pressure from either side—though later in the year the Poles were forced to commence an offensive-defensive war against the Soviet. The remaining three, Estonia, Latvia and Lithuania, were not in the same happy position. They were threatened in the East and South by Soviet Russia, and in the West by Baltic Germans. They were backward in political development because for centuries the people had lived as subject races under Tsarist Russia or the German Baltic Barons.

They had no constitutional experience to guide them, no army or navy and no money, but they had, in common with their neighbour Finland on the opposite side of the gulf, three valuable assets, a natural desire and discipline for law and order, a love of their land and most important, a seaboard.

It was this access to the sea which formed the basis of their freedom and economic life, without it they inevitably would be strangled by one or both of their powerful neighbours. Defence of their ports and harbours therefore, and freedom to import and export what they wanted, was obviously the first essential on which these Baltic States could start a new national life, and it was left to the British Navy to help them carry it out by keeping the ring clear of intruders.

This problem although a strategic one, was complicated by other political factors not least of which were the cross currents of political opinions in England. The bulk of the British public, for want of official guidance, was under the delusion that because part of the British fleet remained in Baltic waters, our ships were sent there *solely* to support the White Russian interests against Red Soviet Russia and restore the old régime.

There was, in consequence, in England, one faction of the public and Press led by Mr. Churchill which strongly held this view and urged Great Britain to support her old Ally of 1914 and escort the White Russians back to Petrograd by force. The Labour Party and the extreme Left however were loud in their demands for 'hands off Russia'.

This conflict of opinion served only to weaken our Government's policy and turn it into one of expediency instead of objectivity, which in its turn reacted on the position of the Admiral, whose task in the Baltic was to keep the sea free.

People at home were much too engrossed with their immediate problems of demobilization and the khaki election to worry about what was happening in the Baltic. All they cared about was that Britain should not be dragged into another war and the Baltic seemed to many a not unlikely place if we were to involve ourselves too deeply in Russian affairs, whatever sentiments we might have

had for an old ally of 1914. The accusing fingers of the
White Russian emigrées in London and Paris who felt we
were deserting them in their hour of need, were not taken
too seriously. After all, we had done our best in Archangel
and were helping Kolchak the White Russian leader with
money and equipment. More than that they could not
possibly expect.

I will not weary the reader with a long technical analysis of
the strategic set-up: a brief summary only should suffice to
show the basis on which the Admiral had to make his
decisions having regard always to the size of the force he
had at his disposal and the political cross-currents in
London, Paris and Helsingfors, where the White Russian
General Yudenitch had his headquarters.

In the Baltic Sea which runs north-east and south-west
there are three gulfs of strategic interest. The Gulf of
Finland in the north, the Gulf of Danzig in the south and
the Gulf of Riga in the centre. Communication from one
end to the other lies along a line of approximately a thousand
miles from Copenhagen to the Gulf of Finland. From
this vital line of sea communication sidelines run out to
the ports of those States who have sea-boards converging
more or less on the Gulf of Riga in the centre.

The whole area was strewn with thousands of mines laid
indiscriminately during the war by both Russians and
Germans, many adrift from their moorings. So the first
task of the Navy was to ensure a safe route along this line
and its subsidiaries to the principal ports of the Baltic
States. No mean task when the Admiral had only limited
forces and few mine-sweepers, but it was accomplished
before the end of the summer not without losing several
ships and two cruisers seriously damaged. The channel thus
made was known as the Red Route because it ended in
Petrograd and opened up Finland and the Baltic States to
trade and commerce with the rest of the world.

This was the first step towards economic independence of
the people living in these Baltic countries, and their

national life from then on should have progressed on normal lines had it not been for the unfortunate treaty of Brest-Litovsk made after the revolution between Bolshevik Russia and Germany. This permitted German troops to occupy Lithuania and Latvia, including Mitau, the coastal towns of Memel and Libau and the entire Gulf of Riga, while the Russians accepted a new frontier farther to the east.

With the Armistice in November 1918 and the defeat of Germany in the West, the Baltic States were left in a state of flux, the Russian Bolsheviks ready to march in and regain what they had lost at Brest-Litovsk as the Germans withdrew in places back to their old frontiers, each side looting as they advanced or retired until nothing was left to the people except bare earth.

It mattered little to the Balts, Letts or Lithuanians who were their masters as both overlords were equally hated, but to the Allies it mattered a great deal because Allied policy of the *Cordon Sanitaire* confined Russia strictly to her old frontiers to stop the spread of Communism to the West. Britain and France therefore struck a mild bargain with the Germans in the Armistice terms of surrender by allowing them to remain in occupation, "until such time as we decided they should leave": and at this point there enters the picture the sinister figure of General Von der Goltz, Commander in Chief of the German forces in the Baltic, including the famous Iron Division.

Von der Goltz, like other high ranking German generals refused to admit that Germany lost the War. To them they were defeated *on the western front only*. They argued that the Armistice terms did not apply to the eastern front where they were free to recoup themselves for the loss of their colonies at the expense of the Baltic States, particularly Latvia and Lithuania. German troops were in actual possession of all the Baltic ports except Revel, which had been rescued from the Bolsheviks only in the nick of time by a British cruiser squadron as early as February 1919, and restored to the Estonians, who afterwards renamed the town Tallin as the capital of their country.

Von der Goltz, ignoring his War Minister, Herr Noske, and the central government in Berlin, was determined to hold these ports and create for some future time a *Balticum* for Germany. Knowing that to suit a temporary convenience of their own the Allies were using his occupation troops inland to keep the Russians out, he used every artifice his mind could devise through prevarication and delay to hold the ports, as they were his only means of communication and therefore vital for the occupation forces. As a general he was extremely competent, but in his self-imposed task he had perforce to resort to double dealing and unscrupulous methods which made him a thorn in the side of our Admiral. However, Von der Goltz had found his match. The Admiral was equally determined that the ports should be handed back to their rightful owners as starting points for their new governments.

The first clash came in April at Libau where Von der Goltz seized the town and harbour after turning out Ulmanis and his local Council. The process was repeated at Memel, Windau and Riga but with the solid argument of British cruisers deployed off the ports, the Admiral obtained from Von der Goltz towards the end of May an undertaking to hand over Libau, Memel and Riga to the local people, and arrangements were put in hand to help them govern and defend themselves. Much depended, however, on the value of the German general's word. It was at this time that ice conditions in the gulf of Finland began to ease sufficiently to allow ships of the Russian Baltic fleet to leave Kronstadt: and once again destroyers of the Red fleet supported by heavier units came out and bombarded the Estonian coast between Narva and Revel. The Admiral moved his light cruiser squadron immediately to Revel to meet this new challenge on the spot, leaving Von der Goltz to keep his word about the ports, and a series of naval activities now commenced in the form of 'tip and run' raids from Kron-

stadt. Each time the Russian destroyers and cruiser *Oleg*
appeared, our ships went after them when either one or
both of their battleships *Petropavlosk* and *Andre Perosvanni*
emerged from behind their minefields, and after engaging
our ships at long range, retired again. Occasionally they
scored a hit but not often and after several skirmishes—
the last being on 31st May—gave up this form of tactic
hoping we would lose ships patrolling off the minefields.

At this point, as I have already explained, the Admiral
decided to move to the more advanced base at Biorko to
keep a closer watch on the Russian Fleet lest any of their
units should come out. This was now his main problem
and further complicated by the activities of two Russian
submarines one of which was lost on their own minefields.
We lost one of ours the L.55 which the Russians claimed to
have sunk.

It might be said that our Admiral ran grave risks by
moving his fleet so far away from the Baltic ports. He was
inferior in strength to the Russian fleet in any event as they
had battleships and he had none, but he would have been
weaker still if he had divided his cruisers between the
Baltic ports and Kronstadt. He chose instead the bolder
course of blockading the Russian fleet in Kronstadt while
he waited for a further reinforcement of cruisers. They
arrived from home later in the summer and were detached
under Commodore A. M. Duff to Libau and the Baltic
ports to deal with Von der Goltz who, as might be expected,
was making trouble all round. Meanwhile, thanks to the
efforts of our Minister in Helsingfors Mr. H. M. Bell, the
Admiral with the help of the Finns turned Biorko into a
base safe from submarines by placing a boom across the
entrance, and it was from here that he directed all sea
operations in the Baltic.

His responsibilities increased daily; organizing safe routes
to the ports and the supply of arms and food; providing
support for Allied Military Missions and sub-missions at
Danzig and Helsingfors; and watching the Germans in the

East and the Russian fleet in Kronstadt. Not a day passed without a call for help or naval assistance from some direction or another, and whether it was made from an allied military mission or a friendly Baltic State such support as the Admiral could give was invariably forth-coming.

With the arrival of General Sir Hubert Gough's Military Mission in June some of the load was taken off his shoulders, especially dealings with Generals Von der Goltz and Yudenitch; but in the end whenever action was required it had to be decided and taken by the Admiral himself who wryly remarked to me on one occasion that these generals could never stay in the same place. They always want to move from one port to another, preferably in a British cruiser!

Such then were the principal factors upon which the Admiral had to take his decisions, and he decided quite rightly that his best plan was to settle accounts with the Red Fleet first and to deal with the Germans in the Western Baltic afterwards.

* * *

It was during this period of the 'white nights' when I was fitting my boat with a new propeller shaft in the Finnish naval arsenal at Helsingfors and Sindall refitting the other boat at Biorko, that I received an urgent summons from the Admiral.

This time the interview concerned the possibility of getting from England a whole flotilla of C.M.B.s and using them, as I did against the *Oleg*, in a full-scale attack on the Russian fleet in Kronstadt harbour who were tying up his ships to Biorko. He wanted the answer to many questions. Were the boats and crews available? How long would it take to get them out? How would they come? What type of boat would be best? etc. etc. Sporadic raids by one or even two boats he said were not good enough. Something on a larger scale was wanted if the Bolshevik fleet was to be put out of action, and to be successful that something had to be unexpected. He had thought about this ever since I had sunk the *Oleg* with one small boat.

The brilliant attack on Zeebrugge harbour carried out with such success by Admiral Sir Roger Keyes on St. George's Day, 1918, had shown what good results could be obtained by carrying out a surprise attack against a defended harbour, provided there is perfect co-operation between the air and sea forces. It was with this in his mind that Sir Walter Cowan decided to plan an operation on similar lines against the ships lying inside the naval base at Kronstadt. Aircraft were of course required in addition to the C.M.B.s.

"You see Agar," he kept on repeating," I want this to be a blow, a kind of raid, the same as Roger did in Zeebrugge but without landing troops and demolition parties who only clutter up the main striking force with paraphernalia . . . etc. etc.," and so on in similar vein.

Walter Cowan had a gift of coming to the point quickly. He disliked verbosity and hated technical details. To him the function of an aeroplane was to fly; the engine and propeller were just 'things' and so to a certain extent were our boats, only his seamen's sense understood their value and capabilities. His brain was amazingly quick and alert and so was also that of the commander of his flagship, Commander Chichester Clark, whom he always brought into his confidence when discussing his plans as he did on this occasion.

SECRECY he said was an essential as it was at Zeebruge. "I don't mind the Russians knowing about our Aircraft as we can't hide them in the sky," he said, "but they must not know about the C.M.B. Flotilla as that is to be the *striking* weapon."

I suggested towing them out with destroyers a pair at a time, as Stuart in the *Voyager* towed our boats. Walter thought this an excellent idea since nobody could know they were in the Baltic until they arrived in Biorko and it would be quicker than sending them as cargo freight. The interval between their arrival and the Operation must be as short as possible.

Chichester-Clark and myself with the help of Charles Morgan,* the flagship's navigator, set to work and drew up a plan of action for the Admiral of which the main points were as follows: —

1. The basis of the operation was to be complete *Surprise*, and therefore it must be carried out at a time when least expected by the Kronstadt garrison.

2. The main attack to be delivered by a flotilla of coastal motor boats which were to approach the forts in the way I had done when making our contacts with ST25, and by the same route.

3. When the vicinity of the forts had been reached, an air bombardment to be carried out on the garrison town and inner forts of Kronstadt with the object of diverting the attention of the shore batteries.

4. Under cover of this diversion, the C.M.B. flotilla acting as a Striking Force to penetrate inside the naval harbour and attack the Bolshevik capital ships with torpedoes. Should there be a boom across the entrance a passage must be blown through it.

5. In the event of the operation proving successful and the Bolshevik heavy ships being immobilized, an inner and outer barrage of mines to be laid at the entrance of the main channel of Kronstadt sealing the exit into the Gulf of Finland.

Such then was the broad plan of this Operation which if successful, would leave the Admiral free to detach part of his fleet to the Western Baltic to deal more effectively with the German occupation troops in Latvia and Lithuania, and the remainder of his fleet to support the White Russian General Yudenitch in his plan to capture Petrograd with his North West Corps by advancing through Estonia—a plan about which Walter Cowan had many misgivings.

* At that time Lieutenant Charles Morgan, and in War II Admiral Sir Charles Morgan, K.C.B., D.S.O.

The additional ships required for the Kronstadt operation were immediately asked for from England and were promised by the Admiralty. They consisted of: One flotilla of C.M.B.s—if possible the 55 ft. type; one composite Aircraft Carrier (H.M.S. *Vindictive*); one large minelayer and some minelaying destroyers.

Speed was essential and when the Admiral stressed this in his cipher telegrams, the Admiralty replied that everything possible would be done but owing to shortage of mechanics the boats could not possibly arrive before the end of July. They arrived as promised and a fine performance on the part of the Admiralty and Captain French in Osea Island. Walter Cowan never complained of lack of support from the Admiralty especially with the C.M.B.s, which like many other naval and military units at home, were in course of reduction to a peace time establishment.

When it was known definitely that the flotilla was on its way, orders were given to stage the operation for the second or third week in August when the moon was waning, and it would be dark enough for the boats to reach their objective unobserved, deliver their attack just before early dawn, and make their escape afterwards before it was broad daylight. This allowed for a week or ten days at Biorko for the personnel of both aeroplanes and C.M.B.s to rehearse their individual parts.

Meanwhile much preparatory work was done in Biorko itself to the astonishment of the inhabitants of the tiny village of Koivisto. This was the only pocket of civilization in the whole large inlet, where the Russian fleet in pre-war days did their summer manoeuvres after an inspection and review by the Tsar.

The Finnish Government gave every possible assistance in these preparations for defending the base and under the energetic direction of their liaison officer, Lieutenant Foch. Trees were cut in the forest close by to make an anti-submarine boom. It was put in place by sailors from the ships, who also made a temporary aerodrome ashore by the same process, while a slipway was constructed, and moorings laid down off a small island near the harbour entrance for use as a seaplane base.

Life for our sailors was a repetition of Scapa Flow in the Great War, where they had waited and watched for the German High Sea Fleet for four years but with this difference, that the enemy were less than forty miles away instead of four hundred and there was much more activity for them on shore in Biorko with the comforting thought that in any case they had to leave the place before the ice came in January.

*   *   *

During this period from the third week in June until the third week in July while my two boats were being repaired and refitted, I divided my time between Helsingfors and Biorko, paying one visit to Revel for the purpose of completing our contacts in Estonia and making further plans for our next contact with ST25. Hampsheir was in the Sanatorium and although making some progress towards recovery, was still unfit for duty.

So far, our Terrioki activities were known only to a very few and the secret was still preserved. In Finnish official quarters in Helsingfors, all that was known about us was that a certain Lieutenant Agar had sunk the Bolshevik armoured cruiser *Oleg* in the Finnish Gulf when acting on the orders of the British Admiral, Sir Walter Cowan, which was of course true. Beyond that nothing was known about our C.M.B.s and the Admiralty took great care to allow our activities to remain in complete obscurity for the next two months, which is the reason why I was known later on as the 'Mystery V.C.'

In Helsingfors, I had, like my biblical prototype Agag, to "tread delicately", as it was obviously unwise for me to be seen about in public, either at our Legation or with our contacts. ST30, who occupied a certain semi-official position in Helsingfors, had returned there. It was through him and his good influence with the Finnish officials that I was able to have my boat repaired at the Finnish Naval Arsenal.

Peter and I saw quite a lot of each other during this time, and early in July I made acquaintance with my second courier, whose fortunes later on were to be so directly linked up with mine and ST25. His name was Gefter, at one time a midshipman in the Russian Navy, and besides being a good seaman he was well experienced in boats of all types.

In character and appearance he was quite different from Peter. He was short, thickset and stocky. That he was brave and cool, especially in a tight corner, I had abundant proof later on, but in contrast to Peter who was carefree natural and gay, Gefter was of a cold, cool and calculating disposition. In addition, he was an artist of no mean ability both as a painter and actor. Seldom have I met two men so dissimilar in disposition, yet who possessed in such large measure the quality of personal courage and absence of fear. Both could be trusted absolutely in an emergency to give of their best and never lose their heads, and although they were handsomely rewarded in money for their services their motive was solely patriotism. Peter was my age and we became (and actually now remain) very great friends. Gefter was much older. We never discovered their origin or if they had any family. These things they kept strictly to themselves, except that Gefter once mentioned the existence of a son he had never seen, who might perhaps have been the reason why he volunteered for this kind of work. In any case for the type of men we required ST25 could not have chosen two better suited for the job.

I had also, during this short interlude, interviews with interesting people. A few particularly stand out in my memory.

The first was with General Sir Hubert Gough, G.C.B., who had just arrived in Helsingfors as Head of the Allied Military Missions with his headquarters in Finland. His was no easy task as in addition to handling Von der Goltz, he was charged with the unenviable one of galvanizing Yudenitch and his White Russian North-West Army into life, and in consequence was beset on all sides by political intrigues.

It was amusing to note that the three generals Gough, Von der Goltz, and Yudenitch, flew their national flags on top of the three principal hotels in Helsingfors which housed them and their large staffs, and were dubbed by the Finns the Three Fortresses. There was much competition amongst the kitchen staffs to get into the British fortress as they called General Gough's hotel, as the German mark and Russian rouble were such soft currency that eventually our consulate paid their bills. A midshipman from one of our destroyers during a skylark on shore unrove the halyards of the ensign staffs at the German hotel one night causing considerable amusement to us, and annoyance to Von der Goltz before the flag could be flown again.

It was hoped in some quarters that General Gough's very presence in Finland would influence the Finnish Government to place their Volunteer Army at the disposal of the Allies, for a concerted move against Petrograd from both sides of the Finnish Gulf which would catch the city in a fiercer grip. These proved to be pious hopes only, because the Finns, without a definite declaration of military and financial support from Great Britain and the Allies, would not move. They had no money, and having removed the 'Red Terror' from their country earlier in the year, desired nothing more but to be left in peace.

General Gough, of the Curragh fame, and Walter Cowan were of the same type and breed. Both were men of action and when not on active service they lived for horses (skins, as Walter called them) and hunting. Both had the same shrewd judgment and tastes, with the result that they got on together splendidly in all the difficult cross-currents of Baltic intrigues which might have upset other men. There was little the General could do for me except give me his blessing, which he did in that kind and generous way which only large-hearted and great men have, and I shall never forget his personality or his kindness.

There were no less than three successive British Ministers in Helsingfors while I was in the Baltic but I knew best our Acting Minister when I first arrived, His Excellency Mr. H. M. Bell, C.V.O., C.B.E. He described himself as a 'war diplomat' without any knowledge of Foreign Office procedure or custom, but Bell's handling of British and Allied interests in Finland was a masterpiece of common sense and tact, which produced invaluable practical results; permission of the Finnish Government for the British Fleet to use Biorko as a base; facilities to use the Naval Arsenal in Helsingfors, and in many other smaller matters where the sympathetic help of the Finns enabled us to overcome our difficulties.

In private life a plain business man, Bell tackled his job with businesslike thoroughness and efficiency. In the Legation offices he was known as a slave driver because he gave as his definition of an 'off day' one on which the staff in his office did not look in after dinner. It was Bell who paved the way, and laid the groundwork, for the close trade and economic relations which have flourished between Finland and Great Britain from the date of our recognition of her Independence up to the present day. He was much beloved and respected in that country, especially by General Mannerheim, the Finnish Regent, and in consequence his influence was very great. He had, moreover, the advantage of being able to speak the Finnish language as well as both Russian and German.

Bell's accounts of his experience in Finland when he arrived as the first British Consul are most interesting.* It must be remembered that prior to the Armistice, Germany was in virtual occupation of the country and that when the Germans left and the Bolsheviks came in, General Mannerheim had to rely solely on what German

* See: *Land of Lakes* by H. M. Bell (Robert Hale).

support he could get to drive the Bolsheviks out again. He had no other choice.

The Germans, Bell told me, made the mist ke of treating the Finns as a subject race and looked upon Finland as a source of loot. They removed to Germany everything they could lay their hands upon, butter, iron, copper and any useful article they had need of. They riddled the Government services with their own officials whom the Finnish Government had great difficulty in getting rid of. It is interesting to note that in 1918 and before the war was over a German prince—Prince Friedrich Carl, Landgrave of Hessen-Cassel (married to a grand-daughter of Queen Victoria) had actually been offered and had accepted the throne of Finland. Finland was thankful enough that the Germans came when they did, and equally happy when they left.

When I told him about my flight in the Finnish aeroplane over the Tolbukin lighthouse, Bell was highly amused and recounted a most interesting story concerning it.

Shortly before the Germans left Finland, a copy of a telegram came into his possession which had been sent by the German General Staff in Helsingfors to the German General Staff in Revel and signed "Von Below". In translation it read as follows:—

'Send by three steamers—STURZ, NOODIGACHT, and MAGDEBURG—three aeroplanes and three hydroplanes. They will be shipped to Koivisto (Biorko) with instructions to fly over the Karelian-Finnish frontier. They will be painted with enemy colours (Englischen).'

The idea I suppose was that they should drop bombs or propaganda on the Finnish villages in Karelia (where British troops of General Ironsides Archangel Force were already fighting against the Bolsheviks) so as to create the impression that the machines were British and had come from Murmansk. Fortunately this project never materialized because the Finns confiscated the machines and used them for their own purposes. It must have been in one of these that I had made my flight with Arthur Reichel.

Bell left Helsingfors early in August when he was relieved as British Minister by Sir Coleridge Kennard who was attached to our Legation in Stockholm and from whom I received at all times the same kind help and advice. He, unlike Bell, was a professional diplomat and had an intimate knowledge based on experience in Russia, of the character and psychology of the Russian people. Where Bell through his businesslike diplomacy and special knowledge of the Finns and Germans, had so successfully handled Allied and British interests in Finland during the German occupation and withdrawal, his successor arrived at a time when the Finns were facing a different political problem, and his knowledge of Russia and Russian was of particular use in helping the Finns to solve it.

Having got rid of the German influence, the Finnish Government now began to show signs of anxiety regarding the large number of Russians in their midst and particularly of the activities in Finland of General Yudenitch, who was not only Kolchak's official representative but also had British support; and whereas the British Government had already recognized Finland's independence *de facto* and had done so *de jure* in May, Kolchak had done neither. The Finnish attitude towards the Russian emigrés is not therefore surprising.

Our Minister then had the difficult task of allaying Finnish suspicions and at the same time of giving official British recognition and support to Yudenitch. His natural tact and charm stood him in good stead in this delicate situation.

He was a delightful host and occasionally gave small parties at his house to which he would invite a few special friends. They were the only parties I ever attended in Finland, as I had to avoid all functions. One in particular will live in my memory. After dinner a Tzigane Gipsy

H

orchestra made its appearance and played to us from a
balcony just outside his dining room. It was the first time I
had heard this real gipsy music, not its imitation. For me
it was a melancholy thought that only a year ago in the
early hours of the morning this same orchestra was playing
in its true native setting in an open-air restaurant in
Krestovsky Island; the very place I had just visited a fortnight
ago in my boat under very different conditions. We sat
for hours with the lights turned out, listening to the
strains of that sad music, quite oblivious of the time. It
was broad daylight when we left his house. I can recall the
dark, handsome features of the gipsy orchestra leader who,
when told (without mentioning my name) that I was a
naval officer, immediately played the same tunes which
he used to play before the Revolution to his patrons who
were often Russian naval officers. He recounted a most
amusing story of the Tsarist Navy which Sir Coleridge
translated.

Apparently at one time the leader used to play at the
kuban restaurant in Petrograd famous for its cellar and
good food. Its clientèle were, for the most part well-
known aristocrats. He recalled an occasion when a Russian
Admiral entered the restaurant and sat down alone to
dinner. Sitting a few tables away was a party of rowdy
young people. They were gay and drinking champagne,
which in those days in Russia was only just beginning
to be the fashionable drink amongst the *Jeunesse dorée*.
Summoning the head waiter, the Admiral ordered his
dinner and with it a bottle of Vodka, at the same time
emphasizing that the bottle must be one with a white ring
round the neck signifying that it was first class quality.
Meanwhile, the party at the other table started to poke
fun at the old man by pointing to his bottle of Vodka.

Dinner proceeded apace, the old man not paying any
attention to the young party. Halfway through, he finished
the bottle and ordered another, whereupon the youngsters
waxed even more hilarious and sent across to his table a

bottle of champagne which he ignored. Then after finishing his meal—and with it his second bottle of Vodka,—the old Admiral called for the head waiter in a loud voice and ordered a soup tureen into which he poured the bottle of champagne in front of him, and, bowing to the members of the 'gay party', washed his hands in it, and after drying them on his napkin, stumped out of the room. The humour of the episode is undeniable and typically Russian.

*   *   *

I cannot omit at this point a reference, if only a passing one, to another personality—a lady—who was quite a figure on the political horizon of Helsingfors in those days.

Madame W.—for thus she was known—was an outstanding personality and kept a most interesting 'salon'. She had a good cook and, what was still more important at that time in Finland since the country was dry, a good cellar. Her five o'clock teas were famous—one met at her house politicians, naval and military officers, emigré Russians, Estonians, Lithuanians, Latvians, but no Germans —in fact anybody who had a political axe to grind. Most of her guests were NOT, to use a Russian colloquial expression 'politicheski blagonadiozhni' (politically reliable). Although very well-to-do, her husband had taken part in the 1918 Red Rebellion and was imprisoned in the Sveaborg fortress. He had been actually under sentence of death but was pardoned later by the Finnish Government largely, it was said, through the good influence of Bell.

She was a clever woman, a marvellous linguist and had great personal charm. I personally did not visit her salon, but in spite of the fact that the Finns regarded her as being far from 'politicheski blagonadiozhni' nearly all foreigners, including the British, were to be seen there. Months afterwards she rendered me a valuable service.

*   *   *

For me those three weeks passed only too quickly. There

was much to do as regards our Secret Service plans, in addition to refitting and preparing our two C.M.B.s for service. My own boat (No. 4) was soon ready at the Finnish Arsenal Yard, and did a test run around the islands off Helsingfors in which I took Sir Park Goff as a passenger. (He was visiting the Baltic States on a Parliamentary Mission), after which I arranged for the boat to be towed back to Biorko by a destroyer. Peter was my frequent companion. He was getting depressed at our enforced delay, for to his highly strung nature action meant everything. Together we paid two visits to Hampsheir in his Sanatorium tucked away in the pine forests many miles north of Helsingfors.

We travelled in the oddest of trains driven by the oldest of engines, and I doubt if our speed ever reached twenty miles an hour, but there was a wonderful fascination in the journey. The beautiful green colourings of the fields and pine forests must, I felt sure, act as a sedative to Hampsheir's broken nerves. We were in the depths of a primitive and unspoilt country. At each little wayside halt, flowers, both wild and planted, grew in profusion. After the few passengers had alighted from the train and packages for the next halt had been placed in the van, the guard, who wore a quaint, old-fashioned uniform not unlike those worn by German foresters, never failed to visit our compartment in the train and, with head respectfully uncovered, ask permission for the train to proceed to the next halt.

I enquired the reason for this, and was told that according to an old Finnish custom only officials or the Tsarist aristocracy were allowed to travel first class, and as we occupied the only first class carriage in the train we were in consequence regarded by the guard and local inhabitants as privileged travellers.

Darkness disappeared completely only for a very short while as the train progressed northwards; and the whole unspoiled countryside seemed to be transformed by nature into one immense conservatory open to the sky. Innumerable lakes of all shapes and sizes (known in the Finnish language as 'ponds') showed up in beautiful relief against the background of green formed by the forests and fields.

The rickety old train, grinding along the rough permanent way, was a symbol of the simplicity of country life and the privations and hardships the people had passed through, since it was all that was left for them to use after the Bolshevik ravages and German exodus. It was easy then for me to understand, after one or two of these journeys into the interior, that the Finnish people desired nothing more than to be left in peace and be given time and facilities to reconstruct their country according to their own ideas of national independence. The last thing they wanted was another war or a war party no matter what price the reward for their services might be.

On the morning of the 17th July I was back in Biorko, where Sindall and Marshall had prepared the boats in readiness for our next venture. It was arranged in Helsingfors that Peter was to join us at Terrioki by an overland route on the 19th July, and that I was to take him into Petrograd that very night. Gefter was to join us on the 22nd July and be taken to Petrograd in the same boat which was to bring Peter out. Gefter's special task was to accompany ST25 out, as by now London's demands for the return of the head of our British intelligence organization in Russia were insistent. Our programme was an ambitious one, for we had no means of knowing how much—if any—information of our activities had reached the Bolsheviks. It was impossible for ST25 to have sent any messages through to Terrioki and in any case he was away in Moscow. We did know, from the few refugees who had escaped across the Finnish frontier, that as a result of the sinking of the *Oleg*, Bolshevik vigilance had increased. But I felt sure it would be directed towards the opposite side of the Gulf, i.e., the Krasnaya Gorka end and not towards the Finnish coast.

Before leaving Helsingfors I co-opted yet a third courier who was ready and willing to come with us and accept our risks. He was a young man called Vladimir Konstatinoff, who had served in a Russian Guards Regiment early in the war and was sometime afterwards employed by the B.B.C. as a translator. He was to be our 'stand-by' and I arranged for him to live with us in the *datcha* at Terrioki.

We all liked Vlad, as we called him. He was a cheerful soul and good companion; obviously of high social standing and taught me the finer points of chess. Unfortunately he was unaccustomed to boat work, so I gave him the job of house-manager in the *datcha* which he willingly accepted *pro tem*. Perhaps later on he suggested he might be able to get through the Russian barbed wire entanglements on the Finnish side of the frontier, and for that I kept him on our pay roll as he was a useful asset.

We set out from Biorko late on the evening of the 17th and made the trip round the coast (as before) by night. By now we knew our landmarks exactly and had no difficulty in locating the small harbour at Terrioki at night, though we had of course to risk the Russian minefields and the chance of hitting a mine loose from its moorings, but it was better to accept this risk than betray the presence of our boats to the lookouts in the Kronstadt forts by a daylight passage.

ST31, who had preceded us independently by land, again flashed his signal from the end of the small yacht club stone jetty and had everything arranged in the *datcha* where Peter had already arrived. We found that our supplies of petrol and oil were intact at the yacht club exactly as we had left them. Our night landing and disembarkation went without a hitch and there was no change in the little harbour tucked amongst the pine trees. Even the fishing boat was there anchored in its old place in the middle of the harbour and ready again to be used as a mooring buoy for our C.M.B.s. The only differences were the Finnish sentries who seemed astonished to see us but evidently had orders to let us through.

Next morning I renewed acquaintance with the Commandant, who greeted me like an old friend. He said that no event of importance had happened since we had left Terrioki, and that he had received an official order from Helsingfors to co-operate with any British naval personnel visiting the district under his command, especially those in torpedo boats. (I saw in this the helping hand of Bell.) A telephone line was installed in our *datcha* which placed us in direct communication with the signal station at Stirrs Point lighthouse. I could now at any time pass my messages direct to Biorko via the lighthouse. The Commandant renewed the orders to the Finnish guards to allow no one to approach the harbour or yacht club building except ourselves. I told him that I would be out on patrol that night in the neighbourhood of Kronstadt and would inform him of the result the following morning.

The arrangement I had come to with Peter was to land him that night at the same place off Krestovsky Island as before. Sindall was to take Gefter there on either the 3rd or 7th subsequent nights. His trip was dependent on weather conditions and also on what success we had with ours. Peter then was to come out, if possible by the same boat which landed Gefter, and was to keep the small 'pram' in which he landed, hidden in the rushes. His despatch consisted of only one tiny thin slip of paper with times and dates written on it, nothing more. It would have been fatal to ST25 if Peter had been searched and found in possession of documents. He also took in money. This money was in the form of copies made of the old rouble notes but the perforations and colour were so badly printed that they were easily detected and therefore useless to ST25 who had to burn them. It was most unfortunate as he needed money badly. London was to blame for this unfortunate error.

All was set. Once again the Commandant and I ascended the church steeple to our look-out platform and surveyed the familiar chain of forts and the batteries on the northern shore of Kronstadt Island. There was no apparent change.

Smoke could be seen rising from the far side in the direction of the naval dockyard which was blotted out from our view by the shore, but this might have meant anything. Later in the evening our smuggler pilot turned up. He said that he had heard rumours that the Red Commander in Kronstadt had given orders for patrol boats to watch the approach to Petrograd behind the forts during the dark hours. He would not say where the information came from or what the patrol boats were, and I rather suspected that this piece of news was given as a preliminary to a demand for an increased fee for his services. Anyway, we would find that out for certain ourselves within a few hours. I had decided in my mind that if we encountered any of these patrol boats we could easily shake them off with our high speed and machine guns.

By nine o'clock we were in our boat ready to slip away. Twilight had descended. By ten o'clock it was dark and once again we were off on our errand.

There were five of us in the boat—myself, Marshall, Beeley, the smuggler pilot and Peter and within half an hour we were approaching those horrible looking black objects, the forts, which grew larger every minute as we advanced towards them. Soon we had to slow down, and again that awful feeling of tension arose as we crept past. At last we were through—unchallenged—there was no sign of any patrol craft. Full speed ahead now for our rendezvous at the river mouth.

We arrived at the same place as before. There was no delay. Peter jumped into the 'pram' as soon as we had it in the water—a grip of the hand and he was gone. Five minutes later we saw his signal of three short flashes given on his electric torch and I knew he was safe on shore. But what of ST25? Was he safe? Had he escaped the Red purges? These thoughts and others flashed through my mind as we sped back towards Terrioki. At all costs we must not be seen as that might compromise the Admiral's plans, but I had to fulfil my mission first.

Fortune favoured us again for we passed through the forts unchallenged, neither were there any signs of Red patrol boats. I took a wide sweep towards Kronstadt Island on the way back but there was nothing to be seen afloat; the only signs of any were a few wisps of smoke coming from the direction of the naval dockyard. We then made our way back to Terrioki where we arrived in the early hours of the morning well pleased with our work.

I told the Commandant that there was nothing to report and that we would be going out again in two days' time. This time I had promised Sindall the trip and was left myself to wait on shore. Gefter arrived from Helsingfors the following morning as arranged. We went over the route and plan with him most carefully on the chart as this was his first landing in Petrograd from a C.M.B. He carried one tiny despatch, an even smaller one than Peter's, informing ST25 that he was to do his utmost to return in our boat to Terrioki and he took more money.

ST30, Beeley and myself took up our stand for the night at the end of the stone jetty by the harbour and watched Sindall's boat disappear in the direction of the forts. I now realized for the first time the anxiety of waiting. It was just as nerve-racking as the tension we felt in the boat when passing through the forts. The time seemed to pass so slowly. Instinctively our eyes were glued to the passage at which we knew Sindall's boat was aiming. We watched him as long as we could with our glasses, through which the forts now appeared only as tiny black dots.

What was that?—a gun flash—yes, followed by another, and then several more in rapid succession. Then silence. What had happened? The strain during this period of waiting was awful, but, thank heaven, it did not last long. Soon the familiar hum of the boat's motor could be heard and to our relief shortly afterwards she nosed her way back into the little harbour apparently undamaged.

Sindall explained in a few brief words what had happened. They had evidently been seen by one of the larger fortresses on the far side nearer Kronstadt, which had opened fire on them.* Luckily the gunner's aim was inaccurate and the firing very wild; the boat was not hit and it was also fortunate that no searchlight had been trained on to them. Sindall decided to turn back at once and make towards the Tolbukin lighthouse in order to leave the impression upon those who had seen the outline of the boat that he was a patrol boat from Biorko side and not from Terrioki. Had he kept on towards Petrograd trusting to the speed of the boat to get through, he would most certainly have had a rough reception on his way back.

Sindall showed by his action in returning at once, a cool judgment and grasp of the situation which was beyond all praise. He said that Gefter had behaved extraordinarily well and had shown no sign of fear while they were under fire, but he was not quite so sure about the smuggler pilot. Both Gefter and Sindall were determined to try again on the seventh day from zero as arranged, and were not in the least upset. "It was," he said, "only a small set-back and nothing to worry over."

Thinking things over alone, I came to the conclusion that the secret of our base was still preserved—this was the most important point of all. Sindall probably approached the forts at too high a speed and a shade too early. I noticed at the time when he left that it was not completely dark. There would be better conditions in four days' time. The smuggler pilot had already showed me, on our Russian chart, another passage through which he assured me the boat could pass. This gap was nearer the Finnish shore and farther away from the forts which had opened fire on Sindall, and I therefore decided to try it. Taking things all round it seemed to me that our prospects were far from hopeless. We must treat this as a piece of bad luck and no more. As for the pilot, all he demanded was extra payment—"danger money"—as he naïvely put it. In any case we should have

---

* This would have been one of the fortresses close to KOTLIN Island and not one of the 'chain' forts.

had to pay him—to buy his silence, but this time not in money. I promised rum, which to him, and his fellow contrabandists, was much more acceptable in dry Finland, but payment was not to be made until the boat returned home safely. His eyes glistened with anticipation.

Life went on quietly in the *datcha* during the next three days. ST31 was with us and we kept Gefter indoors out of sight. Konstantinoff, in his role of house manager, busied himself with our bodily needs and in his spare time played chess with me and invariably won. Hampsheir turned up one day from the Sanatorium. I cannot imagine how he persuaded the doctors to allow him to leave, as he looked extremely ill and had lost a lot of weight; but was full of pluck and eager to do his bit with the others, but I had to send him home.

Major Scale (ST27) our co-ordinator in Stockholm sent us two young civilians qualified as radio operators, but what apparatus they were to operate remained a mystery. They had assumed names and passports as Vic Jones and John Bush and were a cheery addition to our party in the *datcha* which now numbered ten, after including the Finnish female cook and Constantinoff.

We were visited occasionally on the sly by Mr. King our vice-consul in Viborg and his loyal Finnish assistant, Mr. V. Läapass (a businessman in Viborg, devoted to the British and executed by the Soviet Russians in the Second World War in 1940). It was through them that we kept contact with Stockholm by telegraph and thence with London, but I was already beginning to feel nervous about the size of our party, as the last thing we wanted was to be the centre of inquisitive eyes on this small but important frontier post so close to Petrograd.

Sindall and the mechanics made friends with a few Russian refugees living in the other *datchas*. These refugees had long since been through the quarantine camp, formed two miles inland by the simple expedient of enclosing a cluster of small *datchas* with barbed wire. Having done their

quarantine they were allowed to take up their quarters in
the larger *datchas* nearer the seashore, of which ours was
one. For want of money they lived a primitive life of near
starvation with dreadful memories: a wife waiting for a
missing husband, another for her son, or perhaps sons and
daughters for their parents. With few exceptions they were
people who had been born in good circumstances and were
accustomed to a comfortable life in pre-revolutionary
Russia. They had no money except what they obtained
from time to time by selling a treasured family possession
and their plight was incredibly pathetic.

Terrioki attracted these aristocratic refugees like a magnet.
One and all were imbued with the firm belief that the
British Navy had arrived to succour them, and that therefore
Petrograd must fall and they would soon be able to regain
possession of their estates. Little did they realize how
slender were the chances on which these hopes were
founded. Each fresh arrival brought more stories of the
Red purges, of friends arrested as counter-revolutionary
hostages, executed, or even tortured by the Chinese mer-
cenaries of the Cheka, stories which lost nothing in the
telling and so terrible that one old Russian nobleman
summed them up by saying that "Petrograd is now in the
hands of the Devil." They were all 'suspect' to a certain
degree by the Finns who knew that Bolshevik agents were
spreading propaganda in Finland. Their one and only
consolation was the beautiful Russian church where at least
they could practise their religion.

Not far away, at Rajajokhi, Repin, the famous Russian
artist was painting his masterpieces in a villa, quite oblivious to what was going on around him and to the fact
that his world had been turned upside down. Mr. King,
our British Consul in Viborg, passed many of his pictures
through to New York and London via Stockholm, where
they were bought for trifling sums and today are worth
fortunes. While our Finnish vice-consul and good friend,
Mons Läapass, showed me a most wonderful collection of

Fabergé objets d'art and jewellery he was keeping under safe cover biding the day when their owners would return to Petrograd.

Everywhere there were signs only of neglect and decay in these 'once-upon-a-time' charming and lovely summer *datchas* in this pine forest. The sadness of it all was incredible and impossible to forget.

For ourselves, we could not possibly have chosen a 'hide-out' more suitable for our secret work, since such occupants as there were in the villas near by, spent their days brooding on their own problems—Russian fashion—over a *samovar* of unsweetened weak tea, with no inclination to bother about others (like ourselves) in the vicinity. They seemed to live in an atmosphere charged only with hopes, doubts, fears—no purpose in sight!

CHAPTER V

CHANGE OF PLAN

IT was late on the night of the 23rd July—the day before Sindall was due to make his second attempt to land Gefter and return with Peter—when we were suddenly disturbed. We had settled in for the night at the *datcha*; Sindall and the mechanics had turned in, Konstantinoff and I were finishing our game of chess with Marshall and ST31 looking on. It was, I suppose, about eleven o'clock at night when suddenly we heard a tapping at the window. In an instant, as if by instinct, Konstantinoff had the lights out and, drawing his revolver, went to see who it was. We were unaccustomed to visitors at the *datcha*, let alone visitors at night, and I remember it flashed through my mind how typical this scene must be of a piece of Russian melodrama, as it had its comic side; but who should our visitor turn out to be but no less a person than Peter himself!

He had a strange tale to tell. After landing in the 'pram' and flashing his signal back to me to indicate that he was safe on shore, he had started off towards Petrograd, when suddenly he was challenged by a patrol. He made a bolt for it, and managed to elude his pursuers in the darkness. But, he said, he was quite certain they had now discovered his landing place and would certainly find the 'pram', all further ideas of using Krestovsky Island as a rendezvous must be abandoned.

Arriving in the city in the early hours of the morning, he managed to establish contact with ST25 who, as soon as he realized the danger to which we would be exposed if we returned in our boat to the same rendezvous as arranged on the 4th day, begged Peter to return to us immediately as there was not an hour to be lost. ST25 had chosen another rendezvous farther down and nearer the Finnish frontier.

The place selected was on the shore opposite the Lachta light vessel. This would entail a longer row out in the boat from the shore to the C.M.B. which was unavoidable. It also meant that a larger and heavier boat than the small 'pram' would have to be procured which Gefter was confident he could manage.

Peter decided that the quickest return route to us in Terrioki was the direct one across the Russian frontier to Finland. It was also by far the most dangerous, as was well known by those who had tried it, unless one went as a refugee Russian which meant incarceration in the Finnish quarantine camp. Taking the Russian train running to the frontier post of Rakoki he jumped off when it slowed down at a crossing and hid in the woods until nightfall when he chanced his luck near a check point. The odds were thousands to one against him but he got through safely and was exhausted when he reached the *datcha*.

We revived him with some food, hot tea and rum, and getting out the charts, went over the new route most carefully. All of us realized what an amazingly providential stroke fortune had dealt us when Sindall was turned back by the forts, for if he had gone on he would most certainly have been trapped off Krestovsky Island. ST31 had already purchased a small skiff, slightly larger than the 'pram' Peter had left hidden in the reeds, and therefore better suited for the longer row towards the Lachta shore. Gefter said he did not mind this at all as he was accustomed to handling boats, and indeed subsequently proved to be an expert.

I myself did not like the idea of stopping the C.M.B. so far out to sea, but Peter said that ST25 did not want us any closer in as it was too dangerous and suggested as an alternative that we should go right up to the light vessel itself, on which he had a friend, but I thought this proposal even more risky still, for it would give away our secret to more people. I decided against it and told Sindall to stop the C.M.B. about a quarter of a mile off the light vessel and let Gefter row the boat in.

In my message to ST25 taken in by Peter I had told him of the Admiral's plans for the big attack on Kronstadt and therefore of the urgency for him to come out before the end of the second week in August failing which he must wait until the first week in September to let things quieten down. Dates were left for him to choose together with alternatives. In his reply back to me, hastily scribbled in a cemetery, he gave the dates as the 4th and 8th August, failing which he would wait until the 1st week in September. In the meanwhile he had to take a quick journey to Moscow. Peter said there would be a lot of stuff to carry, meaning of course documents and samples of Bolshevik memoranda, so ST25 must have a companion to help carry things. This ruled out the 'pram' which could take two people only so Sindall would have to take in a skiff to hold three. With this information now at hand from ST25 I postponed his trip for another six days, i.e., the 28th July when he was to take in as arranged Gefter plus skiff, and again I told Gefter to urge ST25 how important it was for him to report to London.

*　　*　　*

Next day I had a telephone call from the officer in charge of our naval signal station at Stirrs Point lighthouse and was told that a few of our own aeroplanes had arrived at Biorko and would in a few days' time be carrying out reconnaisance flights over Kronstadt to obtain photographs of the naval harbour and ascertain the exact location of the Bolshevik heavy ships there. He said that there were several Red submarines operating against us in the Gulf. This was no news to us as ST25 had already sent out a warning that preparations were being hastened in Kronstadt to put their submarines into action sooner with German personnel manning them.

The Soviet wireless stations at Petrograd and Moscow were also very active with propaganda about this time and were ceaselessly broadcasting messages to our sailors in

Biorko urging them to refuse duty and hasten the cause of World Revolution. One message in particular was of interest to me. It stated that the British had sunk the cruiser *Oleg* by a submarine in revenge for the loss of our own submarine L.55 which had been sunk late in May by two Red destroyers.

It is interesting to note that this was the first time that wireless stations were using radio for propaganda purposes, and from this message I concluded that the Bolsheviks were still in ignorance of the nature of the attack on the *Oleg* and that therefore the presence of our two C.M.B.s at Terrioki was still unknown to them. A comforting thought, but at the same time I realized that it would be impossible to keep our base at Terrioki secret for much longer—at the most a few weeks—especially now in view of the coming activity of our aeroplanes at Biorko.

The two couriers spent hours together comparing notes, routes, dates, times, etc. Not a detail was overlooked. I had fixed the 28th July as the date for Sindall to try again. This time he was successful, but to give the reader a clearer though somewhat highly coloured account of their trip through the forts, let us turn to Gefter's own version of it as published by him in a German magazine several years afterwards, the main facts of which are both accurate and correct:—

"About nine in the evening in the dining room of a *datcha* at Terrioki which was occupied by English and foreign sailors, a few of us had gathered. On the dining room table were spread out sea charts of the narrow part of the Finnish Gulf, known as Markisova Luzhei.

"Everything had already been worked out and checked up, time and again. Distances had been carefully measured, while the depths and the dangerous spots were known by heart; and yet one wanted to look again and again at the little tracks marked on the chart in pencil which we had to follow so as first, not to be beaten to pieces by the frantic

I

speed of the boat, which exceeded seventy kilometres an hour, and second, not to hit one of our own Russian mines, of which there were many in the Gulf.

"A Finnish pilot—contrabandist—who said he knew these waters like the fingers of his hand was brought into the room several times and consulted.

"He was a local fisherman and had done some smuggling during the winter.

"Food and a bottle of cognac was on the table, but no one paid any attention to them, so engrossed were we in the task that lay before us. We spoke like conspirators, only in whispers, as if a dangerous secret seemed to lurk in the corners of the room. Serious business was at hand.

"We had to pass in a speedboat through the numbered Kronstadt forts to the neighbourhood of Lakhta; from there I was to be let down from the speedboat in a small yachting skiff dressed in a Red army tunic. I had to row in this small boat to the Lakhta reeds and hide in them until the morning and when (in the early morning) the whistle of the first train was heard, I was to go to the station, get on to the train, and travel to Petrograd where I was to find another Englishman who would be known to me only by a password.

"A week later I was to return with this Englishman to the same spot by the reeds, get into my yachting skiff and row out to a position one mile south of the Elagin lightship. At that hour the English speedboat should arrive from Terrioki, and exchanging flashlight signals, take us from the skiff and carry us back to Finland.

"A few days previously I had made a trial run in this motor boat with one of the English sailors which had been quite successful. It is true that a few shots were fired at us from the forts, but at such a speed and at night there was nothing to be feared, I felt, from this shooting.

"Eleven o'clock approached. The fresh and gentle coolness of an August night came in through the open window. In a neighbouring *datcha* the strains of a piano being played could be heard clearly and softly. From the other side of the Finnish Gulf, away near Krasnaya Gorka, I could see in the distance the faint beam of a searchlight, like a spear plunging into the darkness searching the sky. It was time to start. We got up.

"A young sailor was in command of this little band. He was tall and fair and spoke in a short, crisp voice of authority strange in one so young.

" 'Sindall will take you in tonight,' he said. 'I will accompany you myself as far as the yacht club and watch you start.'

" 'It may be a little cold waiting in the reeds until the morning so take this,' handing me a flask of cognac, 'it may help you.'

"I had on several occasions crossed the Finnish Gulf in boats and on the ice in winter under much more difficult conditions, so that the coming trip in a 250 h.p. boat in the pleasant company of such young people did not seem to me to be specially dangerous. The trip which I had made a few days before in the same boat up to the chain of forts and back impressed me so much by the rapidity with which it was done, that I was in quite an optimistic mood. I tried not to think of what was to happen when I should be put off from the deck of the motor boat in the little skiff. The beginning of this adventure reminded me much more of a sporting escapade; something like races in motor boats, than a venture in which our very lives were at stake.

" 'Let us go.' Two mechanics went on ahead and the tall sailor and I descended the steps of the *datcha* and sank into the darkness of the garden. It was warm and damp, with the warmth of an August night that brings on sadness. I was reminded of the last few minutes of a love meeting, so reluctant was I to leave this peaceful setting.

"Four of us were going in the boat and as many accompanied us to say goodbye. We walked stealthily in pairs through the woods, afraid to be seen, and some little distance apart; the tall, fair young sailor and myself bringing up the rear. Sometimes the front pair lit up the ground with an electric torch as it was quite dark and there was difficulty in finding our way.

"Soon one smelt the dampness of a great expanse of water. The sea was near. When we came out from under the trees, it was much lighter, and far away to the left the little golden lights of Kronstadt twinkled. To the right, as before, the beam of the searchlight over Krasnya Gorka still pierced the sky. The waves splashed up on to the bare sandy shore with a noise that reminded me of a fugue on a great string orchestra. Our feet sank into the deep sand. It was very quiet.

"Round the corner appeared a little light. It was the yacht club with its white walls showing up against the dark background of the forest. In the small harbour there rocked lightly a sailing boat of Swedish type riding at anchor. From time to time on the other side of the breakwater one could hear the growl of a motor out of the darkness like the neighing of a gigantic horse waiting for a gallop.

"There the mechanic was turning over his engines.

"We took leave of each other. The young and gay Sindall joked as he sat in the small rowing boat which took us from the beach to the motor boat; so small that it could only hold three people so I waited for its return.

" 'The night is very good,' the tall young sailor in command said to me. 'There is no moon and no stars, and only a slight wind. I am sure Sindall will get you there safely in an hour and a half. Remember that in a week I shall come to fetch you out in the speedboat myself. These are the dates. You must make no mistake about the time because there is three hours' difference between our time and Bolshevik time. Don't forget I shall look for your signal of three flashes which I will answer from my boat. When you find the Englishman inside you must give the password first and now—goodbye.'

"The row-boat returned from the motor boat. It was time to get in. The merry young mechanic, Piper, whom I remembered on our last dash in the speedboat, greeted me.

" 'Happy journey,' I heard from the shore. 'Au revoir for a week, bon voyage.'

"A few minutes later, a big, flat object loomed up. It was the motor boat, painted in protective colours. The boat was of hydroplane type with a wooden keel. As it gathered speed its prow rose higher and higher above the surface of the water. The boat did not float, but skimmed over the surface of the water, sometimes almost rising above it. In rough weather it seemed that the boat would be destroyed by its own speed.

" 'Today we are travelling light,' said Sindall. 'We could not carry both torpedo and skiff.' Indeed, in the long torpedo tunnel, there was nothing but the skiff. We set out straight from shore to avoid submerged rocks. The motor was running at half speed which was a good thirty-five kilometres an hour. Behind the stern, the wash of the boat formed a deep pit in the water, while at the sides two bow waves formed like high glass walls. The whole boat trembled with a shiver as if making a monstrous effort.

"From time to time as we met a wave, we bumped upwards as if the boat was lifted by the hand of a giant. Sindall turned the wheel, and the lights of Kronstadt began to grow and approach. I stood in the torpedo tunnel, clinging to the skiff. I thought of two things. Was it true that between the first and second forts there were torpedo boats of an old type on watch, and what could they do to us? The second thought was, were the reeds at Lakhta really so high as the pilot said, so that it would be easy for both myself and the boat to hide in them? Doubts about this began to eat into my heart. If it turned out that there was nowhere to hide, my situation would not be so happy, especially as I knew there were many Red patrols in the neighbourhood of Lakhta.

"From the right, from Kronstadt, flashes like lightning burst out of the blackness. We were being fired upon. It

was like shooting practice, only the shooting was from the
guns of the forts instead of from revolvers. Sindall increased
speed. The boat raised herself up with its prow and began to
fly over the water. I was wet through with spray so threw a
tarpaulin over myself. Sindall did not change the course and
must have deceived the Kronstadt forts who thought we
were going towards them instead of towards the black line
of inner forts situated nearer the mainland and between
which we were able to slip.

"Sindall went in exactly between two of them. I wondered
to myself what was taking place inside them. Were the old
torpedo boats on the watch? All was dark and there were no
lights on the forts. A minute later the boat lined up to them.
What an endless minute! Again the boat leapt ahead and
upwards, but still, how slowly those black masses seemed to
crawl towards us. Mechanically I stood on tiptoe, gripping
the woodwork with my fingers as if to push the boat
forward myself. At last we were through and the mad speed
of the boat now became noticeable.

"The forts flew by as the passing stations fly by the
windows of an express train. I looked around. Several more
flashes of lightning burst from the forts. Too late! A wide
expanse of water now spread itself before us. In the distance
one could see the glimmering lights of the city of Petrograd,
to me once friendly, but now hostile.

"Sindall reduced speed. Straight ahead I could see the
Elagin lightship and to the left, the lights of Lakhta. All
seemed calm and peaceful except for the noise of the boat as
she sped along the water like a graceful bird. A short
distance now only remained. Sindall reduced speed still
more and it became possible to carry on a conversation. In a
few minutes he stopped.

"Everyone on board now became gay. We had accomplished
successfully the first part of our journey. We shook hands
with one another and clapped each other on the back.
Sindall left the helm, the motor sighed and became silent.
All around was quiet and from the shore I could hear the

whistle of a railway train. I looked around. On the dark grey expanse of water the line of forts looked like black stripes. No torpedo boats were visible. Near Lakhta the reeds showed in black clumps. How far were they from the shore?

"The dark strip of the shore might be bushes in which case the boat must be near, or it might be forest, in which case the shore must be ten times farther away. As if by design, there was not a light on shore to be seen. Sindall and a sailor lowered the skiff into the water; they put the oars into it and everything was ready. Now I had to begin my job. I shook hands with everyone and climbed into the skiff. Goodbye . . .

"Again the motor snorted, but this time it was not for me! 'They' were going back to rest and the comfort of the datcha, while for me there awaited the reeds and whatever there might be behind them. I had been told that for more than three weeks, no couriers had crossed the frontier in safety. I pulled a few strokes ahead and looked back to see the speedboat turning in a graceful curve towards the forts. I was left alone.

"It was a beautiful scene around me, for a late moon appeared on the horizon behind some clouds. I did not need this moon and hoped it would not show me up against the water. Here, protected by the Lissy Nos there was not a ripple on the water and the sea was like a sleepy inland pond. I rowed, trying not to make any sound with the oars. Who knows how near the shore may be and sound always carries a long way across the water when it is calm. The clouds were reflected in the water, and for a moment or so, overcast the light of the moon; suddenly the skiff hit something. It was weeds below the surface of the water and soon the skiff began to scrape more and more on these weeds. It was difficult to make progress. But I saw ahead a clump of reeds for which I made, and behind it, several more. After a while, I found myself in what I can only describe as a perfect corridor of them.

"Alas, they were not above two feet high. The shore was about half a verst away, so it became necessary, it seemed, to discard the boat. The moon now showed up bright and clear and I was apprehensive again that I would be seen and a rifle from a patrol might even at that moment be pointing at me. However, the painful journey was over at last and the skiff dug its nose into the soft sand right in the shade of a big tree surrounded by high soft grass. I jumped out and shook my feet and as ever in such escapades as these, to which I was quite used, I threw aside thought of what was yet to come and busied myself about the moment. The boat had to be pulled up higher and hidden in the bushes, but as I could only pull it up about half-way, I was forced to leave it where it was. I took out the rowlocks and oars and hid them in the grass.

"I thought it would be dangerous to stay there on the shore in case any patrols came along, so I went into the bushes to await the morning, when I could go along to the station and take a train for Petrograd. Out of the boat I took my small leather portfolio containing some drawing materials as I wanted to make a plan of the coast defences.

'Bushes and bog reached down to the water's edge. I had to get strength for the morrow and needed rest, so I found a dry place, took off my red tunic, and lay down on it. Sleep would not come, as my nerves were too highly strung. I fancied I could still hear the roar of the motor and then I relived that long and nerve-racking rowing trip from the speedboat to the shore. But I must sleep. This was essential. I remembered the flask of cognac given to me by the tall, fair sailor. I uncorked it and took a few pulls.

"All around was perfect calm and peace. I seem to re-collect this very spot. Yes, eight years before when I was a young student I used to take part here in picnics from boats we used to sail out from Lakhta. At that time, the country was our own, now alas, it was in the possession of outsiders.

"I took another drink, lay down, and fell asleep.

"I was awakened at dawn by the birds. The weather was

good, warm and calm; my body was tired, I had no inclination whatever to get up, as I felt so drowsy. Indeed, I had chosen an excellent place in which to rest. There were bushes all around which hid me like a high wall.

"It would be suspicious, I thought, if I went at once to the station to catch the first train, so why not wait for the second or third train, when civil servants would be going back to their daily task? Then I could mix with the crowd. I decided to do so and have two more hours' rest and fell asleep again. The sun was up when I awoke; it was eight o'clock. I got up, directed myself by my little compass to the station at Razdielnaya, walking through the bushes so as to avoid the open spaces. It was necessary to avoid any road where I might encounter a patrol.

"The railway was nearer than I thought and I was soon out of danger. When I got to Razdielnaya, quite a crowd of business people had already arrived. But what a change in the looks of these Petersburgers. They were haggard and in rags. Many looked at me with envious eyes, mistaking me for a Commissar and I overheard one old woman say, 'Look at that glutton, see how he has been fed.' I was glad of this, as it showed that my appearance would excite no suspicion and I reached Petrograd quite safely. The only nervous moment I had was when passing through the barrier at the station, as each one had to show their documents. I had been provided with these in Finland which stated that I belonged to a certain institution, but in the end, I did not show them because I managed to make use of a side entrance at the station.

"The first part of my undertaking was over and I had now to make my contact with the mysterious Englishman in Petrograd and transfer to him the despatches which I had sewn in my tunic. Then, God willing, exactly a week later, I must procure another boat, if I could not find the one I had left behind me, and row out to the Elagin lightship at midnight to meet the speedboat, if it managed again to get safely through the forts.

"Then for Europe once more, safety and comfort. There were lots of 'ifs' in the matter."

*   *   *

On 30th July the Admiral carried out operation D.B. (the initials of the late Earl Beatty). It was the first time that British aircraft made their appearance over the Kronstadt fortresses. The object of the operation was to bomb the Bolshevik submarines, their dry dock, and their depot ship in the inner naval harbour of Kronstadt. Photographs had already been obtained. It was, as the Admiral termed it, "blooding the new arrivals", but also served the purpose for them of a dress rehearsal for the big attack that was to come later when the C.M.B. flotilla arrived.

The operation was timed for early dawn and was carried out with much skill and gallantry by the pilots. To our surprise the anti-aircraft fire put up by the Bolsheviks was both heavy and well directed and drove our machines to well over 4,000 feet but in spite of it they returned safely to Biorko without any casualties. Sindall and I took our boats out during the night and waited at a pre-arranged position near the Tolbuhin lighthouse at early dawn. We had been asked to do this by the Admiral in order to support the attack by lying in wait for any Red warships which might come out from Kronstadt or rescue crews who might come to grief. Nothing came out, however, except one small patrol vessel which Sindall attacked, but owing to her light draught, the torpedo passed under the ship and was unfortunately wasted.

Next day I travelled overland to Biorko to see the Admiral and tell him of our plans to go into Petrograd on 4th August and 8th August and the submarine warning ST25 had sent out. Biorko had now taken on all the appearances of an active naval base. The boom defences were laid with gate vessel in place, and the number of ships at anchor presented quite an imposing spectacle. The *Vindictive*, a new composite aircraft carrier had arrived and with her peculiar flying-off deck presented quite a contrast to the light cruisers and destroyers. She was detailed to act as 'parent ship' to the C.M.B. flotilla, one of which had arrived (Lieutenant W. H. Bremner, D.S.C.); the remainder were at Copenhagen and now *en route* for Revel in tow of destroyers and were expected at Biorko in ten days' time at the latest.

The aerodrome, although primitive, was safe enough for the machines to take off but not with a full load of bombs; a good deal of work remained to be done to enlarge the runways, which entailed cutting down more trees. In addition there were anchored inshore of the cruisers close to Koivisto a number of fleet auxiliaries, oilers, store carriers, etc., and a flotilla of Finnish motor launches who took their share in the defence of the base by carrying out patrols close to the shore. Altogether, Biorko was a Scapa Flow in miniature.

The Admiral transferred his flag from H.M.S. *Cleopatra* to H.M.S. *Delhi*. He told me he was still most anxious about the activities of Bolshevik submarines and said he knew that there were at least three working in the vicinity and he was certain that German naval officers were operating them. We had already lost one of our own, the L.55. Absence of darkness, calm weather and narrow waters did not altogether favour them, but they were a real danger all the same. What I had heard confirmed the warning sent out by ST25 and the Admiral in consequence had ordered an increase in the strength of our patrol destroyers. Luckily two of them (H.M.S. *Valorous* and H.M.S. *Vancouver*) encountered one of these submarines on 27th July (the *Ersh*) and claimed to have sunk her.* This success, he said, plus the air bombardment on 30th July, should curtail any future Bolshevik submarine activity, but it was the most he could hope for. Everything now depended on the results of the large-scale C.M.B. operation which was planned for the third week in August.

It was arranged that if we succeeded in bringing ST25 out on the night of 4th August, I was to take him straight to

* The *Ersh* although badly damaged succeeded in getting back to Kronstadt.

the flagship where the Admiral would arrange for his
passage home in a man-o'-war, and his final word to me
just before I took leave of him was to tell me that I had
been commended for gallantry in sinking the *Oleg*, and that
after consulting the Captains in the Fleet my name had
been submitted to the King by the Admiralty for the award
of the Victoria Cross.

*   *   *

After the Air bombardment of 30th July we could see
from our look-out position further indications of activity at
Kronstadt. Small tugs, with lighters in tow, could be seen
every day plying between the forts, and large columns of
smoke issuing frequently from the direction of the naval
base indicated that ships were raising steam.

We wondered what was afoot, and if the Bolsheviks were
busy improving their defences and placing boom obstacles
between the forts. ST31 suggested that they were probably
mounting more anti-aircraft batteries and searchlights on the
outer forts. This proved to be true, as the volume of anti-
aircraft fire directed against our reconnaissance machines
increased daily, and made the task of our pilots difficult and
hazardous. In addition they were further handicapped
because the machines sent out from England were of an
obsolete type and unsuitable for the work, owing to the
small size of the aerodrome at Biorko from which they had
to take off and land. The Finnish aeroplanes gave us what
assistance they could, but their activities were confined
solely to patrolling the Gulf. One brave man—Lieutenant
Hungell—had to make a forced landing on the sea on the
10th August and lost his life. Three days later on 13th
August we suffered our our first British air casualty—
Lieutenant Taylor—who crashed his machine when taking
off from the aerodrome.

The Terrioki Commandant was now getting very nervous
about this air activity and was apprehensive that it might
invite counter measures from Kronstadt. This, he said,

would take the form of a bombardment of Terrioki itself;
(he reminded me that the harbour was supposed to be
within range of the Kronstadt guns), or possibly of an air
bombardment of Terrioki Village by Red aircraft. He knew
the Bolsheviks had several ready for service at Oranienbaum
where there was an aerodrome on the other side of the Gulf,
less than thirty miles away with German pilots. He suggested
that as we now had our own aeroplanes carrying out the
reconnaissance of the Gulf and Kronstadt, it would perhaps
be safer for me to take my two C.M.B.s to Biorko.

This was a poser. I could see that he meant well and was
concerned only for our safety, and I liked him all the more
for it, but I realized that unless I fobbed him off again with
some excuse, the time had now arrived for me to make a
clean breast of our Secret Service activities with Petrograd.
In any case I had now to explain away the presence of Peter
unless the latter was prepared to allow himself to be kept in
close confinement in our *datcha* for days on end. ST31
agreed and said that as we were now dealing with a man who
liked us and was a friend it would be better for our story
to come direct from myself than for the Commandant to
hear of it in a roundabout manner, through a third person.
Had our couriers been Finns the situation would have been
quite different. The trouble was that all three were Russians,
and dislike of anything Russian was growing daily in Finland.
Even General Mannerheim himself was losing his popu-
larity.

*   *   *

It was a long and difficult interview. I could see the
Commandant's face assume an expression first of surprise
and afterwards of seriousness as I unfolded the full story of
our Petrograd activities covering a period of eight weeks
since our first arrival in the beginning of June. They were of
course a flagrant breach of the country's laws. ST31 interpreted for me and occasionally put in a word on his own
account, when reference was made to the couriers. We kept

nothing back, except our connection between Helsingfors and London as that was a matter that did not concern the Commandant. We had to make out a good case and in the opening gambit I think we did. When I had finished my explanations there followed an awkward pause.

"What you have told me," said the Commandant, "may have serious consequences both for you gentlemen and myself. You have compromised my position, because I am responsible for the examination of every person who enters Finland across my section of the frontier, which extends from sea to Lake Ladoga. Even you yourselves must be under suspicion if you have, as you admit, crossed this frontier on several occasions.'

I pointed to the map hanging on his wall, and indicated that when I had crossed the frontier, the route I had chosen was a sea passage, and I stressed the point that, although he was technically correct in saying that I had crossed and recrossed the Russo-Finnish border from Terrioki, I could equally well have done so from Biorko, which was not within the Commandant's control, and from which base the British Admiral had already obtained permission from the Government of Finland to operate. I added that my principal concern was the status of the 'couriers', since it was more convenient for me to run them into Petrograd from Terrioki than from Biorko.

"Yes," he replied, "that is precisely the point. These men, about whom I know nothing, should have been brought before me for examination. My instructions are to arrest, and detain in quarantine for a period of fourteen days at least, every person arriving in Finnish Territory from Soviet Russia, and whether they arrive by land or by sea it is the same thing. What guarantee have I," he asked, "that your couriers are not Red agents who, unknown to you, are spreading propaganda in Finland. You may say they are not, and you may be right, but how can you judge?"

I saw at once the force of the Commandant's argument. If we had stuck literally to the regulations, both Peter and

Gefter had to be interned in the quarantine camp for a fort-night at least; their whole position would be compromised, our activities disclosed to many officials, and the prospect of keeping our future plans secret would be wrecked. We had to win the Commandant over to our view.

I explained at length that we had enlisted the services of only three couriers. It was true that they were Russians and all of them ex-officers, but before taking them into our service, ST31 had made the strictest enquiries as regards their characters and history prior to the Revolution. If necessary, we could get the highest British authority in Helsingfors—namely the British Minister—to vouch for them. I myself would vouch for their conduct in Terrioki and asked the Commandant to accept my word of honour on this point. I pointed out to him that in the work we were doing two factors were of vital importance, namely time and secrecy and surely he must see that if we were to continue our work with these couriers, it would be im-possible to do so if they had to conform to the regulations made for those Russian refugees who had the good fortune to escape into Finland across the frontier.

I could see that the Commandant was still unconvinced. He added for our information, that to his own certain knowledge several Soviet agents had also crossed the frontier into Finland during the last two months and were now doing his country a lot of harm with Communist propa-ganda.

"Already," he said, "due to their pernicious agitation, our people are beginning to react against our liberator and Regent—General Mannerheim."

I told him that, of the three couriers, we had only passed two into Petrograd and, of these two, so far only one had come out—Peter. He was now in my *datcha* and I invited the Commandant to interview him at once. I also gave an undertaking that when I had brought the second courier out I would bring him to the Commandant for a personal inter-view. But I wished at all costs to avoid his subordinate officers being told of the identity and activities of these two men.

"By your own showing, Commandant, if there are Red agents in Finland, surely we are the very people against whom those agents will direct their activities."

At this point I could see the Commandant begin to hesitate. Pressing our case I begged him to treat it as a special one. I said that up to now our secret had been preserved, and asked him to remember that we had already given him full proof of our common cause of the defence of the Finnish coast against Bolshevik aggression, by our action in sinking the cruiser *Oleg* and also in our reconnaissance trips off Kronstadt island.

"As regards these two couriers," I said, "they are two brave Russian patriots who have risked their lives in what they believe to be the cause of their country and have no other interests. I alone am responsible for their presence here. You may blame me if you like for not giving you our *full confidence* when we first arrived here. Had I done so you would have had no option—not knowing our peculiar circumstances as you do now—but to place the couriers in your quarantine camp." He nodded assent and I continued.

"The position now is quite different as we have been able, during this period of two months, to complete our own British Intelligence Organization with a brave Englishman at the head of it, who is now in Petrograd. I myself have a responsibility towards this man, who in serving the British Government is also serving the best interests of Finland. You have been a good friend to us in the past and our Minister in Helsingfors will not forget the assistance you have given us. All I ask from you now is permission to carry on from Terrioki until this Englishman of ours in Petrograd is safe."

ST31, who interpreted word for word as I went on, put more than extra vehemence into this last sentence. I could see the Commandant was not only impressed with our sincerity but had also made up his mind. Turning to me, he asked, "When are you going next to Petrograd in your boat?"

"Tonight," I replied.

"And your couriers?"

I explained to him that one was already there whom I hoped to bring out with ST25. The other was being left behind.

"This man then, whom you are leaving behind," he went on, "I understand he has been with you backwards and forwards at least on two or three occasions."

"Yes," I replied, "that is so."

"Very well, then," he said decisively, "my instructions from Helsingfors are to the effect that I am to assist you to operate your boats in every way I can. This I will do—but as regards your Russian courier, I cannot permit him to go with you unless I see him first. Upon this interview will depend whether or not I grant him the necessary permission.

"Now, as regards your boats, if you choose to go to Petrograd, that is your own business and your own risk, but remember I must see myself anyone you bring back here. That is clearly my duty. To oblige you I will not send them into the quarantine camp if they are known to you personally but they must not leave this area without my permission. I myself have the responsibility of your personal safety. Sooner or later your counter-revolutionary activities against the Communists will become known. There is first your sinking of the cruiser *Oleg* and secondly the activities of your British aeroplanes. Neither of these can be kept secret from the Bolsheviks much longer. For the moment you are safe, but as soon as your presence at Terrioki is known you may be sure that the Communists will send special Red agents to put an end to your activities. Some of them are here in Finland even at this moment and however much we watch them, sometimes they escape us."

I thanked him for his consideration and kindness. I could almost hear the sigh of relief from ST31 as he interpreted those final words, and promising to send Peter to report at

K

his office that afternoon, I took my departure. Once again
Colonel Sarin proved himself to be a true friend.

Peter, when told that he had to report at once to the
Commandant's office, was at first terribly nervous. We
explained to him that it was the best thing to do in the
circumstances and reassured him that all would be well; that
he was not to invent any cock and bull story, but just relate
the fact that he was entirely in our employ and had no
interest as regards Finland. His Finnish papers were in order.

He acquitted himself well in his interview with the
Commandant and was given permission to stay on in
Terrioki provided he lived at our *datcha* and did not go
elsewhere. He was, he said, most anxious to accompany me
on the trip to the new rendezvous, pointing out that in case
of any accident to us in the boat he might be able to help
us, as he knew one of the crew on board the Elagin lightship
off Lakhta. In the end I agreed to take him, not that I
wanted to have any communication with the lightship but
because I knew he would never be a liability, and might, if
things went wrong with us, prove to be a great asset.

We calculated that ST25 had now returned from Moscow
as it was 8th August and the date arranged to fetch him out.
Gefter was in Petrograd and had had ample time (ten days)
in which to complete all his preparations, the most important of which consisted of the provision of a shore boat to
take both himself and ST25 from the shore to where my
boat was waiting, a distance of just over one mile. Sindall
had explained to me the exact place where he had stopped,
and where Gefter had landed.

It was to be our last trip in as I had already sent a message
to ST25, verbally, by Gefter, that after this date it would be
impossible for me to come in for him on account of the naval
operations which the Admiral would probably be taking
against Kronstadt, and that these operations would not be
complete before the third week in August, after which date,
if necessary I could come in again, but that the risks would
be greater.

I must confess I had more anxiety about our chances of getting through the chain of forts successfully on this trip than on the previous one. I could not dismiss from my mind the ominous movements of tugs with lighters in tow plying to and fro between the island forts, which we had seen from our watch-tower during the last week. Peter, as usual, was full of optimism. He wanted to be the first man to greet ST25 on his return to safety and on this occasion I was positively glad of his cheerful company.

We left the harbour as usual, just before 10 p.m. and made towards the forts. This time we aimed at the gap between numbers nine and eleven, instead of between numbers ten and eight. I had in the boat besides myself Peter, Beeley, and the Finnish smuggler pilot.

There was an early moon which did not tend to help us, but luckily the night was cloudy and there was every indication of a local storm. This, however, would only be in our favour and was no cause for us to abandon our enterprise. A heavy rain squall came down just as we were approaching the forts and completely blotted them out from view. I carried on at slow speed, steering by compass and had negotiated the passage successfully without being seen by the time the storm had passed. We soon found ourselves leaving the forts behind us, steering east towards Petrograd. It was a lucky break and now for the rendezvous which was only five miles away on our left, off Lissy Nos Point. We turned towards the lightship and, passing it on our starboard side, about half a mile away, stopped engines about half a mile from the shore and waited.

There was no sign of a boat or any signal. I waited a quarter of an hour and crept closer towards the shore. Still no sign, and in the meanwhile another squall came down on us. In desperation I made the pre-arranged signal on an electric torch *towards the shore* again and again, thinking perhaps that there had been some mistake and Gefter had missed his way; although by doing so I knew that not only we ourselves, but also our two men on shore would be running risk of discovery. We waited another half hour and there was still no sign of any boat. Peter suggested going up to the lightship and asking them if they had seen a rowing boat about, but I would not hear of this as we would have to come out again. He then offered to swim to the lightship alone and from there to the shore, but I disliked and mistrusted any idea of communication with the lightship, which obviously must have at least one Communist on board (even if Peter knew the remainder of the crew) and decided that the only thing to do now was to go back and come in again another night. It was already getting on towards dawn and there was only just time to get through the forts before daybreak. Reluctantly we headed the boat back.

What could have happened to ST25? Little did we know that during that terrible period of waiting, both he and Gefter were quite close to us and had seen our boat. Neither did we realize (until months later, when he recounted to me the full story of his experiences during that awful night) that through a series of misfortunes they had to forsake their small rowing boat and swim towards the shore to save their lives, and were lying exhausted on the shore, actually in sight of our signal.*

We were so depressed at our failure that we hardly gave a thought to the risk we ran on our way back through the forts until we looked round to find them well behind us and the boat heading towards Terrioki. The first streaks of dawn were already showing and I remember remarking to Beeley that Gefter might have had some difficulty in his rowing boat in the heavy rain squalls which we had encountered on our way in and out.

Taking stock of our position, I thought things were not so bad after all, since we had overcome our principal difficulty,

* For a full account of this episode see *The Story of ST25* by Sir Paul Dukes published by Cassell. It was a terrible experience for them both. Gefter, to be on the safe side evidently purloined a small fishing boat lying on the beach, but forgot to close the 'fish well', with the result that the boat slowly and steadily filled with water as they rowed from the shore towards us. Within a short while they were forced to go back to save their lives and lay exhausted in the reeds while they watched my C.M.B. return to the forts.

which was the passage of the forts, and therefore the tug and lighter activity which we had seen could not have been directed against us nor had any booms been placed in our path. Then again, I reflected, ST25 probably had reasons of his own for not coming out on this occasion. Having made the passage once under the new conditions, we could do it again. This at least was a comforting thought.

On arriving back at the *datcha* ST31, Peter and I discussed the pros and cons of the whole position. We strongly suspected that ST25's plan had miscarried. I felt certain that he would have come out on that night if it had been humanly possible to do so, and if he had been arrested, then I felt sure that Gefter would have come out to give us the news. So the very fact that *neither* of them appeared pointed to the conclusion that they were both safe and would try again. Fresh dates and places had to be arranged. Peter must go in again to do this. He needed no persuasion. So it was agreed that I should take him in on the following night as there was no time to be lost. I selected another rendezvous midway between Lissy Nos Point and Krestovsky island — that is between our first two rendezvous, and a little closer to the shore to give the rowing boat as short a pull in as possible. Meanwhile I received a message from Biorko to the effect that most of the C.M.B. flotilla had arrived and that the Kronstadt Raid would take place very shortly.

In view of this, I told Peter to tell ST25 that he must stay in Petrograd a little while longer or escape across the Estonian frontier as I could not be certain of bringing him out until after the attack. I gave him two alternative dates, the 23rd and 25th August. Failing this, Peter must take his chance again of getting through the Finnish frontier lines.

I saw the Commandant the next morning and told him of our failure, adding that I was taking in Peter again that evening. I said that after that I would be having no further communication with Petrograd for at least a fortnight and would follow his advice and withdraw my boats to Biorko. He was very friendly indeed; hoped that I would be successful and assured me he would always be ready and willing to do anything he could to help me if and when I returned.

We managed, by paying a large sum of money, to procure a small boat at Terrioki from one of the Finnish fishermen for Peter to row himself ashore. It was too large to carry on board the C.M.B. and I had no choice but to tow it behind reducing both our manoeuvrability and speed. We set out again at the same time that night and once more reached our rendezvous unobserved. The place which we had selected lay about half a mile from the shore, but as the rowing boat was leaky, we went in closer before stopping engines to give Peter a better chance of getting safely on shore, and, more important still, to give him a chance to escape if there happened to be any patrols about. I told him that if he got into difficulties on landing, he was either to row back quickly to me, or swim back, and that until I received his safety signal of three flashes I would stay in the C.M.B. where I was. This subsequently nearly proved to be our undoing.

We had to wait over half an hour before seeing Peter's 'safe' signal. Beeley at once proceeded to start up the engine for the return journey, when to our dismay he discovered that the small cylinder of compressed air which we used for starting up the engines had been leaking on our way out and there was now very little pressure left. To add to this difficulty the engine had cooled off a trifle during the long wait. I should explain here that without these cylinders it was impossible to give the cranks of our powerful Thornycroft motor (which had never failed us) sufficient impulse to start. Normally we carried two, but I had already used the spare cylinder on our trip the day before. Would there be sufficient pressure in this one left just for one more start? If there wasn't we were completely done in. Our lives depended on that cylinder and nothing else.

I could see Beeley's face in the light of my electric torch as I held it for him near the bottom of the boat while he changed over the cylinders. The sweat stood out on his forehead, but his hands were perfectly steady. He knew as well as I knew what that cylinder meant. Not a word was said and I experienced the same feeling as when we lay in the boat rolling about between those two Bolshevik destroyers, in our attack on the *Oleg* when Hampsheir was trying to load the second cordite charge. One gets a certain tightening of the collar during these moments and there is a difficulty in swallowing. Beeley made the adjustments slowly and carefully, leaving nothing to chance. "All ready, sir," he said, to which I replied as quietly and calmly as I could, "All right, start up, Beeley." There was a hiss at first as the air went into the cylinder, then a splutter. For a split second I thought that that was the last of the charge and the cylinder had given out. But there was just sufficient kick behind it to turn the cranks, and, with a final cough, the engine started.

It was a close thing, and the nearest Beeley and I had been to a Bolshevik prison up to then. Our luck was in though, and still held for the return journey. We accomplished it without incident as far as the small breakwater off Terrioki harbour. But just as the boat was making the entrance, the steering wheel jammed, causing the boat to make a sharp turn. Our stern swung round and hit a projecting rock. This accident lost us our propeller and shaft, which was fractured, and the boat put out of action. It was lucky, though, that it happened at the end of our journey and not in the middle when we were making the passage of the forts. We still had C.M.B. No. 7 left intact and in this boat Sindall and I left for Biorko early next morning to take our part in operation 'R.K.' (Roger Keyes).

* * *

CHAPTER VI

KRONSTADT

"A report has been received from the British senior naval officer in the Baltic that a naval engagement took place in the Gulf of Finland early on August 18th.

"Two Russian battleships, the Petropavlovsk *and the* Andrei Pervosvanni *and one destroyer were sunk. A cruiser was also seriously damaged.*

"The British losses were three coastal-motor boats."

Admiralty statement, August 19th, 1919.

HISTORICALLY the C.M.B. Operation to which this brief statement refers is called 'The Kronstadt Raid' as that was the title given to it by the British Press at the time. It was not very wide of the mark, because it was a surprise raid on an enemy harbour with the sole object of destroying certain warships in it.

Walter Cowan had no intention of attacking such a well fortified place as Kronstadt, still less of putting landing parties on shore to destroy fortifications, harbour installations and so on. Any ideas of this kind would have required forces far beyond what he asked for or had available at Biorko. He wanted simply and solely to immobilize for the remainder of the year, the two Russian battleships and submarine depot ship lying there, after which winter ice would complete the business by sealing up the harbour until the following April.

To him it was as simple as all that, since his cruisers were well capable of dealing with any ships left intact after the raid, such as the destroyer division of the *Gavriel* class and the minelaying cruiser *Rurik*. He had exact intelligence from his own reconnaissance planes as to the strength and position of the Red Fleet in Kronstadt, and from the reports of

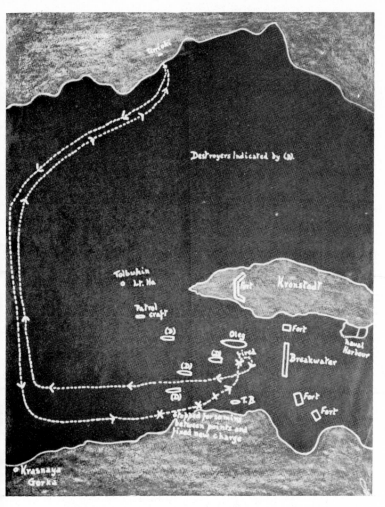

Author's plan of the sinking of *Oleg* (made at the time)

BALTIC 1919   KRONSTADT   26 JULY 1919

Before our Aeroplanes and
Coastal Motor Boats be-
came active

← *Petropavlovsk*
    (torpedoed)

← *Andrei Pervozann*
    (torpedoed 3 times got into
    dock)

Outpost Destroyer →
(3 torpedoes missed under)

Pamyat Azova →
(torpedoed and sunk)

Destroyer Depot Ship →
(disappeared after bombing
raid)

After Coastal Motor Boat
raid of 18–19 Aug. 19

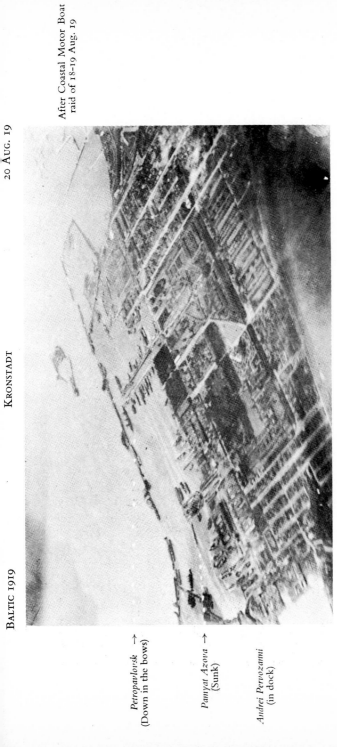

Petropavlovsk →
(Down in the bows)

Pamyat Azova →
(Sunk)

Andrei Pervozanni
(in dock)

Kronstadt Harbour after the raid

C.M.B. 4 now on view in the building yard of Messrs.
J. Thornycroft at Hampton-on-Thames

C.M.B.s in Terrioki Harbour with yacht club in background

ST25 via myself as to the efficiency and morale of the shore
defences under the command of Commissar Gordienko, but
which were actually being directed by Trotsky in person.

Walter Cowan was under no illusions as to what he was
up against and the risks involved, but like all great leaders
refused to be unduly influenced by the odds against him.
He based his plan on the element of *surprise*, that element
in war rated by Nelson, Napoleon and other renowned
Commanders as the highest of all tactical and strategical
requirement essential for success.

I remember so well during one of our walks on shore, the
Admiral expounding to me this principle based on a lifetime
of active service. "To give your enemy advance notice of
your intentions, as we did at the Dardanelles, Agar, is to
invite failure." He followed this with a eulogy on his friend,
Admiral Sir Roger Keyes, and his surprise blockship operation in Zeebrugge harbour. "Yes, Agar," he continued.
"complete surprise and I shall do the same thing here . . ."

Never was a man more confident and full of enthusiasm,
and he promptly labelled the raid 'Operation R.K.' after
the initials of his friend whose example he emulated.

While I was waiting in Biorko, he often took me for his
afternoon walk on shore, the only exercise he allowed himself,
striding out as fast as his short legs could carry him. It
was a job for anyone to keep up, especially the marine
orderly who followed half walking, half running. He
insisted on being accompanied always by his special orderly
armed only with a stick and bayonet (side arms) because he
said it was bad manners to carry a revolver in Finland, a
friendly country. It was on one of these outings when he
broke the news that after consulting his captains in the
Fleet he had sent in my name for an award of the Victoria
Cross and had received a message that King George V had
approved, together with a D.S.C. for Hampsheir and
Conspicuous Gallantry Medal for faithful Beeley, my
mechanic. The official citation was not made until much later
so I remained something of a 'Mystery V.C.' in the same

manner as Commander Gordon Campbell. I was over-whelmed with congratulations from my old friends from Osea when they arrived in the C.M.B. Flotilla.

Biorko had by now taken on a 'new look' altogether, and the harbour was a hive of activity compared with the solitary sheet of water with one small oiler in the corner when we first arrived nine weeks previously. It was now the first week in August, and by local standards the end of the summer and beginning of autumn. No longer could we expect day after day of lovely calm weather as the autumn storms would soon begin. H.M.S. *Vindictive*, a brand new composite carrier, e.g., half-cruiser, half-carrier, was at anchor acting as parent ship to the C.M.B. Flotilla of which six boats had already arrived and were berthed alongside. One was lost in the North Sea and one still due.

She was commanded by Captain Edgar Grace (generally known as 'Dasher') and son of the late Dr. W. G. of cricket fame. He incurred, alas, the Admiral's wrath by getting his ship stuck on a shoal when about to enter Revel harbour on the way to Biorko. Walter Cowan ordered her to be cleared at once of all ammunition and stores to lighten the ship and a division of destroyers to steam at full speed as close as possible to where she lay aground; hoping that the wash of the destroyers plus the lightening of the ship would free her while he connected up tows from his flagship and another cruiser. The Baltic being tideless, no other method was possible.

Luckily the weather continued calm, and after frantic efforts on the part of everyone under the eye of an angry and impatient Admiral, the *Vindictive* was towed clear of the shoal, but poor old 'Dasher' Grace remained under a cloud for quite a time before regaining the Admiral's good books after his excellent work at Biorko in getting the C.M.B.s ready for the Raid. 'Dasher', as his nickname implies, was a most energetic and forceful captain and extremely popular with our young chaps in the boats while they were berthed alongside his ship, as well as with the airmen, under

Squadron-Leader Donald, who for the first time were carrying out an operation under the newly established R.A.F. instead of the old R.N.A.S.

Besides the *Vindictive*, an additional flotilla of destroyers, and a group of inshore mine-sweepers added to the number of ships in the bay which already held oilers, storeships and fleet auxiliaries on a modest scale, but nevertheless gave the anchorage an impressive appearance. The sailors obviously knew that something was in the wind, followed of course by much speculation and buzzing on the mess decks of the cruisers, but nobody knew quite what it was until the day before the Operation.

Fortunately Walter Cowan allowed no press correspondents with the fleet, giving Pollock of *The Times* one interview only, with half a page of notes which he showed me beforehand and no more; adding, that he would treat all other press callers exactly the same. I'm afraid Pollock went away somewhat disgruntled, but those were the days before Press conferences afloat and Press hand-outs. Hughie Muir of the *Daily Express* fared much better by remaining in Helsingfors and discreetly tapping the gossip-mongers in the Hotel Societenhusen (H.Q. of Yudenitch) who knew everything except the movements of the British fleet which remained—as Walter intended that it should—wrapped in mystery while he commanded in the Gulf of Finland.

On shore, besides the aerodrome already referred to, Donald set up a small seaplane base on the foreshore on the opposite side of the bay where there was a cove with a nice sandy beach. It was in full view of the cruisers at anchor which made it easy to pass signals from one base to the other using a cruiser as repeating ship. The sandy beach was popular with the signalmen because the local villagers used it for their daily dip which in Finland is taken by both sexes in the nude. So there was no excuse for the 'bunting-tossers' (sailors' slang for signalmen) *not* keeping a good look-out on the seaplane station from the cruiser's flag decks which were specially fitted with high-powered naval telescopes.

Human nature being what it is, one cannot blame the zealous signalmen; but this Finnish sea-bathing custom was soon adopted by the seaplane crews without in any way causing comment or offence to the villagers, which shows how silly we are sometimes with our ideas of sex.

As one of my C.M.B.s was a lame duck I could offer the Admiral the use of one only, and was thrilled and honoured when he asked me to lead the C.M.B. flotilla through the chain of forts before the boats took up their final positions for the attack on Kronstadt harbour. He said it was just what he wanted as the others, following me in the larger boats, would have more confidence in getting through knowing I had done the passage successfully several times already. Technically we were not under his orders, but I was certain that 'C' in London would warmly approve our taking part. Captain French who had organized so well and at such short notice the despatch of the Flotilla from Osea Island, had placed it under the command of a more senior officer in Commander C. C. Dobson, an ex-submariner, and 'Dobbie' to the flotilla. French gave him one of our most experienced C.M.B. officers—Lieutenant Russell ('Beans') MacBean, D.S.O.—to handle his boat and they made a splendid combination, 'Dobbie' running the Flotilla and 'Beans' his boat.

The Admiral wasted no time making his plans and final decisions. In a man like him there were no elaborate orders or reams of paper work known as 'bumph' by soldiers, an expression which Walter disliked as an ugly word. Leaving Squadron-Leader Donald and Commander Dobson to settle between themselves details about the aircraft and C.M.B. Flotilla and the exact timing of each other's movements, he insisted on the attack being carried out as soon as possible. Every day's delay he warned us meant less chances of the advantages of a 'surprise blow'. There was therefore to be the utmost speed in preparation, and if a boat or aircraft was not ready on the day ordered for the operation, it must be left behind and that was that. Mindful of the mistake we made at the Dardanelles and the success of Roger Keyes at Zeebrugge, Walter Cowan would brook no delay at all except that of weather. Actually, after their long trip across the North Sea the C.M.B.s certainly did need engine overhauls, but a week was the maximum time allowed with an extra day for rehearsals, which were carried out off the *Vindictive*.

We had reached the second week of August and, as the moon conditions would be just about right between the 17th and 21st, the Admiral ordered Operation R.K. between those dates on the first night suitable. It was not to be confined only to C.M.B.s and Aircraft, but a strong backing up force of cruisers and destroyers were also to take part by patrolling outside the minefield. Apart from the obvious foresight in having his bigger guns ready in case things went wrong and we were chased out of Kronstadt harbour, it was a fine morale booster for the ships' companies to feel that they also were part of the big attack and not just sitting pretty in Biorko, while the skimmers and aircraft were stealing the show. It was a gesture of recognition for the services of the men in the larger ships after all their hard work on patrol duties and sweeping channels clear of mines in dangerous zones, work which was usually out of sight yet always hazardous, but with Walter Cowan never forgotten. It was his way of showing the sailors that everyone in his Fleet regardless of what ships they served in, was part of the team.

The Admiral's idea of an air diversion while the C.M.B.s were making their way through the passages of the forts required the most careful timing. Taking basis zero hour as the time the first C.M.B. should be due at the entrance to the basin of the Naval Dockyard where the Russian battleships were berthed or, as the younger chaps put it, the time when the balloon goes up, I reckoned that given a successful run through the forts at slow speed, and allowing for a certain amount of delay, it would take about half an hour to find our way round to the dockyard basin entrance.

It was this vital half hour which was the crux of the whole plan, and if our airboys could keep the Russian gunners and searchlights busy during this period, there was, I thought, a good chance of the C.M.B.s getting through as far as the basin before their presence could be known; and therefore if the passage of the forts could be made at 1 a.m., the period during which the C.M.B.s would need help from the air would be between 1 a.m. and 1.30 a.m. Our supporters would drop at regular intervals as many *small bombs* as possible, the effect of which would be to keep the garrison gunners underground and under cover. From this Dobson reckoned that the main attack on the battleships should be round about 1.30 a.m. (0130), drawing from Walter Cowan the remark that in all his experience on shore during land operations—and his experience in China, the Sudan, and Boer Wars was by no means inconsiderable—the best time for an attack was always between 1 a.m. and 3 a.m. when human nature reduces the morale of sentries and men on look-out duties to its lowest. Apart from this, we hoped that one effect of the Air bombardment would be to force the sailors on board the Russian ships to take cover between decks which indeed proved to be the case.

Dobson and Donald therefore each co-ordinated the time of arrival of their units so that the aircraft would drop their bombs as the C.M.B.s arrived off the inner line of forts and continued to do so for half an hour, by which time it was expected that the leading 55ft. C.M.B. would be off the main dockyard basin entrance (150 feet wide). This was the main idea. As for the rest, chance must always play an important part as Nelson never failed to remind his captains before he went into battle, with the famous order:

> "In close actions at sea and hazardous operations on shore, something must always be left to chance . . .
> "But in case signals can neither be seen or perfectly understood, no captain can do wrong if he places his ship alongside one of the enemy."

Walter Cowan showed me a faded copy of this order written in his own handwriting and carried in a thin leather cover in the inside pocket of his reefer jacket which he wore at sea during five years of War.

With the addition of our small 40 footer in which the Admiral had asked me to lead the C.M.B.s through the chain of forts, Dobson's flotilla consisted of seven 55ft. boats, four of which carried two torpedoes and the remainder one each. When fully loaded they were slower than the forty footers but they carried in addition more machine guns and depth charges. I must explain here that all C.M.B.s had a large turning circle, and while they were easy to manoeuvre at high speed, they required plenty of sea room. The restricted space inside the dockyard basin therefore handicapped the crews considerably when handling their boats, as they had to turn before firing torpedoes and declutch one engine to reduce speed while manoeuvring in such a confined space. Luckily the 55ft. type had two engines and two propellers which made things a trifle easier for them, but nevertheless it was going to be an extremely tricky job to handle a C.M.B. once inside.

For technical reasons the engines were not fitted with reversing gear so we could not stop our boats by going astern. The most that could be done was to take out the clutch (a rather crude affair), to slow down the boat and hope for the best. Normally when berthing after a run, we shut off the engine at a point allowing sufficient room for the boat to lose her way, after which all hands grabbed boat hooks and check lines to bring her to a stop, assisted perhaps by a friendly hand on shore or by the gangway of a ship. Otherwise the boat would overshoot the mark as would an aircraft on landing and the technique was much the same. Occasionally the clutch stuck and refused to come out. This usually happened after a fast run when the engine was very hot and it made things more than awkward.

Faithful Beeley my mechanic in C.M.B. No. 4 had a

wonderful dodge which worked most successfully. He kept
handy a carpenter's wooden mallet well weighted with lead
with which he beat the clutch fly wheel as hard as he could
before pulling out the lever. My passengers, when they
watched him do this for the first time, thought he had gone
mad but he never failed to get the clutch out. And now we
must examine more closely the problem posed for Dobson
—how best to organize his seven boats to make sure of
hitting the targets selected by the Admiral.:

By priority they were:

1. *Andrei Pervosvanni*—battleship commanded by Senior
   Commissar Raskolnikov.
2. *Petropavlovsk*—battleship.
3. *Pamiat Azova*—Submarine parent ship with two S/M.s
   alongside.
4. *Rurik*—an old cruiser fitted for minelaying.
5. The dry dock—in one corner of the basin.

These were the principal targets, but our airmen had seen a
destroyer guardship usually at anchor just outside the basin
which would require attention.

There was as might be expected amongst the C.M.B.
personnel much discussion as to choice of targets, and a
natural eagerness all round to be one of the boats selected
for the basin. As for our small forty-footer, my job ended
after we had led the flotilla through the chain of forts, but
Dobson asked me to remain on patrol between the forts
and the next basin, known as the military harbour, where
tugs and smaller vessels were berthed, to intercept any
patrol craft coming out, but at all costs to keep clear of the
attacking C.M.B.s. The cruiser *Rurik* was included in the
targets because an agent (through ST25) reported she was
loaded with 300 live mines, always the Russians' favourite
weapon from which our ships had suffered several casualties;
a matter which induced the Admiral to stress a point
that if there was a torpedo to spare he would be pleased

for her to have it, but the battleships must come first.

I don't think 'Dobbie' cared much about the prospect of 300 Russian mines exploding with one large bang inside the basin, nor did the others but the Admiral would have enjoyed the fireworks which no doubt would have been a wonderful spectacle, but hardly a comforting one for the C.M.B. crews close to the *Rurik*. Anyway, it was hoped to use any extra torpedoes on the battleships and one against the dry dock before giving the last—*and positively the last one* —to the *Rurik* as a parting shot by the last boat leaving the basin.

Dobson's final target plan (see plan on pages 168-9) was settled after the airmen had carefully made an air survey picture of the basin with all the ships in place, from which it will be seen that the most difficult targets were the two battleships berthed together in one corner of the basin, and the easiest target, the submarine depot ship *Pamiat Azova*. The destroyer guard ship berthed outside was also a reasonably easy target depending which way she was swung to the wind. Finally to make certain of how they lay, Donald arranged for two planes to make a final recce of the basin on the afternoon before the attack, one carrying Dobson and the other Bill Bremner, (Lieut. W. H. Bremner, D.S.O., R.N.), a most experienced C.M.B. officer who was to lead the C.M.B.s into the basin. He carried in his boat a set of net cutters and gun cotton charges with which, in the event of there being a boom laid across the entrance he was to blow a gap before attacking the *Pamiat Azova*.

With seven C.M.B.s at his disposal Dobson assigned one (Lieut. Napier, R.N.) to attack the destroyer guard ship outside the basin and the remaining six to go for targets *inside* with Bill Bremner leading as No. 1 after which he was to be followed by five boats as follows:

		Target
C. Dobson		
&	No. 2	*Andrei Pervosvanni*
R. MacBean		(2 Torpedoes)

L

A. Dayrell-Reed
      &   }   No. 3   *Petropavlovsk*
G. Steele   (2 *Torpedoes*)

There was to be a short pause of ten to fifteen minutes
between the first three boats and the next three, who were
to go for the battleships again if the first attacks failed, or
alternatively the *Rurik* and dry dock. The idea of the pause
was to allow time for the first three boats to reach two
waiting billets inside the basin, so as to avoid a collision
with the next three C.M.B.s following them.

This risk of collision between boats was uppermost in the
minds of everyone, the Admiral included. One certain way
of avoiding them was to insist on a longer interval of twenty
to thirty minutes between the first three boats entering the
basin and the rest.

Dobson rather favoured this idea, but it was not popular
with the crews who thought that if they had to wait for the
first three to clear the basin the next three would stand a poor
chance of getting in their attacks, so the pause and waiting
billet idea was adopted. Two places were chosen ahead and
astern of a hospital ship, berthed at the southern end, and
we accepted risks of collision if the timing went wrong;
risks which were very real in a restricted space with six
boats running at night at high speed without lights, apart
from the opposition of battery and machine gun fire and the
blinding glare of searchlights on the boats' crews.

Looking back on the plan, it might perhaps have been
better if four boats only were allowed inside and the
remainder kept out until the guard-ship had been disposed of
and the attack on the battleships delivered, but it is easy
to be wise afterwards especially when taking into account
that a C.M.B. cannot fire a torpedo except when travelling
at high speed. At lesser speed the torpedo takes a dive known
technically as 'the initial dive' and strikes the bottom,
which stands the boat a fair chance of being blown up with
the torpedo. Nor had we any aircraft or C.M.B. flares to

illuminate the basin and help the C.M.B.s find their targets. We had to make our plans with what material there was available on the spot.

Lt. A. Dayrell-Reed, D.S.O., R.N.R., who was due to follow 'Dobbie', was popularly called 'Mossy' because of his large black beard. He had the other battleship *Petropavlosk* as his target (but actually we did not know which was which), and afterwards was to go on to a waiting billet. He had a splendid crew including Gordon Steele, his second in command, who was awarded afterwards a Victoria Cross, and Sub-Lieutenant Morley, who had been shipmates with Gordon in the *Iron Duke*. They were perhaps the best team in the flotilla. The next party which was due to enter (Nos. 4; 5 and 6) was commanded by Lieutenant-Comdr. J. Brade, R.N.R., Sub-Lieutenants F. Howard, R.N.R. and E. R. Bodley, R.N.R. They also had the battleships as their target so had likewise to follow the same line of approach as Dobson (see map and diagram) but as already explained were given the two alternatives of the dry dock and the *Rurik* in the event of the battleships being successfully hit by 'Dobbie' and 'Mossy' Reed.

I have often thought on reflection that those C.M.B.s who were due to follow the first three, had more difficult tasks than their leaders although at the time of the discussions on board H.M.S. *Vindictive;* it was thought that if the first three succeeded in getting inside the rest would be easy. But when crews are unable to see things in their immediate vicinity, and know that the alarm had been raised and the enemy thoroughly alerted against them as they entered the basin, the strain of keeping a cool head and judging aright what action to take to damage the enemy without damaging their own side is more heavy. The first-comers, although the first to face the music, at least had a good sporting chance of catching their enemy unprepared and a better one of getting clear away. We were hoping that by the time the first torpedo attacks had been delivered there would be so much confusion in the basin that the second party would have little difficulty in getting away, and so it would have been, except for an unfortunate mishap.

Having settled on the targets and timing of the operation all that remained was a final briefing of the crews and our order of departure from Biorko towards the first obstacle, the now familiar chain of forts on the North side. The Admiral considered it a better one to tackle, since we had negotiated it several times ourselves. It would be safer than trying a new route at the southern end of Kronstadt which entered the main channel to Petrograd and was certain to be better watched and more strongly defended than the others.

We settled unanimously on the passages through the chain of forts, and to make certain of them I engaged through ST30, who was living in the *datcha* at Terrioki, two contra-bandist pilots, one of whom had done the passage with me before. This one I gave to Dobson who took him in his boat, while I took the other myself, but when it was explained to them that after passing through the forts we intended to turn to the *right* and make for the naval basin in Kronstadt to attack the Russian fleet at their berths, and not to the *left* towards our previous R/V off Krestovsky Island, the smuggler-pilots got cold feet and wanted to back out. They were, however, finally persuaded to come with us on promise of double pay of £25 each for the trip, plus a double ration of rum (two quarts instead of one); H.M.S. *Delhi*'s paymaster providing both money and rum as well as answers after-wards to Treasury inquiries.

One extraordinary piece of good luck came our way. On the 15th August the fine Baltic summer weather broke and instead of lovely calm weather the eastern part had two to three days of westerly gales in succession accompanied by frequent squalls of heavy rain and leaden skies. This bad weather caused a piling up of water in the Gulf of Finland, and a general rise in the level of two to three feet at least. The advantage of this to the shallow draft C.M.B.s was obvious and not to be missed. The weather cleared on the

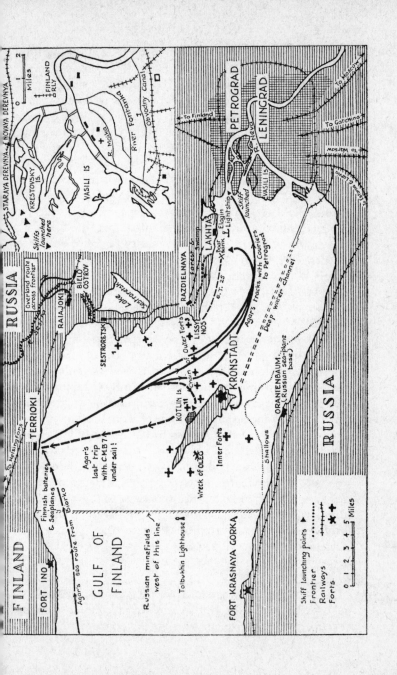

17th and without waiting for another day the Admiral ordered the Operation R.K. to take place that very night.

Dobson and Bremner were given by the airmen a final bird's-eye view of the basin, and the crews were all ready to go after a few last minute preparations and a splendid address from the Admiral. As might be expected from a man like Walter Cowan, there were no fireworks or pep-stuff in it, but just plain, good common sense advice as to what to do and what he expected of them. At the same time it was most inspiring. It was arranged that after leaving Biorko all boats were to R/V off Inonini Point at 10 p.m. and wait for the final signal from Dobson on flashlight to 'Go On'. Napier was to follow immediately astern of me to deal with the destroyer guard-ship. Dobson and 'Mossy' Reed were to follow Bill Bremner after which came the last three. If there was heavy fire from the forts we were to split up and use two passages, rather than form one long line.

With so much to do, there was little for the crews to think about during the afternoon except to get on with the job of preparing their boats and engines. The day had been a long and busy one which was just as well as it took their minds away from speculating what might happen after midnight. One remembers now the youth of those taking part including the mechanics, some of whom had never been under enemy fire before; Russell MacBean, Bill Bremner and 'Mossy' Reed were old hands who had seen a lot of C.M.B. service on the Belgian coast, and because of this, gave bags of confidence to the youngsters. 'Dobbie' of course was a tower of strength and all were eager to follow his lead. It was with this happy spirit that the flotilla set forth on the Raid on what was reported to be one of the best defended fortresses in the world, KRONSTADT.

*   *   *

The story of the events of that night as seen by those in my own boat would be very far from complete; but to obtain a connected narrative of the whole sequence of events, however, I was able afterwards to receive first-hand verbal and written accounts from nearly all who took part in it and survived. Besides Commander Dobson and our airmen under Squadron-Leader Donald,* these include Lieutenants Bremner, MacBean, Steele, Napier and Giddy. For the sake of simplicity I have condensed them into one single story which is as factual as I can ascertain for the purpose of historical accuracy, and confirmed later when Lieutenant Webster, R.N.V.R., and myself interrogated six survivors of the crew of the Russian guard-ship *Gavriel* who escaped ashore in Narva Bay after their ship had been blown up on one of our C.M.B. mines in October that year.

It was quite dark and nearly 10.30 p.m. by the time Dobson made his flashlight signal to 'Go on'. I could see Napier quite clearly behind me, and another boat behind him whose exhaust pipes were giving out terrific flashes as one engine back-fired at intervals. Not a happy start I thought but she soon quietened down. We were doing an easy twenty knots as we approached the forts, and had lost sight of those astern except Napier. We thought we could see three of them half a mile away on our starboard side throwing up spray from their bow waves. Napier behind us was also throwing up a lot of spray and I was certain there was little chance of our making the passages through the forts unobserved, as the boat behind him had a badly tuned engine making a fearful din and spitting out flames from her exhaust. It was just too bad, but nothing could be done about it except crack on speed when the forts opened fire which they did. Luckily their searchlights were not switched on and the fire, which was light battery and machine gun stuff, was extremely haphazard and did no damage except to our smuggler-pilot's morale. We went on a wide circle towards the Petrograd main channel before turning towards Kronstadt dockyard having lost sight of those on our starboard side whom we assumed had gone through the other passage of the inner forts.

* Now Air Marshal Sir Grahame Donald, retired, K.C.B., D.F.C., A.F.C., M.A.

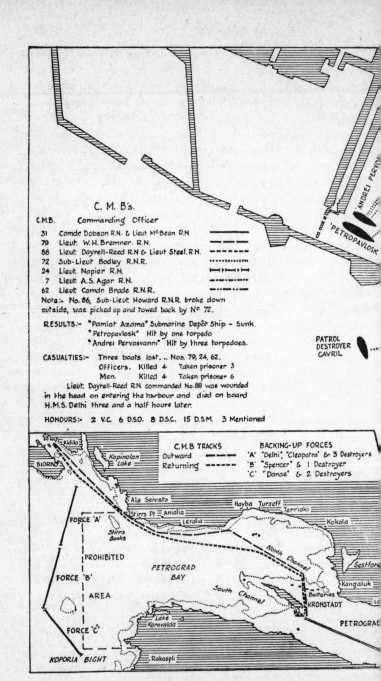

C. M. B's.

C.M.B.	Commanding Officer
31	Comdr. Dobson R.N. & Lieut. McBean R.N
79	Lieut. W.H. Bremner. R.N.
88	Lieut. Dayrell-Reed R.N & Lieut. Steel. R.N.
72	Sub-Lieut. Bodley R.N.R.
24	Lieut. Napier R.N.
7	Lieut. A.S. Agar R.N.
62	Lieut. Comdr. Brade R.N.R.

Nota:- No. 86, Sub-Lieut. Howard R.N.R. broke down outside, was picked up and towed back by No 72.

RESULTS:- "Pamiat Azama" Submarine Depôt Ship - Sunk.
"Petropavlosk" Hit by one torpedo
"Andrei Pervosvanni" Hit by three torpedoes.

CASUALTIES:- Three boats lost... Nos. 79, 24, 62.
Officers. Killed 4 Taken prisoner 3
Men. Killed 4 Taken prisoner 6
Lieut. Dayrell-Reed R.N. commanded No.88 was wounded in the head on entering the harbour and died on board H.M.S. Delhi three and a half hours later.

HONOURS:- 2 V.C. 6 D.S.O. 8 D.S.C. 15 D.S.M. 3 Mentioned

C.M.B TRACKS
Outward ———
Returning ------

BACKING-UP FORCES
'A' "Delhi", "Cleopatra" & 3 Destroyers
'B' "Spencer" & 1 Destroyer
'C' "Danae" & 2 Destroyers

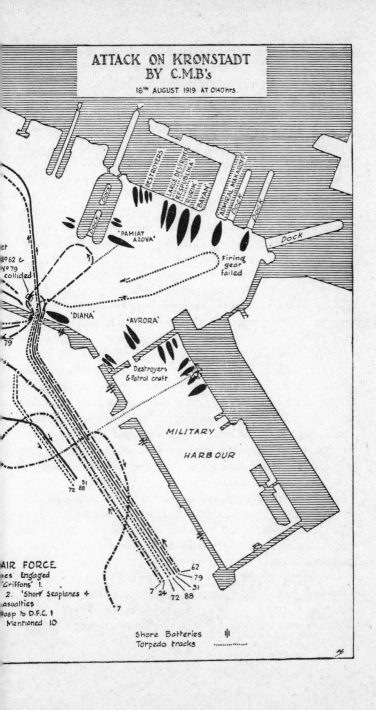

ATTACK ON KRONSTADT
BY C.M.B's

18th AUGUST 1919 AT 0140 hrs.

Dock

Dock

Dock

DESTROYERS

LARGE DESTROYER
RESPUBLIKA
RURIK
"BAYAN"

ADMIRAL MAKAROFF

Dock

Dock

Dock

'PAMIAT AZOVA'

Firing
gear
failed

No 62 &
No 79
collided

79

'DIANA'

'AVRORA'

Destroyers
& Patrol craft

MILITARY

HARBOUR

31
88
72

62
79
31
7 24 72 88

7

AIR FORCE
...es Engaged
'Griffons' 1.
2. 'Short' Seaplanes 4
...asualties
...osp to D.F.C. 1
...Mentioned 10

Shore Batteries
Torpedo tracks

It transpired afterwards that Dobson and the two boats following him (Bremner and Dayrell-Reed) lost sight of us in the darkness. His smuggler-pilot finding himself too close to the northern end of the Kronstadt shore, turned parallel to the chain of forts slipping in close to either Nos. 7 or 10, a gap we had not previously used, on which they would certainly have stuck, had it not been for the extra three feet of water under their propellers.

Actually because of their spray they were sighted by the large fortress of Kotlin guarding the northern shore, and were given several bursts of fire but again, as with our party, there was no damage because Kotlin failed to switch on their searchlights and all C.M.B.s except No. 6 (Howard) successfully got through the passages. Howard had to be left behind and was picked up later by Bodley (No. 7) on his way back from the basin when both came under heavy fire: a splendid combination of bravery and seamanship and a lucky escape for the *Rurik* which was Howard's target.

So far luck was on our side. First, because of the Pilot's mistake, Dobson with his first three attacking boats was able to cut the corner and get a shorter passage to the basin. This placed him well ahead of the second party to follow and he arrived at the entrance to the basin with time to spare. Secondly, the extra water level had certainly helped his boats to get through a passage we had never tried before, and lastly the Russians never used their searchlights which could have been our undoing, perhaps because they were not ready-manned or because they did not want to give away their position to our airmen. It is impossible to say. They were certainly in good working order, as was proved the following day and afterwards. Luck however is two sided and it later broke back on us.

On arrival off the basin entrance *complete surprise* was thus achieved and Walter Cowan's plan succeeded beyond expectations, the rest was up to the C.M.B.s. There was no boom in place or obstruction to be blown up and no outward opposition whatsoever. Our R.A.F. friends the airboys were doing their stuff most gallantly upstairs, zooming around and dropping their small bombs as near as possible to the batteries on the breakwaters whose gunners were obviously taking cover. We could see the red flashes of the bombs as they exploded. Bill Bremner (No. 1) had a clear run in and a straight target for the *Pamiat Azova* which he got with his one and only torpedo—a bull's-eye—followed as he described, by a crunching roar as the sound of the explosion reverberated across the water to where we were waiting, a quarter of a mile off the Military Harbour to stop any patrol craft that might come out.

Bremner then went over to his waiting billet and was soon followed into the basin by Dobson (No. 2). His was a very difficult manoeuvre because, to get into position to fire his torpedoes, he had to stop one engine, turn the boat, and gather speed rapidly before firing, a task which required much skill and judgment, but 'Beans' at the wheel was an experienced hand and had the boat steadied and on course exactly at the right moment when Dobson fired, scoring two bull's-eyes on the *Andrei Pervosvanni* followed by two terrific explosions and then proceeded to his waiting billet near the hospital ship to wait for Dayrell-Reed (No. 3). By this time the basin had thoroughly woken up and was alive with general pandemonium and confusion. Searchlights were sweeping the water indiscriminately and Russian machine guns making their horrible typewriter sounds were click-clacking all over the place regardless of where they were firing provided it was a moving target. Into this came 'Mossy' Reed (No. 3) and Brade (No. 4). Our boats replied with their Lewis guns which were fitted with belts of R.A.F. tracer ammunition, though this turned out to be a liability as the tracer bullets gave away their position.

'Mossy' had been in C.M.B.s ever since their start in late 1917 and had been well trained in boat handling by Eric Wellman. Nothing ever moved him and I can see him now with his head sticking over the canvas screen shielding the torpedo firing instrument and steering wheel. Following the same technique as Dobson and Russell MacBean his boat had to make an even sharper turn towards his target before gathering speed to fire, but with expert skill and superb judgment he had the turn started perfectly, when something happened, and instead of righting the wheel to allow for the swing, the boat continued on turning with 'Mossy' slumped over the wheel making no effort at all to check it.

Real moments of crisis are rare and this was one of them. To act swiftly and correctly on split second judgment with a cool head, when bullets and shells are flying around and any moment may be the last on this earth, requires both physical courage and temperament which few possess. In Gordon Steele,* his second in command, 'Mossy' had such a one. Turning round from the shoulder of his Lewis gun, Gordon realized at once that the boat was off course and out of control. 'Mossy' had been shot through the head. Jumping to the wheel and levers, he brought the boat under control again and carried out the attack against the *Petropavlosk* as originally planned, firing his torpedoes so close that one hit the heavy cable by which the battleship was made fast to the wharf, part of the yellow picric powder from the explosion of the torpedo falling on the stern of the C.M.B. The other torpedo struck the forward part of the huge ship underneath a turret, putting her out of action.

Gordon then joined Dobson at the waiting billet following him out of the basin entrance, and through the chain of forts which by this time were ready for the boats on their return journey with searchlights as well as their Q.F. staff. But by making a smoke screen ahead, and with the aid of our airmen who came to their support diving fearlessly onto the forts with their tracer bullets going full blast, the C.M.B.s managed to get through without serious damage. Both Dobson's and Steele's boats (Nos. 2 and 3) were intercepted by the flagship on their way to Biorko and the

---

* Now Commander Gordon Steele, V.C., R.N. Retired, to whom I am indebted for a description of his boat's part in the attack.

wounded 'Mossy' transferred to the cruiser's sick-bay. He died soon afterwards but not before the Admiral spoke to him and shook his hand, as did all members of his crew. Gordon told me that he was conscious enough to know the boat had done well which to him was all that mattered, and so ends Phase 1 of our narrative.

* * *

For Phase 2 we must return to the scene at the entrance to the dockyard basin after Dobson and Gordon Steele had successfully made good their escape and were about to tackle their return passage through the forts. Good fortune which had certainly been on our side with all three important targets put out of action at no loss to ourselves, was now to turn against us. Outside the dockyard breakwaters, while Dobson's party were doing their stuff inside, Napier (No. 7) attacked the destroyer guard-ship *Gavriel*. It was a straight run and also a surprise attack which should have succeeded, but his torpedo missed: it was either deflected or ran underneath the target. A real piece of hard luck.

In our own boat, we closed the military harbour according to plan. This was a smaller basin with a narrow entrance, where a group of patrol craft and tugs could be distinguished berthed in a bunch close together. We fired our torpedo through the entrance into the middle of them. The explosion was clearly visible and must have caused considerable damage and commotion but, mindful of Dobson's repeated warnings to keep clear of the main path of the retiring C.M.B.s, we returned immediately to our position near the Petrograd Channel to watch events, and could see the terrific explosions in the naval basin as Dobson and his first party (Nos. 1, 2 and 3) scored their hits on the battleships and *Pamiat Azova*, after which we noted what we thought was their wake as they cleared the breakwater on their escape route. More explosions on shore livened up the scene accompanied by red flames showing that our supporters, the airmen, were still busy with their bombs.

By now we had lost sight of Napier and the *Gavriel*, and could see nothing of the others of the Second Party (Nos. 4, 5 and 6). Brade (No. 4) unknown to us had arrived off the naval dockyard basin entrance but without Howard (No. 5), whose boat had broken down with engine trouble on the other side of the forts, and Bodley (No. 6) who was also having trouble with the forts and batteries. The firing gear of his boat was shot away by a small calibre shell putting him out of action in so far as his target was concerned; so instead of carrying on towards the inside of the basin he returned to the chain of forts to Howard's rescue, and after considerable difficulty towed him clear of the line of fire, a most gallant action on his part.

We are now left with Bill Bremner (No. 1) inside the basin and John Brade (No. 4) about to enter and repeat Dobson's attack on the battleships. Napier's C.M.B., after attacking the *Gavriel*, was hit by a large calibre shell from one of the batteries or from the *Gavriel* herself. His boat was split in half and sank within a few hundred yards of her target.

It was a cruel disaster and is best described in the words of his second in command, Lieutenant O. Giddy, R.N.:*

" . . . As Agar's boat, which was leading us, turned in its tracks opposite the basin entrance—this was the pre-arranged signal that we were in position—a score or so of batteries opened fire from what appeared to be every possible direction. We swung hard over to the right and headed straight for the outline of the guard-ship. We must have been quite close because Napier fired his torpedo as soon as we came out of the turn. We had no chance to watch for its success; there was a sudden rush of flame and a noise which split the surrounding pandemonium into nothing. I felt a sharp jab in my back and fell across the cockpit.

"There followed the most amazing silence broken ridiculously by the voice of our Welsh mechanic, 'That's

* Now Commander Osmund Giddy, D.S.O., R.N., retired, who has kindly allowed me to quote from his experiences published in *Blackwood's Magazine*.

sugared it.' Although I did not know it, Napier had been
blown into the water. I was about to jump below to get the
engines restarted when I saw that our boat had been split
in half longitudinally. With my two seamen I tried to free
the two Kapok fenders to form a raft and was about to do
so when C.M.B. 24A (official number of our boat) subsided
gently under our feet and we stepped off the disappearing
hull into the waters of the Gulf of Finland.

" . . . So much had happened in the last five minutes that
I felt little interest in my own situation, but with eagerness
I watched the harbour mouth into which our C.M.B.s had
disappeared. Soon a huge flare rose above the searchlights
which was followed by heavy explosions and implied that
things were getting really busy. I could see the destroyer
guard-ship more plainly anchored off the entrance, and I
realised our torpedo had missed. She must have seen our
bobbing heads in the water for soon a machine gun sprayed
bullets around us. We made comic attempts to dive underwater but I soon discovered my body was dead below the
waist. No one was hit and the destroyer's attention diverted
by the exit of two of our boats from the basin at full speed
with tracer bullets from their machine guns turned on the
destroyer like meteors fired from the sky . . . It was a grand
sight from the water . . . I became semi-conscious in the
water, but was supported by my life jacket to be awakened
about two hours later by the form of a grey row-boat with
white figures in her (Russian sailors). For all I cared they
might have been the boatmen of the Styx . . .''

The loss of Napier's boat was bad enough, but worse
was to follow. Brade's C.M.B. (No. 4) on his way into the
basin collided with Bremner's (No. 1) on his way out. Both
boats were travelling at high speed. Brade's boat rammed
Bremner's at right angles, cutting it almost in half. It was
the one thing we had planned to avoid. Brade evidently was
blinded by searchlights on entering the basin and, instead of
keeping straight on to attack his target, took a sharp turn

to the left. Both boats remained locked together in the centre of the entrance, a target for the Bolshevik fleet inside and the batteries on the breakwater.

Brade kept his engines going at full speed and by doing so forced both boats bodily clear of the entrance, giving them a temporary respite and time for Bremner with his gun cotton charges, which had some use after all, to blow up his boat (No. 1) and transfer the crew to No. 4. They now came under fire from the *Gavriel*, so Brade most courageously attacked her with his two torpedoes, both of which also missed the target. The *Gavriel* thus survived no less than three torpedoes, and would have had ours as well had we not already sent it into the basin of the military harbour.

Misfortune however refused to stop here for these two brave C.M.B. captains and their crews. A shell from the *Gavriel* put the boat's engines out of action after which she remained stopped and was eventually sunk by gunfire. From our position near the Petrograd channel we could see a large area of flames on the water as the petrol tanks of both boats blew up, and mistook them for the *Gavriel* herself. Brade lost his life, but Bremner survived although badly wounded. Both showed a wonderful example of courage, as did also Napier and his crew when things went wrong.

This brief narrative describes the sequence of events as we saw them. The part played by our airmen, without whom it would have been impossible to carry out the operation, was magnificent. Beginning with the diversion created when dropping their small bombs at zero hour, they drove the garrison to cover. Without this, our first three C.M.B.s could never have reached the dockyard basin undetected. Bombing from the air *at night* was a technique unknown during War I, and their difficulties can well be imagined. Following this diversion, our airmen in their semi-obsolete machines, Griffins, 'one and a half strutters', and Camels, kept repeatedly diving on the searchlights to attract their attention to the sky and away from the sea. Time and again they dived on to our old enemies, the chain of forts near the entrance, and without doubt accounted for the surprise entry of Dobson's first three C.M.B.s into the basin.

When they saw the difficulties we had on the return journey they came to our rescue again in the most unselfish and noble way. We, in our small forty footer, were I believe the last to leave the scene; by which time all the forts were ready for full action and dawn beginning to break. Those who had passed through, Dobson, Steele, Bodley with Howard in tow, had had a rough time; the latter two still being under fire at a distance; but seeing us a long way behind, and about to make our dash through the passage at high speed, one of the airmen (Flight-Lieut. Fletcher) turned back to give the two forts on either side of us a final strafe of tracer bullets in wasp-like dives. It enabled us to get through safely to Terrioki, where we arrived at daylight to refuel before going on to Biorko to report to the Admiral. How they took off in the darkness with a full bomb load on their makeshift runway and landed in the early dawn after their petrol had given out is just proof of the guts and courage of these young airmen. We certainly gave them full marks.

Photographs taken by them early next morning revealed the extent of the damage done. Both battleships lay on their side at the wharves obviously out of action, and the *Pamiat Azova*, the submarine depot ship, heeled over resting on the bottom. All these ships would require extensive docking and repair before being fit for service again. These were of course the main targets. The *Rurik* and dry dock escaped damage as did also the *Gavriel*, cause of the losses of our three C.M.B.s. But a retribution followed her two months later when she blew up on one of a cluster of C.M.B. mines laid by Russell MacBean and myself in the main Petrograd Channel (*See page* 199).

The Admiral spoke to every one who had taken part in

M

the action, airmen and C.M.B. crews, on their return to harbour the next morning, praising them for their gallantry and courage. He said that the result of the action meant the end of any Russian threat by sea to Finland and freedom for the Baltic States which was what we had been sent out to accomplish. But above all things he said the action would rank as an example of British courage of which the Navy would always be proud. They were simple words, but came from the heart of this flag officer; small in stature but great in leadership, and the sailors understood him even if they did not understand the complicated policies of governments.

We buried 'Mossy' Reed next day in the tiny Finnish cemetery at Koivisto with full naval honours from the Fleet. It was most moving for us all, especially when two little girls ran out from the crowd of village spectators with posies of wild flowers for his grave. We learned afterwards that the Russians in Kronstadt also buried with honours those bodies they recovered from our C.M.B.s, due largely to Gordienko the Bolshevik chief commissar who had been a Petty Officer in the Tsar's Royal Yacht *Standart*.

Of the honours given for the Operation, 'Dobbie' was awarded a Victoria Cross for gallantry and his splendid leadership. A V.C. was also awarded to Gordon Steele for gallantry and resource in action. Both honours were richly deserved and extremely popular in the Fleet and with all who took part in the Raid.

Our airmen supporters were awarded decorations for gallantry in action as well as every C.M.B. captain and some of the mechanics and seamen. But far more heart-warming than honours was the general thanksgiving in Finland and the Baltic States when the news became known that the Russian Fleet had at long last been immobilized, and was no longer the threat it had been for centuries to the coast and harbours of Finland and Estonia. There was much rejoicing in Helsingfors and Revel, as well as apprehension amongst the German occupying forces in the Western Baltic whose

turn would come next, now that the British Admiral had
dealt effectively with the Russians in the Gulf of Finland.

*   *   *

CHAPTER VII

END OF MY MISSION

WHEN I took Peter into the new rendezvous on the 3rd August, I had arranged quite definitely with him that we would make one more attempt to fetch ST25 out of Petrograd in the third week of August (i.e., after the naval attack). This was to be our last and final trip and we settled on two alternative dates, namely 23rd and 25th August. Our small party at Terrioki realized that the presence of our C.M.B.s and their activities at Biorko must be known to the Communists, and that the risks we had now to run to get through the chain of forts were considerably increased; our chances then of arriving at the rendezvous must be proportionately reduced.

We received an unpleasant reminder of this two days after the naval attack on Kronstadt, when a couple of aeroplanes flew over Terrioki in the early hours of the morning, and dropped seven bombs on the village without causing any damage except to give the villagers a bad scare and make ourselves and our boats unpopular with them. Obviously then, our hide-out at Terrioki as well must be known to them.

Searchlights could be seen every night at Kronstadt, sweeping the sky for aircraft and the approaches to the forts for fear of another attack. These lights were particularly in evidence in the neighbourhood of Forts numbers 8 and 10 and the large battery close to the northern shore of the island. As far as we could observe they were being operated with only very short intervals throughout the dark hours. It was certainly a case of closing the stable door after the horse had bolted—but, in our own case at Terrioki, we had to pay yet one more visit to the stable.

In the face of these precautions taken by the Kronstadt garrison, it seemed sheer madness to make any attempt to get through. It was hopeless to attempt to creep through unobserved as we had done before, and our only chance to do so now under these conditions lay in making a dash at high speed through one of the three gaps in the chain, repeating the same thing on our way back, and trusting to luck that the engines of the boat would not be hit by a bullet or shell in a vital spot while we were running the gauntlet. The whole thing was now a worse gamble than before.

Gefter had returned to Terrioki across the Estonian frontier by an overland route, and gave us a vivid description of the harrowing experience he and ST25 had been through on the night of the 8th August when they were both nearly drowned at Lakhta within sight of my boat and I had to return to Terrioki empty-handed. This time, he said, he was quite sure that Peter would procure a good boat from one of the fishermen, and if only we could get through the forts in the C.M.B. he was confident ST25 would be at the rendezvous to meet us. He begged me to take him as he knew where their rowing boat would be.

Having given my word to Peter, I felt in honour bound to make the attempt and made up my mind to go, come what may. That being the case, what was our best chance now that the forts were keeping a special look-out for us? And through which gap?

We knew at least three gaps* through the forts, possibly four, and obviously, I thought, it would take several days —if not a week—for the Russians to block up every one and therefore the sooner the trip was made the better our chances would be of escaping these traps. The batteries and searchlights had to be reckoned with in any case and this risk we must accept and counter by speed. Unfortunately, having already settled on the 23rd, there was three days enforced delay ahead of us during which nets or floating logs could be placed across the passages. This delay was

* Although we did not know it, the reasons for these gaps in the submerged breakwaters linking the forts, lay in the duplicity of the contractors who constructed them, a common enough fault in the days of Tsarist Russia.

maddening, especially when one is keyed up to make an effort and nerves in consequence highly strung.

Both the Admiral and Dobbie tried to persuade me to abandon the enterprise—at least for some weeks until things perhaps might quieten down—but I replied that as this was the very purpose for which our boats were sent out to the Baltic, it was clearly our duty to go as long as we had a boat ready for service. We still had number 7 intact—number 4 was undergoing repairs at Biorko and was not quite ready. The Admiral, realizing this, said that as our role in the Kronstadt Raid was solely that of volunteers I must decide for myself whether to make the attempt or not.

Marshall and Beeley offered to come as crew and I consented to take Gefter as well, although there was no real necessity for it. He said, it was for him a case of fulfilling his duty, which meant, I suppose, that it was his way of trying to make amends to ST25 for the mistake he had made on the night of the 8th August, in taking him out in a small fishing boat to meet me, without first making certain that the fish well was empty.

There was also another reason why it was so important that I should make this last trip. 'C' was still sending urgent messages that for political reasons ST25 must return at once to London. He was wanted by the Government as an eye-witness, to give to the public a true account of the real facts and conditions of life in Soviet Russia, particularly as regards the activities and methods of the 'Komintern'. This was urgently required to offset the accounts of the Labour Party, members of which had paid recent visits to Moscow and were vociferously urging a policy of 'Hands off Russia'. Talking it all over in our little *datcha* at Terrioki, we agreed that this was not the time to throw up the sponge when things were difficult. We must make every endeavour to get them out.

To my surprise, one of the Finnish smugglers offered to come with us. They had been earning good money at our expense, as I paid them well and, what was more important to them, I paid them in good British money. On this occasion I said I would pay the fee they had had for the Kronstadt raid, as the risks were equal, and I have no doubt that it was the promise of this reward, plus a belief in my luck, which induced this smuggler to offer his services, well knowing the risk he would run if we were caught.

I was firmly convinced myself that my luck would hold and that we would, in the end, pull through, and I can say quite frankly that this optimism, or whatever one may term it, was shared by the others of our party. I had, however, at the back of my mind, a vague sense of foreboding—a premonition—that something untoward would happen. There were five of us in the boat, myself, Marshall, Beeley, Gefter and the smuggler pilot. It was to be the LAST TIME and in fact was our thirteenth passage of the forts. My lucky number.

Fortune favoured us once more with splendid weather. The night was calm and there was no moon. A long head swell resulting from the reaction of the westerly winds which had prevailed for the last two days, bumped the boat about a great deal, especially when she began to gather speed, but beyond a certain degree of physical discomfort, did not worry us very much. We had set out shortly after ten o'clock at night and made at once for the gap between forts numbers 7 and 8. Searchlights were showing to seaward from either side of fort number 10, two from the large battery on number 4 (rather a long way off) and one which was burning in our direction from the large fort on the northern shore of the island. Nothing from number 8. With any luck, I thought, we might be able to slip through the beam of the light laid from number 10 before it was focussed on to us. This was the light laid parallel to the water and directly across our path.

We gradually worked the boat up to a full 30 knots. Faster and faster she went. Our Thornycroft engine had never once let us down, and I felt sure would not do so on this occasion, for we knew that in speed lay our only chance of success. The engine never went better and Beeley was as proud of it as one is of a favourite hunter and gave it as much care. The long swell caused the boat to throw up a great deal of spray as we were running light without a torpedo, but she rode it well, cushioning with light bumps on the crest of each wave. (At this speed we were hopping from one wave to another.)

Less than half an hour after leaving the harbour at Terrioki, we found ourselves approaching the forts and all seemed to be going splendidly. I was beginning to think we stood a good chance of getting through the beam of that wicked-looking searchlight from fort number 10, now less than a mile on our starboard side. Suddenly, from right ahead, first one, then another, and yet another searchlight beam shot out. The lights shone directly on to us and seemed so close and so powerful that I was blinded completely at the wheel. Bending my head down I tried to rivet my attention on the compass and take a line on the spot where I thought the gap would be between the two forts. We had unfortunately only an old-fashioned piece of smoked glass in the boat with which to ease our eyes from the strain of looking at the lights. We were still running at full speed, throwing up a large amount of spray and the noise of the engine drowned all sound; even the bullets and shells fired from the forts, strangely enough, did not trouble us, so preoccupied were we with those infernal searchlights. Of what happened after that I have only a faint recollection, nor do I know to this day, but either the rudder of the boat, or the wheel ropes must have been damaged by a bullet and I lost all control.

To ease down or stop meant simply inviting disaster. There was nothing to do except to keep the boat going at full speed, hoping by good luck to wriggle out of the beams of the searchlights. Our position was not unlike that of a rabbit trapped between the headlights of a motor car.

It was impossible to see anything and in a few minutes we had lost all sense of direction, so we had not the vaguest idea where we were, nor where we were heading for, but in that short time the boat must have described the complete arc of a semicircle with a radius of at least a mile towards Kronstadt. I knew that at this speed something would happen soon, but was not prepared for what followed. Suddenly the boat received a terrific bump, followed by a bang, and was brought up standing. The sensation was as if one was travelling by car at fifty miles an hour and suddenly ran into a brick wall, though in our case, I suppose, the water must have taken a great deal of the impact. We were thrown forward with a violent shock and I myself was temporarily knocked out. Obviously we had run into something, but what?

The sudden change from the roar of the engine to complete silence seemed most uncanny. One by one we picked ourselves up, Marshall, who was with me in the cockpit, was, I think, the first to come to life. Beeley was lying spread-eagled over the engine and stunned by the impact. I thought for a moment he was dead, but he was only, like myself, badly bruised and shaken and soon got up with the laconic remark, "I'll try and get her going again, Sir." He was always a man of few words.

But what had happened, and where were we?

The scene seemed to me to be suddenly transformed, for instead of being chased by searchlights, all except one had disappeared. The one that remained was burning from a fortress to the right of us, and so close to the boat that the beam swept over our heads as it described its mechanical sweep of the water backwards and forwards. Fortunately for us we were just outside its arc of search. Gefter was standing up behind me searching the shore and opposite coast with my binoculars. I was still somewhat dazed and shaken, as my head and chest hit the spray screen in front of me when I was thrown forward in the cockpit after the impact. Marshall handed round a tot of rum which revived us, after which we were able to take stock of our surroundings.

We had, as I thought, described a wide semi-circle after I had lost control of the boat and eventually ended up by running on to a rocky breakwater somewhere between fort number 5 and the northern shore of Kronstadt island. The large island battery, which we knew as fort number 4, lay between us and Terrioki village. The searchlight from fort number 5 still plied its search above our heads to the east and north of us with agonizing rhythm. The C.M.B. rested on a rocky ledge of this breakwater with her rudder, propeller and propeller shaft stripped off. She had started to make water. How her thin shell managed to remain intact after the severe blow she had received passes my comprehension, but the fact remains that it did and is a tribute to the skill of those who designed and built her.

Everyone in the boat was wonderfully calm and collected, except the smuggler-pilot who lost his nerve and began to shout and gesticulate, but was soon silenced by Gefter (I think with a certain amount of physical force, for he lay moaning in the torpedo trough for the next few hours or so.)

We were in a terrible plight. Only fifteen miles across on the opposite shore could be seen a few faint twinkling lights on the Finnish coast, which to us meant safety. We had before us not more than four hours darkness in which to cross that intervening space and save our lives. To add to our difficulties there were two fortresses between us and that friendly shore. What was to be done?

I spoke to Gefter first. "I am sorry indeed, Gefter," I said, "that our last enterprise should have come to this end. You see for yourself our situation."

Pointing to the Kronstadt shore which was quite close, I continued, "Kronstadt island is there, only a few hundred yards away. You can swim quite easily across to that shore and find safety for yourself. You are a Russian; your Communist papers are in order; perhaps even you may have a friend on the island or someone you know. You have at least a chance to save your life, for there is four hours darkness, so you had better go now, at once, before it is too late and, we are discovered by that searchlight."

He paused a few moments before making any reply, and then quite deliberately and slowly he said in his halting English, "But you—what are you going to do?"

I replied, "I must stay here with my comrades by the boat, and if discovered, blow her up."

Without any hesitation he put out his hand and said, "Then I stay also."

For that action alone I have never ceased to admire his courage. We galvanized ourselves into activity, and the relief of action served to deaden, like an opiate, all thoughts of the horrible fate which would overtake us at daylight if we remained in our present position. Marshall at once set to work to bale the boat out and plug up the hole in our side with pieces of clothing and anything he could find and made a good job of it. I still would not believe that the boat would float if we got her off the breakwater, as I thought she must be smashed to matchwood, but both Marshall and Beeley said it was worth while taking a chance, rather than remain where we were; anything was better than our present situation.

We pushed and shoved with the boathooks and in some peculiar way—I don't quite know how, but I think chiefly because of Marshall's efforts—we managed to get her clear of the rocky breakwater and to our delight, the C.M.B. floated. All hands now set to work baling the water out. Luckily we had at least one bucket in the boat and several empty petrol tins. This took about an hour, during which time the searchlight overhead did not cease to cast its horrible glare over us with almost mechanical regularity once every minute, like the revolving light from the North Foreland lighthouse. At midnight it went out, but whether because of some technical fault in its apparatus; or because its Communist operator wished to go to sleep; it is impossible to say; but for us it was a welcome respite and relief; for we knew that we had at least three hours more life left.

The slight westerly breeze which had started when we left

Terrioki had now died down and the sea was flat calm, but the swell which had caused us so much discomfort on our passage in, now turned out to be our salvation. Slowly and steadily we were drifted by it in a north-westerly direction away from fort number 5 and its searchlight, *and straight towards the Finnish coast*. This swell had been caused by the unusual height of water in the Gulf and it was accompanied by a small current which also set in a north-westerly direction. The combined effect of its action and the current drifted our boat at quite an appreciable speed—I should say a knot and a half, and to our surprise, we found ourselves, without any motive power, in the boat, slowly approaching fort number 4.

It looked as if Providence was deliberately intervening to help us to escape from our predicament. But how long would this last?

My companions were simply splendid. Without one word of complaint or blame, they worked away without ceasing. Our one and only object was to keep the boat afloat, and though our situation was desperate, we knew that if we could do this we would stand some chance—which was better than none—of passing the big battery of fort number 5 and shorten the distance between us and Terrioki. I prayed hard for the swell and current to continue its good work.

We passed—or rather drifted past—the battery without any challenge or notice. It was already half past one in the morning. It crossed my mind that at this hour five days previously we were outside the Kronstadt naval basin. Within an hour the first streaks of dawn would be making their appearance, and with it the discovery by the fortress of the boat and its helpless condition.

As if in answer to prayer, a breeze sprang up from the south-west. This not only blew us in the direction in which we wanted to go, but also added to our progress. We cut away the canvas which was nailed down to the boat's light deck and normally served to keep the fore part of the boat watertight. With this rough-painted piece of cloth, and by lashing the two boathooks together, we improvised a mast and sail which Gefter described so aptly as a 'ragged affair' but which was sufficient to catch the breeze. Gefter, too, hit upon the clever idea of steering the boat by means of the empty petrol tins which he roped together and, veering them astern at the end of a thicker rope, acted as a drogue or sea-anchor which held the boat stern to wind and sea. Our progress increased and in this rough and ready way we were able to steer without a rudder.

I calculated that at this rate, and provided we could still keep afloat, by early dawn we would be three miles distant from the battery. But that was not enough as we should still be well within range of its guns—if only we had one more hour's darkness, we might get clear. I thought of ST25 and wondered, first, if he had been waiting for us at the rendez-vous and secondly, why we should both have had to go through almost the same horrible experience.

The dawn soon approached—for us it seemed only too quickly—but Providence once more came to our rescue because an autumn mist began to form on the water, hiding us from the fortress and giving us the extra hour's reprieve which we had been praying for. This mist, how-ever, soon melted away as the sun began to rise and by the time it had cleared sufficiently for the fortress to see us we were at least five miles further on and only two miles from safety and Terrioki.

I had made up my mind, and so had the others, that if we were fired upon, we would try to swim towards the shore, hoping that Sindall would procure a boat and row out to us, but I knew our chances were slight, as by then, with the exception of the smuggler-pilot (who had now come to life and was also busy baling) we were all fairly exhausted by our efforts to keep the boat afloat. The water seemed to be gaining slowly, but with the chances of our escape rising, we put more vigour into our exertions. The wind, too, had increased which did not help matters, and I realized that if a squall came, as they often did at that time of the year, we were done for, and the boat must founder.

Marshall handed round another tot of rum, and I could not resist a laugh when he proceeded to use his sea boots for baling, as he said it was easier that way than with the empty petrol tin. We noticed two small fishing boats approaching which we had not seen before. These boats, like ourselves, must have been hidden in the mist. There were two men in them who were Red soldiers from one of the forts near Kronstadt, evidently trying to supplement their meagre daily ration by fishing. Their curiosity had overcome their good sense, for they were unarmed.

It was an easy matter for Gefter to order one alongside by frightening them with our machine gun. They said they thought that we were a British aeroplane which had crashed in the water. They completed our salvation, for we were able to make use of their sail instead of our ragged piece of canvas and make them take us in tow towards Terrioki. Our C.M.B. was now rapidly getting waterlogged, but we toiled on, constantly baling, and eventually reached the shoal water near Terrioki breakwater where the boat grounded exactly twelve hours after we had set out.

Our smuggler-pilot now began to assert himself and demanded the arrest of the two Russian fishermen. We were furious and for two pins Marshall and Beeley would have dropped the contrabandist overboard. These two men had served us well and could do little harm to us in the future. We gave them back their sails and all the food plus a little rum which we had left over in the boat, for which they seemed most grateful, and with a *dosvidania* (au revoir) we allowed them to return from whence they came and they sailed off in the opposite direction.

Sindall had already come out in a rowing boat, and it was not long before he had landed our exhausted bodies safely on shore. He said that he had asked for an aeroplane to come out and look for us at dawn and that one had been sent from Biorko but I suppose I must have been too preoccupied to notice it, though Gefter declares that he did.

In spite of the knocks she had received, we managed with the help of the local Finnish fishermen to salve C.M.B. 7 during the next few days, but she was too badly damaged in her hull to be of any use, so I was obliged to destroy her and blew her up with a guncotton charge. It was an untimely end for a C.M.B. which had served us so well and so faithfully, but we had no other choice. Her sister boat, C.M.B. No. 4 in which I won my V.C. now lies as an imposing relic in the boat building yard of Messrs. John Thornycroft at Hampton on Thames where she was built.

* * *

Gefter's account of our adventure that night appeared in the publication I have already referred to, under the heading of *Archives of the Russian Revolution* and published in Germany in 1920. Extracts from it are interesting as he relates it from his point of view as a Russian courier, setting out on a desperate errand:

"Two days later I was again in Terrioki. I had to go to Petrograd again to fetch the mysterious Englishman in the speedboat. This time, with the tall, fair sailor in command — Agar by name.

"Now the circumstances had changed and the condition of the passage was much harder. The matter was that owing to the English attack on Kronstadt with motor boats, the Bolsheviks had put up a number of powerful searchlights on the shore at Lissy Nos, on the batteries near Kronstadt, on Fort Obruchev, at Oranienbaum and at Krasnaya Gorka.

"The whole gulf was in their lighted control.

"They were also much disturbed by the innumerable attacks of the English airmen and were unable to sleep calmly at night. All this tended to disturb Agar's calm confidence which he had before, in making the passage between the forts.

"However, a start had none the less to be made, and the

mysterious Englishman would be waiting at midnight near Kamenny Island.

"On leaving the *datcha*, Agar gave instructions that a bed should be made up in his room for this man. But this was too great a challenge to fate and she replied as will be seen, by a smack on the face.

" 'Do you know, Gefter,' he said, 'I don't at all like the look of those searchlights.' We were walking through the woods, as before, to the little harbour at Terrioki from where we were to embark in his speedboat.

" 'If three of them catch us at the same time, there will be no escape. It will be devilishly easy for them to shoot at us.'

"I, however, was of a different opinion. Who could do us any harm in our wonderful rapid speedboat which flew through the water like a magic carpet? It would have been quite another matter in an old tarred fishing boat, leaking with water.

"When we put to sea, the narrow and seemingly feeble beam of a searchlight could be seen coming from Lissy Nos. Another beam from one of the Kronstadt batteries. But that was not a harmless beam. We had reached a position which I judged to be about abreast of Sestoretsk, when suddenly the motionless beam of light jumped and swayed about over the water. It did not search the sky, it searched only the water.

"Several times it slipped over the speedboat without observing it. Agar gave full speed. The motor groaned and cut the tips of the waves in anger. Suddenly a huge wall of water coloured with all the colours of the rainbow, and dazzling in its brightness blew up on the port side. The eyes could not stand it. Three more searchlights discovered us. Ahead, out of a fort, a horizontal lightning flash flew out, and we heard a low thunder shaking the air.

"We were being fired upon.

"At full speed, Agar turned to the right.

"For a few moments we were out of the beams. They ran

to and fro over the water like the feelers of Wells' Martians, but found the boat again. Agar changed the course once more.

"It was now out of the question to try to get through the forts. We must turn round them and back to Terrioki. For a considerable time Agar succeeded in keeping himself out of the line of the lights and cheating them by changing his course. The searchlights, however, were still on the boat and were also scanning our earlier tracks.

"The speedboat went ahead wonderfully. Its engines worked without a hitch. When suddenly, when somewhere near the large battery guarding the northern shore of Kronstadt, we were all thrown down and we fell off our feet from the blow of a shell. It seemed as if the boat had suffered such a blow that the keel must be knocked out. But everything went off all right.

"Not far from Fort Obruchev we were discovered by another searchlight from Kronstadt. It was so close that it literally blinded us with light.

"Agar turned aside, the beam followed, Agar changed the course again, but could no longer escape the light. The beam hung on to us like a Borzoi on to a wolf. It was too near and we lost the course during this beating about. There was a dreadful blow and the sound of tearing iron accompanied also by the sound of broken glass. The motor stopped, and the beam of the searchlight, travelling with the boat's speed, rushed ahead. It lost us, this time for good, but the boat was sitting on something.

"There was a dead silence.

"I expected every moment that water would burst in and we should all go to the bottom. But that did not happen.

"Where were we? I looked around. There were lights on the right, to the left and behind us.

"I went to the stern. The boat was held by the very end of the stern on a high cement breakwater which it was trying to take like a racehorse takes a jump.

"We pushed the boat with boathooks and after some time

N

she slid into the water and floated. We tried to start the motor but the starter would not work and when the engine was examined by an electric torch wrapped round in a handkerchief, it was found that there was no hope, for it was broken into two parts by the force of the collision.

"It was nearly midnight, and in less than four hours it would be dawn, when we would be taken off by the Bolsheviks.

"Only a little bit of life remained to us and I knew that I should then have to share the lot of the sailors at Kronstadt who had been drowned with weights tied to their feet. My companions expected nothing better either.

"After a short consultation the following resolution was carried: If the Bolsheviks should come to take us in the morning, we should blow up the boat which contained a charge of dynamite for this very purpose.

"I was given a lifebelt with which I might swim to the shore, but I refused it.

"At such moments I was strangely calm and clear-headed. We had four hours, so I suggested that we should rest for an hour or two to get up strength which we might still need to save ourselves later. I lay down and slept sweetly and awoke with the rocking of the boat.

"I rubbed my eyes. Had a miracle happened? Definitely the lights were in a different place, they were farther away.

"Yes, we were drifting, slowly, it is true, but drifting and in the right direction towards the Finnish coast.

"A fresh breeze began to blow from the south, blowing us to safety. It was necessary to make a sail, but first to turn the boat stern to the wind. We had not only no oars, but even no boards or planks with which we could have turned ourselves round.

"A floating anchor!

"We emptied some petrol tins and closed them hermetically. On the long end of a rope the cans were let out from the stern and, gradually pulling up and letting out the end,

I succeeded in making the boat turn round into the line of the waves.

"Then a long mast was hoisted from the deck. Two pieces of cloth were fastened to it and also to the motor. The sail was not a stylish one, but the boat sailed gaily along.

"At sunrise we found ourselves quite a distance from the fortresses, it was a sunny day and the wind was freshening.

"The waves shook apart the damaged keel and the boat was leaking badly. Our nerves began to fail us, and the crew who had not ceased to be on watch all night, working to get the water out of the boat, now began to show signs of weariness.

"The fort hung over the water behind us. It seemed to hang on account of the morning refraction which causes a mirage. This gladdened me, for so must also, I thought, our boat appear from the fort, as a strange object. Besides, the boat was painted with protective colours, and I had confidence that we should escape observation.

"I regained my nerves, but what was bad was that water was coming in in spite of the fact that the crew had kept on pumping and working without a stop. It was unbelievable that, after thus escaping in the night, we should perish during the day, in perfect weather and in sight of the Finnish shore. The sky was clear and cloudless and I saw an aeroplane appear in the sky. Agar lay exhausted at the wheel and the crew who were also exhausted, would now have to fight an aeroplane.

"Mechanically, with expressionless faces, they set to work to get ready the machine guns, but another miracle happened for an aeroplane could be seen quite clearly with the rings of the Allies painted on it. We regained fresh hope and new strength.

"More petrol tins were prepared for baling by knocking out the bottom of the cans and two small fishing boats suddenly appeared. They came a certain distance from us and stopped, but after threatening them with fire from the machine guns, one of them came alongside.

"They said that they had thought our boat was a British aeroplane which had crashed in the water.

"A mast and sail was taken from one of the boats which we hoisted in our own instead of the ragged affair we had been using and the fishing boat was now directed to tow us towards the Finnish shore. Two hours later we were all safely on shore."

It is incredible to think that our small 40ft. C.M.B. unaided by any power except Providence and with two large holes in her bottom sailed sixteen miles across the Gulf of Finland with five souls aboard and reached safety in Terrioki in nine hours.

Was it a 'miracle' like Dunkirk? Or an answer to prayer? I am sure it was *both*.

*   *   *

CHAPTER VIII

LONDON

OUR activities at Terrioki, as regards our boats, were now over. Number seven was destroyed. Number four had still some life left in her and was fit for further service but she was at Biorko undergoing repairs. We had to abandon, for the time being, all ideas of getting ST25 out of Petrograd by sea, and from this point of view I felt that we had not been completely successful in carrying out our original mission. It was comforting to know that Peter was with him, and I felt sure would succeed in helping him to escape overland by the same route that Gefter had taken. It was obvious to us that this was now the safest route, so I sent Gefter to Revel to await his arrival and remained myself at Terrioki.

More rumours were current amongst the Russian emigrés that Kronstadt would surrender, but one soon learned to disregard completely any rumour in the Baltic.

The Bolsheviks visited us once more with two aeroplanes. On this occasion we saw them coming and ran to our Lewis guns which we had mounted on the upper balcony of the yacht club, but we were just too late to catch them as they passed overhead. Three small bombs were dropped and fell in the adjoining woods without doing any damage and the Russian emigrés told us that this was done on purpose because the pilots had White sympathies. Personally I am inclined to believe this because in addition to the three bombs dropped in the woods, two other bombs were dropped, but did not explode as the safety pins were still in them.

One incident on the night of 1st September—a week after our last trip—did give us food for furious thought. Some well-intentioned person threw a hand grenade into the garden of our *datcha*. Whether this was to serve as a warning, or whether the thrower was too timid to throw it into the house, it is impossible to say, but the only result was a few broken panes of glass to the house, and a large hole in the garden. The Commandant was most indignant and distressed at the incident and posted a Finnish sentry permanently on guard outside the *datcha*.

It was evident now that our base had been located by the Bolsheviks and our Secret Service work known to the Communists, so I told the Commandant that I was closing down all our activities and would like, with his permission, to leave one officer at Terrioki in a liaison capacity. This officer would wear uniform and act as liaison officer between Terrioki and the fleet at Biorko. I told him the Admiral was most anxious about our C.M.B. prisoners from Kronstadt and begged him to pass on to our liaison officer any news that might come through about them to which the Commandant readily agreed.

Sindall, therefore, became contact number 35. There was, of course, a remote chance of ST25 and Peter making their escape across the Finnish frontier, in which case Sindall would be there to welcome them. Marshall and Beeley came with me to Biorko in case C.M.B. No. 4 was required for further service.

On arrival at Biorko the Admiral received a cipher message from 'C' instructing us to cease all Secret Service activity with Petrograd and to use Terrioki only for official liaison work which confirmed the arrangements I had already made with Sindall. We were henceforth to come under the Admiral's orders.

News came through on the following day, the 7th September, that ST25 had escaped over the Estonian frontier and was in Stockholm on his way to London; and now for the first time I can reveal his name—Paul Dukes—afterwards Sir Paul Dukes, K.B.E. The story of his journey across the frontier where he narrowly escaped summary execution at the hands of an over-zealous White Russian guard who was convinced he was a Red spy is told in his book *The Story of ST25*. I followed him home three weeks later but not before carrying out one more mission, this time for the Admiral.

With Russell MacBean we went to the south side of Kronstadt in a 55ft. C.M.B. and laid a small cluster of C.M.B. mines in the Main Channel. The mines were carried in the troughs of the C.M.B.s and although small in both size and number effectively served the Admiral's purpose to seal up the exit for the remaining Russian ships.

A curious feature of this small and unrecorded operation was that the destroyer guard-ship *Gavriel* which escaped all our attentions during the Kronstadt raid, came to her end on one of them. She and another destroyer, the *Azard* commanded by Czarist naval officers, decided to come out one night on patrol in the Finnish Gulf, but actually to surrender to the British fleet when they both fell victims to these mines. They had just time before sinking to close the Estonian coast near Luga Bay where seven escaped across the Estonian frontier. They gave us news of the damage done by the raid confirming the estimate made by our airmen and the survivors who had been taken to Moscow.

My original Mission was now at an end and there was little left for me to do. Paul Dukes had got through safely and was now on his way to England. This was all that mattered to us. I telephoned immediately the good news to Sindall and told him to stay where he was and make every effort to obtain information and check it up regarding our prisoners of war.

The Soviet wireless station had broadcast their version of the Kronstadt Raid in a short laconic message omitting all mention of their damaged ships and claiming a Bolshevik success by sinking three British torpedo boats and taking prisoner four officers and six ratings—no names being mentioned. Our anxiety and that of their relatives was soon relieved by our Viborg contact who obtained an unconfirmed report of the names of the survivors, amongst whom was Bremner. This was confirmed a few days later by the Soviet wireless which broadcast in full the names of all ten survivors without making any difference in their rank.

We were terribly grieved to hear of the loss of Brade, Usborne, McLean, and those ratings who were still missing and must now be assumed to have been killed. Nothing more could be done for them except sympathize with their relatives. What was urgently wanted now was more precise information as to the condition of those who were wounded and where they were and I felt that our organization might be able to do something in this respect, especially at Revel. I had already started to put a scheme into effect when I was sent for by the Admiral.

"I am sending you home now," he said, "to get your V.C."

I told him that I was anxious to stay on to get more information about our prisoners, as I thought that by working from Revel with a fresh organization we might be able to do so. He said that in view of the Soviet wireless message offering a reward for me* it was best to shut down for a while and return to England but that if the authorities at home allowed me to return, he would be pleased to have me on his staff as an Intelligence Officer. In the meantime, it was not only best for me to go home, but I was wanted in London.

I left on the 16th September for Helsingfors where I was given the Legation Despatches and a Diplomatic passport. I was to travel this time as an official messenger via Stockholm where I was to receive another Foreign Bag.

Anything more unlike a King's Messenger I cannot

* When he arrived in Helsingfors ST25 reported that the Petrograd Soviet Council were offering a handsome reward for my capture or that of any members of our Terrioki organization. I was assessed at £5,000 in roubles but how the recipient was to dispose of this huge sum in a Communist country remained a mystery. Similarly the Moscow Soviet Council were offering large rewards for any information concerning the British master spy (Dukes himself) but they had no description of him.

imagine. I was still wearing the same brown suit I had bought at Moss Bros. on my departure from London—the only suit of clothes I possessed, and now badly worn—but in spite of my ragged appearance, Sir Coleridge Kennard—as usual, kindness itself—invited me to dinner on my arrival at Helsingfors.

We talked until a late hour, the British Minister and a young lieutenant.

I was able to furnish him with an account of the Kronstadt Raid and the naval situation in the Gulf of Finland, while he, for his part, faithfully exchanged my news for his own political views and the difficulties he had to contend with in Finland.

He described how shortly before the Kronstadt naval attack, General Mannerheim was forced to resign his position as Regent of Finland, partly because a political reaction had set in amongst the people against anything to do with Germany and Sweden, and partly because of suspicions which were completely unfounded, that he was working with the White Russians in Finland to bring about a Russo-Finnish advance on Petrograd with the Finnish Volunteer Army.

In this he suspected either German or Russian intrigue, but the Finnish people were determined not to be drawn into any venture outside their own country. Mannerheim would certainly be a great loss, but no doubt would come back again when these intrigues had blown over.

Yudenitch was still established in his luxurious hotel—the Societenhusen—complete with staff and usual coterie of hangers-on habitual to every White Russian leader. The British Military Mission still flourished in another hotel and had not yet succeeded in galvanizing Yudenitch into action. General Gough had temporarily returned to England.

When the news of the success of our Kronstadt attack reached Helsingfors, there was rejoicing everywhere. Sir Coleridge said that the Finns, more than any other Baltic

State realized how great a threat the Bolshevik fleet had been to the coast of Finland. The knowledge that this threat was now removed made them more than ever grateful to England for their share in the attainment of Finnish national independence, and he himself had received many congratulatory messages from important and influential Finns, as well as from Members of the Government.

A small military clique, however, consisting for the most part of Jaeger Officers had tried to bring pressure to bear on the Finnish Government to make use of this opportunity when the Russian fleet was immobilized to order an immediate advance on Petrograd by the Volunteer Army. Fortunately the Government were wise enough to resist this pressure and intrigue which Mannerheim had strongly disapproved of.

The argument put forward by the Jaeger military clique was that it would only require a small force to march across the Finnish frontier, a distance of twenty-five miles, and occupy Petrograd City and that the surrender of Kronstadt would follow. In these circumstances, they said, it was possible to immobilize the whole of the Bolshevik fleet and Arsenal absolutely and thus not only ensure security for the Finnish coast from any future threat, but also obtain better territorial terms from Soviet Russia for the Finnish eastern frontier.

But what would have been Finland's position afterwards if this argument were put into practice? The Council of Four in Paris had made an open proclamation in support of Admiral Kolchak, who was still recognized by the Allies as the head of the Russian Provisional Government. General Yudenitch in Helsingfors was Kolchak's official representative. Neither Yudenitch nor Kolchak had recognized, either *de facto* or *de jure*, the independence of the Baltic states and Finland, and, in the event of Petrograd or Kronstadt or both falling into the hands of either the Finns, British or Estonians, Yudenitch would have demanded the immediate turning over of the city to himself.

The North-West Corps which was supposed to be under the direction of Yudenitch, was actually at the time carrying out sporadic raids into Soviet territory under the command of General Rodzianko and was certainly not sufficiently organized to take over the maintenance of the defences of either Kronstadt or Petrograd City. It was unthinkable then, that either the Finns or the Estonians would consent to obey the orders of Yudenitch who, at the time, was a guest in Finland. The Finns, having taken Petrograd, would have had to hand it over to Yudenitch on a silver salver and politely withdraw. Such a position was, to say the least of it, intolerable.

Excluding the Finns and Estonians, there was only one military force in the Baltic capable and willing to occupy Petrograd or, for that matter, any other territory in the Baltic States and they were the Germans.

Any advance on Petrograd by Finland would have only been the signal for offers of help with Russo-German troops by the Baltic Germans who had considerable forces organized in Latvia and Lithuania. It was precisely these forces which were causing us so much concern and which, by the terms of the protocol to the Peace Treaty, should have been evacuated back to Germany.

The Finns, Kennard thought, showed much wisdom in resisting these temptations and he put the position in a nutshell when he said, "With Finnish assistance, Yudenitch could easily have reached Petrograd, but he would never have stayed there. In the long run it would only have resulted in harm for Finland."

The whole situation in so far as the British were concerned was full of paradoxes. It was the duty of the British Minister, when asked, to tender advice to the Finnish Government not to advance on Petrograd but to leave it severely alone, which in his opinion was the policy best calculated to serve the interests of Finland. On the other hand, it was the duty of the British Military Mission to do their best in Helsingfors to assist Yudenitch and his staff in taking Petrograd with the help of the Estonians, which, from a military point of view, was a much more difficult task for the Estonians than for the Finnish army.

As a side-line, he explained to me how the British Minister had to deal with the repatriation of the Red Finnish Legion from Murmansk back into Finland. This was an even more curious and paradoxical problem, and was thrust upon Kennard at extremely short notice. These Red Finnish soldiers had been driven out of Finland during the rebellion by General Mannerheim's White Volunteer Army who regarded them as Communists. After Finland's liberation, their only escape route was north into Karelia where they were taken into the service of the British Army and provided with British uniforms, pay and equipment. We enrolled them as volunteers to fight against the Germans and Bolsheviks in the Murmansk area.

With the withdrawal of the British Relief Force from Archangel and Murmansk in August, these unfortunate men were left high and dry. The Russians would have nothing to do with them because they were Finns, and the Finnish Government disowned them because they were Communists. Like the Assyrians, a home had to be found for them, so why not send them back where they came from and hope for the best? They were accordingly placed in a British transport and sent by sea to Finland.

This, however, did not in any way suit the Finnish Government who pointed out a number of these Red Finns (who had not escaped into Karelia) had been sentenced to terms of imprisonment, which they were now serving in the Sveaborg fortress near Helsingfors. The transport, therefore, was diverted to Revel and it was left to our diplomatic representative to arrange for the disposal of these men wearing British uniform and technically under our protection, and to negotiate in the most tactful way he could their re-entry into the domestic family life of the new Finland.

The intricacies of this situation were solved by sorting out

in the troopship the best of these Red Finns and returning
them to Finland. The toughest and worst characters were
absorbed into a newly formed Frei Corps unit consisting
for the most part of ex-Baltic German and Russian soldiers,
plus a good sprinkling of other nationalities with various
coloured political labels white, red, green and pink. They
were placed under the command of a young acting lieutenant-
colonel of the Irish Guards, the Hon. H. Alexander, and
within weeks became renowned as the best disciplined and
fighting troops in the Baltic, acknowledging political and
military loyalty to their young colonel only and nobody else.
This officer in World War Two became Field Marshal Earl
Alexander of Tunis, K.G., P.C., G.C.B., O.M.

*   *   *

The next day I sailed for Stockholm and to my surprise
found amongst the passengers on board the steamer no less a
person than General Mannerheim himself, the late Regent
also bound for Stockholm as a result of his recent resigna-
tion. He looked a sad yet impressive figure standing at the
stern of the small steamer with his gaze fixed towards the
receding shore as we wound our way in and out of the islands
and past the impressive battlements of the fortress of
Sveaborg, where the first Victoria Cross was won by Seaman
David Lucas in the Crimean War for throwing back a
burning canister shell to the fortress gunners during the
attack by the British fleet on the batteries of Bomarsund on
the 21st June, 1854.

It was late in the evening and the setting sun threw up
the red roofs of the summer *datchas* in beautiful relief against
a background of green pine forests giving the same effect
as a searchlight. Not for a moment did that figure standing
in the stern of the ship take his eyes off this exquisite
evening panorama which to him was his native land. He
watched until the coast faded away into a thin black line,
and finally out of sight altogether. Then, as the twilight
disappeared, he gravely removed his hat and bending his

head, stood motionless for a few moments — it seemed to me
that he was saying a prayer — after which he walked straight
down below to his cabin.

To me there was a sense of drama in the whole episode
and I was deeply moved as I watched this man, who should
be classed with the names of great liberators of the past,
such as Simon Bolivar, Garibaldi and Cochrane. What
thoughts, I speculated, were occupying his mind and what
was his future?

We berthed next morning alongside the quay at Stockholm. There was a crowd of people waiting for the ship
consisting for the most part of workmen, stevedores, and
dock-labourers and one could see that they were held behind
a cordon of policemen. A car was waiting for the General
and as he stepped down the gangway into it, the crowd
began a hostile and angry demonstration. They booed and
hissed and waved red flags.

Mannerheim acknowledged this reception in the most
dignified way by paying not the slightest attention to it.

Major Scale came down to meet me. He was the chief of
our area organization and to whom I have referred as ST24.
He told me that Dukes had passed through only a few days
before and was full of praise of our work at Terrioki. He
and his charming wife were most kind to me during the
few hours that I had to wait before catching the train for
Bergen.

I was given another set of despatches by the Embassy and
a First Class carriage all to myself as far as Bergen where I
boarded a steamer for Hull.

The only recollection I have of my return journey home
was arriving at Kings Cross at a very early hour one morning
and going straight to the Foreign Office, where I had some
difficulty in persuading a minor official to relieve me of my
precious despatch bags and give me a receipt for them as I
was badly in need of a bath, shave and breakfast.

*   *   *

Once more I traversed that labyrinth of corridors in the building near Whitehall which was familiar to me before I left London five months ago. Once again I ascended the last flight of steps leading to the top floor and 'C's' sanctum.

The pretty lady secretary was still there and genuinely pleased to see me back. She said that I was expected but would have to wait a few minutes, so I waited in the passage outside. Presently another door opened and a man came out carrying a despatch case. He was tall, dark-haired, and lean. Something about him and his manner arrested my attention and seemed to me to be familiar, but whether it was the eager look in his eyes, or a certain tense expression in his face, I cannot say.

I looked at him again and then in a flash of intuition a thought came to my mind. "Yes," I said to myself, "it must be him."

I was the first to speak.

"Are you Dukes?"

"Yes," he replied . . .

"Well," I said, "how strange that we should meet at last like this, and here of all places. I suppose you know I am Agar."

He laughed. " 'C' has a habit of arranging these little matters like this." At which we both laughed and shook hands and entered 'C's' office together.

'C's' welcome could not possibly have been warmer or more kind. Paul left us alone knowing he had much to say to me and I to him.

I told him everything; all our difficulties, doubts, fears and dealings with Sir Walter Cowan. I gave the full story of the *Oleg*, particularly mentioning Hampsheir who 'C' said was to be sent to the nursing home at Osborne House in the Isle of Wight. He laughed heartily over the amusing episodes and commended us for all we had done and when it came to accounting for the thousand pounds I was given when we started our venture he rang for the accountant and said I was not to bother about accounts but just hand back any balance left over after our expenses were paid.

When I told him the Admiral was most concerned about the C.M.B. prisoners left behind at Kronstadt, he said that matter had been taken up by the Foreign Office with the Danish Red Cross in Copenhagen. The Soviet wireless had given the names of all ten survivors, and he hoped they would soon be exchanged for two important communists held in England. The immediate thing was to make sure they were well treated, and for this an appeal had been made by the Danish authorities to Litvinoff, one of the Soviet Foreign Office Commissars who had spent part of the war in England and had pro-British sympathies as well as a British wife.

When it came to my own immediate plans and future he told me quite frankly that he did not like the idea of my going back although the Admiral had asked for me. If I did go, it must be at my own wish and as a naval officer. My Secret Service work was over unless I wanted to stay with him and his organization, but that was quite a different matter we could discuss later. He had officially to hand me back to the Admiralty who would decide, but in the meantime I had to report to the Admiralty where the First Sea Lord wanted to see me and afterwards to Balmoral to receive my V.C. from the King.

After leaving 'C' I rejoined Paul Dukes in another room and for the first time we compared notes together. It was an odd feeling to realize that in spite of all that had happened during the last four months we were now meeting for the first time.

Bit by bit, the curtain was lifted and events, which had appeared so mysterious to both of us, were now made clear. He described to me the circumstances of his first meeting with Peter in a public park in Petrograd, and the amazing story he related of this man—'Eggar'—who had brought him in to the river Neva and landed him from a boat of miraculous speed.

He found it hard to believe that Peter had made this journey from Terrioki in a few hours instead of in a few days, and thought at first that P. was suffering from the proverbial Russian weakness of exaggeration.

Then he went on to describe how he had spent the interval during the White Nights and Red Terror in various hiding places, he told of his difficulties with money, food and shelter and of the various disguises he was forced to adopt living sometimes in the tomb of a cemetery for fear of detection.

I listened in silence and understood his feelings when he described to me in simple words the terrible ordeal which he and Gefter had gone through on the night of the 8th August off Lissy Nos when their rowing boat foundered. He described how he and Gefter lay exhausted on the shore and saw my boat less than a mile away disappear towards the forts after waiting for them.

He in his turn, heard for the first time of our adventures on the night of the 23rd August off Tolbouhin lighthouse when Providence saved us in the most miraculous way from capture. He explained to me that even if we had reached the new rendezvous that night, our effort would have been in vain as he could not procure a boat to come out to us.

Finally I heard details of his escape with Peter overland into Latvia. This he describes himself in his book, but for my part, I heard it then for the first time and in that strange place in the top floor flat of 'C's' offices from which we had each of us taken our departure separately. It seemed to me so curious and such an odd trick of fortune that we were to meet thus after these experiences and talk to each other at 'C's' very door.

We saw little of each other after this interview as he was much in demand by high State officials and Cabinet Ministers who wanted a first-hand account of conditions in Russia and under the new Soviet Regime.

During my interview with the First Lord—then Sir Walter Long—the Naval Secretary took me aside and

o

warned me that I must be prepared to answer a string of questions, and I felt terribly nervous. Question after question was fired at me in the First Lord's room—they all concerned the Baltic situation. I did my best to reply and make my answers appear to be intelligent as the Admiral had briefed me before leaving Biorko.

Finally the First Lord turned round and said:

"And now, young man, what would you do out there if you had complete powers as a dictator?"

There was a twinkle in his eye and I had a feeling he was pulling my leg and rather helplessly I looked to the Naval Secretary, Admiral Sir R. B., for inspiration. He had always in the past been most kind to me, but on this occasion was very much the Admiral and gave no sign, so I thought perhaps that as the First Lord had asked me such a blunt question, I could do no better than give a frank reply, and said:

"I think, Sir, if Admiral Cowan was in that position he would wash his hands completely of all the Russians, White, Red, Green or Pink. It is really the Germans with whom he has to deal in the Baltic."

Turning to the Naval Secretary the First Lord asked, "And you, Rudolph, what would you do?" To which Admiral Bentinck replied, "I would first crown you Tsar!" Whereupon we all laughed and I felt the ice broken.

Both had in common with Walter Cowan a love of horses and hunting. Walter Long was actually an M.F.H. when he was First Lord, a distinction shared by only one of his predecessors, Earl Spencer. He had a red beard, as did his naval secretary Captain Hammond whom he insisted on accompanying him on his visits to Ireland in case, he said, a Sinn Feiner should try a bullet on him, in which event there was a sporting chance he would shoot the wrong man.

I had two interviews with the First Sea Lord—Admiral Lord Wester Wemyss, or 'Rosie' Wemyss, as he was popularly called in the Service.

It was the first time I found myself in the presence of the head of the Navy, but instead of feeling frightened and nervous, I was at once put at my ease by his kind and human personality. He radiated sympathy and to my surprise I found myself talking to him in the same way as I had been talking to 'C'. He insisted on being told the story of our Secret Service work at Terrioki and of the Kronstadt Raid. He wanted all the details and was full of praise and admiration for our Admiral in the Baltic who was responsible for planning the attack and carrying it out.

He said that no one realized more than he did the difficult position in which Sir Walter Cowan was placed, and how he had to make bricks without straw. The whole question of the Baltic, he explained, was terribly intricate and was really one of government policy, since we were already committed in Paris to the *cordon sanitaire* against Soviet Russia.

Great Britain was torn between sentiment on the one hand in memory of the services Russia had rendered to the Allied cause in the beginning of 1914, and expediency on the other, when we were reminded by the Chancellor that our post-war commitments against the Bolsheviks were costing the taxpayer additional millions every month.

From a practical point of view, only one country was in a position to take action against Soviet Russia. That was Germany, but this was the last thing we wanted. In fact, our main problem in the Baltic now was not so much the action we could take against Soviet Russia, but the action we *must* take to get the Germans back into their own lands. He said that during the last four months, both in the Government and at the Admiralty, those who had the responsibility of handling affairs had had a most difficult task, as they had no set policy to guide them.

It was well known to them that service in the Baltic was unpopular amongst the men, and although they loyally went out there and risked their lives, there was no enthusiasm behind it, which made the task of the man on the spot, who alone had the responsibility and shouldered the burden, even more difficult. He added that because we had ships in the Baltic, the British press and public jumped to the conclusion that the activities of these ships were directed solely against Russia and overlooked our obligation to compel Germany to observe the terms of the Peace Treaty. But the enthusiasm and support which the sailors should have received from home was more than made up by the personality and enthusiasm which the Admiral on the spot inspired in all those around him, and for this, he said, I could tell the Admiral myself, the Admiralty were deeply grateful.

He went on to explain that apart from their anxiety at the Admiralty about a possible break-through by the Bolshevik fleet, now happily averted, their main pre-occupation was the conduct of Germany. With the bulk of Great Britain's army demobilized, it was left to the Navy to see that Germany ratified the Peace terms and complied with the protocol which bound her by Treaty to withdraw her troops from the Baltic States into East Prussia.

Failing this, there was no other answer except to re-institute the blockade on a large scale, but he was doubtful himself whether the Americans would agree to such a drastic course. If Sir Walter Cowan himself with his Baltic force could accomplish this task without the Admiralty having recourse to the larger measure of blockade, he would be doing both England and the Allies a great service. This to his mind was a far more important consideration than the capture of Petrograd by whoever was willing to undertake that task, and now that the Bolshevik fleet had been immobilized, he felt that our Admiral with his drive and energy was the one man who could best settle the larger question of the German troops in Latvia and Lithuania.

History has now proved how right he was in his summary, and how correctly Sir Walter Cowan also appreciated the true position in the Baltic, and maintained the integrity of Great Britain and the Allies.

He asked if there was anything he could do for me; and when I replied that I wanted to be allowed to return to the Baltic, where the Admiral had told me I could be of service to him with Intelligence work, he said I could certainly return if I wanted to but it must be officially and that I was to see him again before I left as he wished to give me a private letter for the Admiral.

Before leaving, Lord Wemyss told me that the King had sent a message that he wished to see me. His Majesty was now at Balmoral, so I said that I would stay with friends at Blairgowrie, which was not far away, and wait there until I was summoned, as there was nothing left for me to do in London.

I had one more short interview with him a week later when he handed me a private letter which I was to deliver to Sir Walter Cowan. He said goodbye and wished me good luck, and I shall never forget his kindness and charm. He looked dreadfully ill and was succeeded by Lord Beatty a few weeks later.

In the meanwhile Paul Dukes was writing a series of leading articles in *The Times* which were attracting a great deal of attention because they were the first accounts of an eye-witness of life in Soviet Russia under the Bolsheviks. After reading them many thinking people in England began to doubt the wisdom of the *cordon sanitaire* on which French policy was based. Paul put the idea forward that the replacement of one set of bad rulers (the Tsarist regime) by another set of bad ones (the White Russians) offered little solution to the Bolshevik problem which in essence was Communist (Marxism); and despite the hatred in Western Europe of everything connected with the Bolsheviks, he thought the true solution would come by opening up Russia's frontiers peacefully between the Baltic States instead of closing them, provided both German and Russian fleets were out of the way.

Opinion in England was hardening against the White Russian Armies which we were supporting with arms and

money and while not 'pro-Bolshevik' the British attitude
seemed to be veering in favour of giving the revolutionaries
a chance as against the French idea of letting them stew in
their own juice until something better came along. There was
little enthusiasm for the Yudenitch Army, except in the
War Office, but plenty for the young Baltic countries one
of whom, Lithuania, not having suffered enough in the past
from two overlords (Russia and Germany), was about to be
bullied by a third, Poland, in a dispute as to who should
possess her capital city, Vilna.

Many people were beginning to think it was a good idea
to open up trade with the Russian Co-operatives who were
springing up in the inland towns as a basis for putting the
Baltic States economically on their feet, as that trade would
have to pass through Riga and the Baltic ports. But
meantime the Von der Goltz problem had still to be
solved.

My stay at Blairgowrie was brief. My friend had just
bought Butterstone House once the home of Gladstone and
like him was in process of cutting down trees. For me this
would have been a nice relaxation for a few days, but I was
summoned back to London by an Admiralty telegram order-
ing me to present myself without delay at Buckingham
Palace. A railway strike was on and as there was only an
emergency service working the train pulled up into a
remote siding somewhere in Yorkshire as evening approached,
but it was all taken in good part with blankets sent from
the local hotels to keep us warm, as there were no
sleepers.

I was extremely nervous on the morning on which I had
to present myself at the Palace. I was to be received by
His Majesty at 10.30 a.m. and as it was still the days of
undress uniform I wore just an ordinary reefer coat but
borrowed a new sword and belt for the occasion from the
resourceful Gieves of Bond Street.

His late Majesty George V received me in a small private
study. Previous to this I was looked after by the Equerry on

duty who, noticing my nervousness told me a most amusing story of the railway strike in which an amateur engine driver on the Great Western line failed to notice the signals against him and did the journey from Reading to London in record time. This partially restored my confidence, but not altogether, and when I entered His Majesty's private room I confess I did not know what to do or say. The room was small and as far as I can remember full of fine ornaments of Indian workmanship. I noticed in particular two beautiful brasses standing on a table near the writing desk. The door closed and we were quite alone.

The King shook hands with me and must have noticed my nervousness at once, for he put his hand on my shoulder and said: "Sit down, I want to hear your story."

My nervousness went and I felt I was again in the same kindly atmosphere as during my first interviews with 'C' and Admiral Wemyss. There is a certain indefinable quality in a man who can create such an atmosphere which forces one to be quite natural and not self-conscious. He was dressed in an ordinary plain frock coat.

The first question His Majesty asked me concerned my parents, and when I told him they were both dead, he said: "I am so sorry—so very sorry, they would have been so proud of you today if they were now alive." He then proceeded to ask questions about our boats and the Kronstadt Raid and insisted on my describing to him every detail of my attack on the *Oleg* for which he was now giving me a Victoria Cross. He spoke for quite a time about our Admiral whom he knew, of course, very well and laughed when I mentioned the nickname 'Little Titch' by which he was known to the sailors, at the same time observing "that it should suit him very well."

He then went on to talk about Paul Dukes, about whom he had just heard a great deal and said that he deserved a V.C. as well as myself, but that the conditions of the award precluded him from receiving it. But, he said, he would make sure that some suitable recognition would be made for the services he had rendered. (Sir Paul Dukes received the honour of knighthood on 1st January, 1920.)

He asked about my future in the Navy and said I must serve him in the Royal Yacht (I was appointed to the *Victoria and Albert* in January 1924), but I said I was returning to the Baltic with the First Sea Lord's permission for further service with our Admiral there and hoped to be able to obtain some information about our C.M.B. prisoners. He asked who they were and remembered Bremner quite well, who, he told me, had entered Osborne at the same time as his son—meaning of course the then Prince of Wales. I had not noticed the time until he said it was time for me to go, as he had a Privy Council meeting at eleven o'clock. His Majesty then presented me with my V.C., taking care to look at the back of the medal to make sure that the date was correctly inscribed on it. Then to my surprise, he presented me also with the D.S.O. for my services in the Kronstadt attack.

It was not until I had left the room that I realized fully, first that my interview (or rather one should say, audience) was over, and secondly that I had been talking to my sovereign for over half an hour, and as I came away I knew that I had been conversing with a wonderfully kind and wise man.

That night 'C' and some of his staff, whom he always referred to as his 'top-mates' (from the fact I suppose that his inner circle lived on the top floor) gave a small dinner party at the Savoy Hotel to Paul Dukes and myself, as I was returning to Finland next morning. There were altogether about a dozen or us, including Sir John Thornycroft, the designer of our C.M.B.s and my Captain at Osea Island, Wilfred French. I was presented with a silver salver, and as the names of the donors could not be recorded on it, 'C' inscribed the gift with these simple words, "From his top-mates." It is now one of my most treasured possessions.

After dinner we adjourned to the supper rooms to watch

the dancing and I can recollect the old man picking out the prettiest girl in the room—to us a complete stranger—and insisting on her dancing with me. He always managed to get his own way.

*   *   *

CHAPTER IX

RETURN TO THE BALTIC

I RETURNED to Finland by sea, again in a small coasting
vessel, but this time we called at Copenhagen where there
was little news at the Danish Red Cross H.Q. about the
O'Grady-Litvinoff negotiations concerning the exchange of
our C.M.B. prisoners except that talks had begun.

The negotiations dragged on for weeks, then months, and
our men did not finally return until April, 1920 after
spending six dreadful weeks with ordinary criminals in the
Schpalernaya prison at Petrograd and five months in the
infamous Androniev monastery at Moscow, which the
Bolsheviks converted into a prison for White Russian
Counter-Revolutionaries and prisoners of other nationalities
including French and British who fell into their hands on
various fronts.

Our C.M.B. men were transferred there from Petrograd
and suffered the most frightful privations. Describing their
transfer, Giddy wrote: "During the three days journey from
Petrograd to Moscow we were given no food, except at one
station where soldiers brought us bread and weak tea. We
were desperate with hunger and at one stop where a farm
cart drew up with potatoes and carrots, we grabbed handfuls
and ate them raw much to our subsequent discomfort . . .

"Eventually we arrived at Moscow where the whole train-
load of prisoners were divided into two parties. The first
went to the Cheka prison; the other, of which we formed
part, were consigned to the Androniev monastery on the
outskirts of the city. We refused to march, as Bremner was
incapable of walking, and after much heated discussion a
cart was found for him.

"Our party consisted mostly of Russians with as many
women as men. We marched in a column. Next to us, an

old lady in a faded black satin dress hobbled along on high-heeled shoes, bent under the weight of a sack bulging with old belongings. When we relieved her of this she thanked us in fluent English. She was born a princess.

"Near us, too, marched a huge man in an old-fashioned frock coat, topped incongruously by a checked cap. He hailed us in American English and was very friendly, but the princess told us to be careful as he was an *agent provocateur* amongst the prisoners . . . few dared to speak to anyone . . .

"The monastery lies on the top of a small hill overlooking the city and is most impressive. We passed through the great gateway and halted inside the walls which enclosed a cemetery and were kept there for some time, until Napier, myself and the six ratings were taken to a separate building containing two large rooms. In the darkness it was some seconds before I realized the rooms were full of people. They were British soldiers.

"We had heard there were British prisoners of war in Moscow, but to stumble on them like this was wonderful. Our depression vanished and our hunger as well, for, crowding round to hear our story, they pressed on us precious food they had carefully hoarded for emergencies . . .

"They were a mixed collection. Several officers captured in a White Russian mutiny at Onega. R.F.C. officers force landed in Odessa and Murmansk. Soldiers serving in regiments in North Russia and so on . . . We spent five months at this monastery. There was a large contingent of French, mainly businessmen, some Germans, a few Hungarians and Central Europeans. Conditions were appalling . . . our personal cleanliness sadly deteriorated and lice never left us until we left Russia. We washed under a pump in the yard until it froze . . .

"With the coming of the New Year the temperature fell to below zero and it was excruciatingly cold. We slept on trestle beds made of straw and had one small stove only, which burned wood. The soldiers' ears were frostbitten as they had no woollen headgear. There was a doctor in the monastery but he had no drugs. Once the temperature dropped to 30 degrees below zero . . . Such were conditions in the new Russia. It was little better outside where the soldiers could walk freely in the city if they wished while officers were restricted to the monastery walls on the principle that privileges were for men only and not for officers. At last relief arrived with our exchange in April."

*   *   *

When I reached Helsingfors on the 10th October, the place was agog with excitement and the wildest rumours in circulation. Yudenitch, after ceaseless prodding from Gough and the British Military Mission, had at long last persuaded part of his army to advance against Petrograd using Estonia as a base. He chose the only disciplined troops he had which were the North-West Corps commanded by General Rodzianko, a cavalry leader and brilliant horseman but with little knowledge or experience of military operations. Rumour was persistent that he had reached the gates of the city itself.

For once rumour was near the mark. Rodzianko in true cavalry style and with much *élan* launched his attack on Petrograd, regardless of obstacles and without any military plan of co-operation with his ally, the Estonian army under General Laidoner, who was persuaded by General Gough to join the attack under the overall direction of Yudenitch. A rough front was formed reaching from Pskov in the south to Narva, and then on to the seaboard of Estonia, with Rodzianko's forces as a spearhead more or less in the centre. His initial impetus carried him through Yamburg, a railway junction south of Petrograd, on to Gatchina and thence to Tsarskoe Selo, a suburb on the very outskirts of the city close to the Tsar's summer palace, where his units came to a halt, and there we must leave them for the time being.

Russian emigrés, not only in Helsingfors but all over Europe, jubilantly bought back from speculators the rouble notes they had parted with earlier in the year in exchange for food. To obtain this worthless currency, they parted with some if not all of their priceless family treasures in the same way as they often before the war in typical Russian fashion, threw their last golden roubles on the gaming tables in Baden Baden or Monte Carlo. The Hotel Societenhusen was more like a casino than the planning headquarters of military operations and the date might have been the eighteenth instead of the twentieth century, were the results not so pathetic and tragic.

I hurried to the flagship in Biorko to deliver the personal letters and messages I carried for the Admiral from Sir Walter Long and Lord Webster Wemyss; and described my interview with King George V at the same time giving Walter the Monarch's congratulatory message on the Kronstadt Raid. The Admiral was very pleased, and explained to me that from now on I was to work directly under his orders officially as an Intelligence Officer. Normally I was to be accommodated in the flagship H.M.S. *Delhi*, but I must choose for myself as circumstances demanded whether to be in Biorko, Helsingfors or the Riga Area where the Germans again were giving much trouble, or to take passages in destroyers as opportunity offered.

There were not going to be many idle moments in my job, and certainly I could not possibly have chosen a better or more considerate master. Our airmen kept a pretty close watch on Kronstadt since the raid and reported no activity at all from the naval dockyard except on one occasion, when a patrol vessel, the *Kitteboi*, the size of a small trawler, emerged to surrender, and was promptly brought into British service with a volunteer crew and a young sub-lieutenant as captain. She proved most useful as a Fleet tender transporting stores to the seaplane base. Another addition to the Fleet was a division of wooden Finnish minesweepers, in readiness to sweep the inshore channels between Kronstadt and Petrograd in anticipation of surrender.

Foch our Finnish Liaison Officer, Webster the interpreter with rank of Lieutenant, R.N.V.R., Claudie

Graham-Watson the Flag Lieutenant, and myself formed ourselves into a team to do the Admiral's staff-work under the guidance of Commander Chichester-Clark, the *Delhi*'s executive officer. None of us had any training at all in staff work, but the Commander had a first-class brain and 'Scratch' (C. C. De Denne), the Admiral's Secretary, was just about the toughest paper-worker in the Navy. One had to be, with a man like Walter Cowan driving all around him with his tremendous energy. Poor old Scratch seldom left the Admiral's office which he shared with Flags and Webster. It was minute in comparison with modern offices afloat today, but was all that could be spared in a ship short of cabin space and not specially fitted out as a flagship. We overflowed into Flags and his own cabins for cipher work and had another small cabin for our meals which should have been taken at the Admiral's table, but Walter because of an old stomach wound, the result, it was said, of a Dervish spear in the Sudan, had peculiar eating habits and preferred having his one meal a day by himself with very occasionally his Flag Captain (Geoffrey Mackworth) for company.

The Admiral promised General Gough naval support when the North West Corps got under way with its advance, and for this reason retained half his cruisers at Biorko after the Kronstadt Raid. The idea was to help the inshore operations on the Estonian coast of Luga and Kaporia bays, using three cruisers, H.M.S. *Dauntless, Danae* and his own flagship to bombard the Bolshevik positions and support the Estonian army which by agreement with Yudenitch had taken over the left sector of the somewhat irregular front. On paper this White Russian front ran for about 100 miles from Pskov to Narva, but in actual practice it occupied a width at most of 40 miles on a thin strip of territory either side of the Narva river occupied by the Inglemanlanders, the only piece of Russian land left on which Yudenitch was not a guest and from where he ordered Rodzianko to make his final thrust.

From this position the left-hand sector of the front extended northwards to the coast and was held by a volunteer Estonian group of peasant soldiers; splendid fighting men with British equipment and well led, but with little or no military training and despised by the White Russians who had always treated the Estonians as a subject race. They made up however, by courage for what they lacked in technique, and faced the Bolsheviks, who had taken up well-entrenched positions on either side of their formidable fortress of Krasnaya Gorka which, as we already know, dominated the entrances to Kronstadt and Petrograd. Meanwhile in the Western Baltic on the shores of the Gulf of Riga the Admiral had to deal with a different kind of situation at the same time as the one in front of him at Narva.

When between early May and June, Von der Goltz failed in his attempts to establish his Iron Division and Baltic *landwehr* in the coastal towns of Latvia and Lithuania because of the strong action taken by the British Navy, his promises to Walter Cowan not to interfere in the political affairs of the Baltic States had to be accepted at their face value, largely because there was no other way of preventing the Bolsheviks from infiltrating into Estonia and Latvia. It suited Allied policy to make use of the German troops as a stop gap, rather than have Soviet revolutionaries over-running the Baltic States. At the same time to guard against the Germans remaining even in semi-occupation for any length of time, Great Britain sent out a strong military mission under General Sir Hubert Gough, whose timely arrival in Helsingfors in June took a great load off the Admiral's shoulders.

Gough's Mission had two objects in view. The first was to support Yudenitch in his effort to capture Petrograd, and the second to hold the Baltic *landwehr* in check and stop the German Iron Division from interfering with the Letts and Lithuanians. Gough had full authority from the Allied Council, and therefore was in a position to bring Von der

Goltz to heel as soon as the Baltic States were in a position to stand on their own.

Von der Goltz's ideas of fresh colonies in the Baltic (Balticum), to offset those Germany had lost by the War, received a further check with Gough's arrival, since he was now faced by a soldier with full authority from Marshal Foch. Nevertheless, he still persisted during July and August to stir up trouble and halt political progress in the Baltic States despite warnings from General Gough. Having lost control and influence in the coastal towns, he turned his attention to Riga in the Gulf of Riga.

This time his opportunity arose through the complicated intrigues of the supporters of Yudenitch, amongst whom was a self-styled Leader, Colonel Avalof-Bermondt, who, having collected a mixed force of Germans and Russians, persuaded Yudenitch to appoint him Supreme Commander of all Russian Forces in Courland (i.e., Latvia and part Lithuania). His army grew rapidly in numbers as Courland was a good recruiting ground, for ex-prisoners of war of both sides, until by September, 1919 he had 15,000 troops unworthy of the name of soldiers, badly equipped and semi-disciplined, billeted in or around Riga.

General Gough, sensing the potential danger, insisted on Yudenitch giving Bermondt orders to separate the Germans of his Force from the Russians by sending the latter to Narva, to form part of the North-West Corps under the orders of General Rodzianko. These orders were reluctantly given by Yudenitch but blithely ignored. Encouraged by Von der Goltz, Bermondt now added the Baltic *Landwehr* to his Army and by tacit consent of Von der Goltz he was promised support from the Iron Division. By and large, by the end of September this new 'Supreme Commander' could call upon a force of 50,000 men for which he was only nominally responsible to Yudenitch.

As his Army grew so did his ideas, and with such a considerable force behind him Bermondt now thought in terms of an advance on Moscow instead of Petrograd, and saw in his own person a future deliverer of Russia from the Bolshevik yoke. But first he required a base, and what better than the fine port of Riga, ideal for his purpose, from where an advance could be staged via Pskov, already in White Russian hands. Bermondt promptly began to attack Riga.

The Latvians and Letts by now had been supplied with arms by the British Admiral. They were fighting on their own ground and were determined to defend Riga against all comers, including Bermondt's irregulars. When tackled about his intentions by General Gough, Von der Goltz again came forward with the excuse that the Iron Division was acting on its own, adding that as most of his troops had now taken out papers of Russian citizenship he could scarcely refuse them permission to join this force, which had the same interests as those of Yudenitch. It was a subtle argument to gain time and see which way Yudenitch would react. The Latvians appealed to the British Navy, whereupon Walter Cowan unhesitatingly took a hand.

The situation confronting the Admiral was complex in the extreme. On the Estonian coast near Narva, his ships had already taken up positions at Kaporia Bay ready to bombard the Bolsheviks in support of the left flank of the Estonian Army, which in turn formed part of the Yudenitch Forces attacking Petrograd.

Here in Riga, he was asked by the Latvians to dislodge by bombardment another set of White Russian troops, who were also supposed to be fighting the Bolsheviks, and therefore part of the Yudenitch Forces. Bearing in mind his obligations to establish the independence of the Latvians and Letts, Walter Cowan with the consent of General Gough, gave Bermondt an ultimatum to clear out of Riga within 48 hours.

Bermondt, ignoring the Admiral's ultimatum, commenced his attack on the Latvians on the 6th October just as Yudenitch was about to launch his long awaited advance with the North-West Corps from Narva. By the 8th October he had taken up a strong position on the south

P

bank of the river Dangava which runs through Riga, when
the British cruisers *Dragon* and *Cleopatra* arrived with a
division of destroyers including the *Abdiel* and *Vanoc*.
Walter Cowan placed the French Commodore Brisson in
command of the operations with orders to dislodge
Bermondt in co-operation with the Latvian troops. His flag
was flown in the French destroyer *L'Aisne*, their only
representative afloat, but a splendid ship of her class and
well disciplined.

Bombardment from this Squadron soon forced Bermondt
to retire from the positions he had taken up, but not before
casualties had been inflicted on the British ships (15 killed
and wounded) by shore artillery, ex-Iron Division, for which
Von der Goltz refused to accept responsibility. Encouraged
by this naval support, the Latvian troops soon followed it
up with a successful attack on the 'Irregulars', driving them
clear of Riga territory and back to their base at Jelgava.

From there the Latvians continued the pursuit, until they
reached Lithuanian territory, where this Army of mushroom
growth drifted into smaller disorganized units, each leaving
behind its trail of loot and murder, and harried by the Letts
until they reached East Prussian territory. It is incredibly
sad to think that some had fought well as soldiers in the
past war against Russia, and were veterans to whom at least
honour was due, but on arrival in Germany were all treated
alike with unrestrained abuse.

Such is the brief tale of the Bermondt Battle for Riga.
Yudenitch, who, on the sly, hoped to gain advantage from
it, received its worst effects because it estranged his North-
West Corps from the Estonians and Latvians who were his
Allies, and who owned the territory from which he was
about to launch his attack on Petrograd. He tried frantically
to dissociate himself from Bermondt's actions, in the same
way as previously he tried to dissociate himself from those
of Von der Goltz, but it was of no avail. He had played each
in turn and lost, with the result that the Estonians were
highly suspicious of everything he did. His final act in

dismissing his own General Balakhovich from the Pskov sector, which had been gained for him by the Estonians in fighting the Bolsheviks, destroyed what little confidence was left.

As for Von der Goltz, his ideas of 'Balticum' and his shameful vacillations between the Russians and the British, discredited him altogether, and the German Defence Minister in Berlin, Herr Noske, couldn't swallow his attempt to turn his soldiers into Russian citizens. Once a well disciplined Germany military force, the Iron Division now drifted from Riga to Memel and Liban, under the strict supervision of Commodore Duff's naval detachment, and from there to a final evacuation by sea to Germany in disgrace.

I watched from the bridge of the French Commodore's ship the final scenes in Riga. The unrelieved expressions of joy at the departure of the Germans and defeat of the 'Irregulars' had to be seen to be believed, coming as they did from a people incredibly poverty stricken from their sufferings of the past few years. By the 24th November, the date on which the French General Nisselle supervised the final evacuation of the German troops from Von der Goltz's Headquarters at Memel, the Baltic States were able at last to enter the first stage towards their development as free people without the supervision of 'overlords'.

Visiting the coastal towns in the destroyers *Vanoc* and *Wanderer*, it was piteous to witness the low economic state of the people after years of trade stagnation caused by occupying forces. Sentries had to be posted along the quays whenever our ships berthed to hold in check *not* people bent on looting, but the large number, many of good families, who brought with them their most precious possessions to be bartered for food and the necessaries of life. Cigarettes, soap, cloth, tins of ships' biscuits could be exchanged for furs, amber necklaces, gold and silver ornaments. I saw a woman offer her wedding ring in return for a sailor's new flannel shirt to make garments for her baby.

Our sailors of course were forbidden to do any trade of this kind, but some got away with it, and secured for their girl friends at home necklaces of amber and furs which were in good supply. Iron crosses were a fair trade for soap (two bars of soap per cross), but the plum went to the stokers of H.M.S. *Dragon* who produced on their mess deck a baby grand piano for 500 cigarettes (price £1).

Captain Colin McClean, senior officer of the British destroyers, spared neither himself nor his ships during those summer and autumn months in the Baltic. His name together with many of those V's and W destroyers were household words on the littoral. Many saw service in World War Two twenty years later at Harwich and Dunkirk. Individually those small ships have provided pages of unwritten naval history, during their twenty-five odd years' span of active life.

The American Relief Commission under Colonel Warwick Greene and the Red Cross under Colonel Ryan, also did splendid work for the populace of Riga and Libau in helping their rehabilitation after the Germans left, but pride of place must go to the sailors of the British ships who gave everything they had, and would have given their midday dinners had it been permitted to take them on shore. Be it remembered also that these men had no leave or relaxation, no extra canteen stores or things of that sort, which made life afloat, even in Scapa Flow, somewhat bearable. Days on end they spent either on patrol, or clearing channels through minefields, where we had casualties including H.M.S. *Vittoria* off Riga, in addition to those from shore batteries. It is in such circumstances that the British sailor excels all others, especially when well led. Meanwhile, we must return to the eastern basin of the Gulf of Finland where, after much persuasion from the British Military Mission, Yudenitch crossed over to Revel from his Headquarters in Helsingfors, and at last gave the orders to the North-West Corps to advance on Petrograd.

*   *   *

The background to this last and final effort to take Petrograd is worth perhaps a short examination. The Yudenitch Army in the main consisted originally of two parts. One part operated in the south in the neighbourhood of Pskov, on the Russian-Lithuanian border, which the Estonians had taken earlier in the year, and handed over to the Yudenitch General Balakhovich. It consisted of 10,000 irregular troops of Russo-Baltic origin. The other part centred around Narva and, as already described, failed to retake Krasnaya-Gorka in June. This portion, the North-West Corps, consisted of 15,000 troops. From May onwards, while waiting for Yudenitch to assume active command, both these portions carried out, independently of each other, fragmentary fighting against the Bolsheviks, during which they frittered away their resources and gained little or nothing by way of morale or training.

General Gough's Military Mission was concerned mainly with the North-West Corps and the Estonian Army whom Gough persuaded to fight for Yudenitch. Their Commander General Laidoner somewhat reluctantly agreed. For reasons of either intrigue or jealousy, Yudenitch decided in August to disband the Balakhovich portion of his Army. These irregulars now styled themselves 'Green Guards' and were ready to attach themselves to anyone with an Anti-Bolshevik tendency including Bermondt. It is difficult to follow the Yudenitch reasoning through the mass of tangled intrigues. Prince Lieven, one of his subordinate leaders, and a descendant of the same soldier of that name who fought with Wellington at Waterloo, declared that Bermondt, to whom the Prince handed over his command, was receiving more help from the Germans (Von der Goltz) than Yudenitch was receiving from the British. It is also conceivable that lest Bermondt should succeed in an advance from Pskov (see map), which was sound military strategy. Yudenitch from motives of jealousy, cut the ground from his feet by abandoning it to the Bolsheviks who got it without fighting, whereas it had cost Estonia many lives to take it earlier in the year.

By such actions Yudenitch at the outset estranged himself and his North-West Corps, on which was placed his final hopes, from the Estonians whose Army, out of friendship and loyalty to the British, was fighting his Anti-Bolshevik battle for him. The Estonians not only heartily disliked his White Russian troops, but distrusted everything he did including this latest coup. Consequently, the Estonian people argued most strongly against giving him assistance of any sort. Why, they asked, should they help this Russian General to defeat the Bolsheviks when, if successful, Russia would swallow them up again? And there was certainly sense in that argument.

Of the 15,000 troops Yudenitch had at Narva, not more than 5,000 were trained and disciplined as regular soldiers. This was the 'spearhead' of the advance which started on the 8th October when Bermondt's force of Russo-Germans malevolently fell upon Riga. Rodzianko's idea of a rapid thrust against Petrograd cavalry-fashion by taking the shortest route from Narva to Yamburg (an important railway junction south of Petrograd) might have succeeded had he anything to back it up with; but the reinforcements promised by Yudenitch never materialized. He had, alas, only his own resources, plus the Estonian Army on his left who refused to budge beyond their frontier.

With Yudenitch it was the gambler's last throw. Everything depended on Rodzianko, his dash, his *élan*. If only his troops could be seen on the outskirts of Petrograd, the rest was easy and the city certain to capitulate. He failed to reckon, however, on the time he had lost that summer frittering away their strength, the antagonism of the Estonians who would fight well to defend their soil but no more, and finally, the defensive preparations made by Trotsky while he was sitting in his hotel in Helsingfors, intriguing with various political leaders.

Rodzianko, continuing his rapid advance in the centre, by-passed the key fortress of Krasnaya Gorka, recaptured Yamburg, which the Corps had lost earlier in the year, and pressing on, reached Gatchina on the outskirts of Petrograd by the 18th October. His troops on that day were in actual occupation of Tsarske Selo, a suburb of Petrograd, where the Tsar had a palace, and might have reached the city the next day, if things had gone well, but they had shot their bolt. Again rumours of surrender of Kronstadt were rife, and everyone including Yudenitch was on tenterhooks to receive the surrender of the city itself, but nothing happened.

An Estonian Army commanded by the Estonian General Tonnisson operated on Rodzianko's left, the extreme flank of which rested on the sea where the British ships were in support. In front of them lay the formidable Krasnaya Gorka. The extreme left flank of this Estonian Army was commanded by a remarkable Estonian sailor by name of John Pitka, a man after Walter Cowan's heart. He might well have been taken out of the pages of Tobias Smollett or Esquemeling.

In pre-war civilian life this man was a humble ships' chandler, earning his living as such on the waterfront of Revel, where he sold stores to local small ships engaged in the coasting and fishing trade of the Gulf. An intense patriot, he saw his country's opportunity at the beginning of the year when the Bolsheviks, advancing along the coast, tried to seize Revel, but were halted by British cruisers. Manning a small trawler with a few water-front desperadoes, he ran her alongside a Russian destroyer, overpowered the crew and hoisting the Estonian National Flag forced a second destroyer to surrender, as well as two more Russian trawlers and a few small craft. Such was the nucleus of the Estonian Navy, which did splendid service inshore behind the Russian lines supported by the guns of Walter Cowan's cruisers H.M.S. *Dauntless*, *Delhi* and *Danae*.

Pitka never did things by halves. With the title of Commander of the Estonian Navy he soon added the words 'in Chief' (!) and in a short time held a key position in Estonian defence Cabinet. He was the toughest and most adorable ruffian one could possibly meet, and could have given points in manners, deportment and courage to many modern dictators. Walter Cowan was particularly fond of him and trusted him completely. Large in stature with a black beard, he dressed himself half-soldier, half-sailor, in riding breeches, peaked sailor cap and reefer coat festooned with pistol, dagger and all that; the whole presenting an imposing appearance.

To add to his importance and prestige, it was not long before he became Admiral Sir John Pitka, K.C.M.G., and while his education was negligible, his brain and judgment was extremely clear and shrewd, and his summing up of people and events more correct than that of many in high positions. His Fleet of odd ships, consisting of two ex-Russian destroyers *Lennuk* and *Yombula*, an old gunboat, three trawlers and several small craft worked wonders all along the Estonian coast behind the Russian lines, right up to the base of Fort Krasnaya Gorka, beyond which he wisely refused to go.

When short of stores or oil he seldom asked. He just demanded and we denied him nothing. From the Admiral downwards everybody in the Fleet loved this rough, courageous character.

The first time I met him was on board the *Delhi* after the Kronstadt Raid. It was a hot day, but he wore a heavy naval overcoat with two pistols strapped round his middle and clutching a large loaf of ships' bread, he tucked it nonchalantly under his left arm when returning my salute. Amongst other things he was no mean performer on horseback, and could sail and handle a boat with anyone. Such was John Pitka who commanded, besides his queerly assorted Fleet, the extreme left flank of the North-West Corps which included an armoured train manned by Estonian sailors.

Meanwhile, Rodzianko having overreached himself in his gallop towards Petrograd, had no option but to fall back once again on Yamburg in the face of Bolshevik counter attacks led by Trotsky, who had not wasted the summer months but had used them to stiffen the defences outside the city and improve morale by persuading ex-Tsarist officers to take command of the troops in the face of what he labelled with some truth 'Foreigners'. Many of them were more than willing, since this secured for their families privileges in the way of food and flats, in a city at near-starvation point which suffered woeful over-crowding, and the dreaded visits from Cheka police and short shrift from an ignorant 'Revolutionary Tribunal' from which there was no appeal.

On 21st October four Russian destroyers emerged from Kronstadt and were seen to be steaming towards our ships in the Gulf, when the leading pair ran into a small minefield laid in the middle of their own swept channel by our C.M.B.s a few days after the big Kronstadt attack. The remaining pair turned back. Webster, another Intelligence officer on the Admiral's Staff, and myself interviewed some of the survivors who reached the Estonian side of the shore near Krasnaya Gorka, and obtained valuable information about the state of morale in Kronstadt which was pretty low. All the crew of the leading destroyer of the *Azard* class perished. The survivors of the second destroyer the *Gavriel* declared that the Captain of the *Azard* intended to surrender once he was clear of the Russian minefield, but it would have been on his own responsibility, and not that of the Commissars of the garrison. It was the *Gavriel* who was anchored at the entrance to the harbour as guard-ship on the night of our C.M.B. attack and sank three of our boats. It was a curious coincidence that I should be one of those to interview her two survivors and obtain their side of the story. The Admiral was most anxious about the fate of our survivors now in Bolshevik hands, and persuaded the Estonians to hand these men over to us so we could use them for exchange purposes, which was done a few months later after prolonged negotiations in Copenhagen with Litvinoff the Russian Foreign Commissar.

The Bolsheviks now turned their counter-attacks on to the
Estonian positions in front of K.G. on the 22nd, 23rd and
24th October to which we replied with further bombardments from our ships; but unfortunately the cruisers could
not get close enough inshore for their fire to be effective so
the Monitor H.M.S. *Erebus* was ordered up from the Riga
operations. Things were getting pretty desperate for them
when she arrived on the 27th, and was able with her 12-inch
guns to reach the fortress itself. Several hits were registered,
but Rodzianko's centre now began to fall back thereby
uncovering Pitka's Force. Pitka made one last effort the
following day, supported by the guns of all available ships,
in the hope that K.G. would capitulate, but of no avail.
His force and those others in the Estonian Army had to fall
back to conform to the White Russian centre. It was the
beginning of the end.

By the 3rd November, all thoughts of advancing against
Petrograd were abandoned by Yudenitch, although an
Estonian division on his right flank and Pitka's force on his
left were holding their ground. On the 15th November
Yamburg was retaken by Soviet troops who continued their
counter-attack until they reached the Estonian frontier,
where on orders from Moscow they came to a voluntary
halt. It was obvious that the Bolsheviks were willing to
hold peace talks with Estonia and Finland. This was the end.

The North-West Corps had no choice but to fall back
into Estonia, and break up into scattered units. Yudenitch
gave up command in the field to General Glazenap who in
turn had to function under an Estonian General—Tonnisson
—with what remained. Typhus, that terrible disease dreaded
by all armies, broke out in Narva where the arrangements
for the wounded were extremely limited. The authorities
were caught unawares and the unfortunate White Russian
soldiers died by the score.

Of the original twenty-five thousand men divided between
Pskov and Narva less than five thousand now remained. For
military convenience, these were now reorganized as part

of the Estonian Army whose Commander-in-Chief was General Laidoner. A thin strip of Russian territory remained (Inglemanland), quite inadequate in area for any military purpose. Narva, hitherto the Russian base, now became a large typhus-stricken camp where hundreds of men died like flies, and had it not been for the generous help given by Colonel Ryan and his workers of the American Red Cross, the death roll would have been higher still.

A British officer who died in this camp wrote in his diary as follows:

"Our aim is to save from what was once an Army a few whole bodies and sane souls ... Hospitals such as we know them do not exist ... Dead, sick, wounded, lie together on dirty straw pallets in cow sheds where no doors or windows exist, with one doctor and one sister to look after a thousand scraps of humanity ... of the remaining combatant troops there exist between four and five thousand, with Bolsheviks in front and Estonians—*to them a subject race* [my italics]—on either side. Behind are Estonian control posts through which they have to pass linked by barbed wire. They cannot move forward, nor can they, as armed men, move back.

"They have to choose either to give up their arms and file through barbed wire into Estonian territory, or seek clemency at the hands of the Bolsheviks. Once on Estonian ground, they are herded into villages where typhus exists, and into rooms unfit for the lowest of human beings. The goodwill of the Estonian military and civil authorities is powerless against local feelings.

All that is now left is a small band of fighting men who must either die, desert or surrender their arms to people who to them were once their servants. A larger mass are left who are sick and disorganized. They continually ask piteously, 'What are we to do? We are forgotten by the world.'"

* * *

All form of fighting between the two sides ceased by the first week in December, when an Armistice was arranged between the Estonians and Soviet Russians by mutual consent. What remained of the North-West Corps then went from bad to worse. About half the rank and file deserted their leaders and returned to Soviet Russia bitter in mind, body, and experience. Rather, they thought, work in the salt mines of Siberia, since that would be their fate, than die on foreign soil. About a thousand officers or ex-officers were left behind in Estonia, with no one to plead their cause except the few British Staff Officers remaining from the Military Mission. They were stateless and drifted like human flotsam across Europe to anyone who would have them as citizens. The curtain was finally rung down on the 22nd January, 1920, in a curious document issued by Yudenitch releasing all personnel of the North-West Corps from further service, which stated amongst other things:

(a) That the Army would continue to receive pay and rations until a date to be decided by the Dispersal Commission.

But without stating how this pay was to be given or who was to give it.

(b) That ship transport was available to take those who wished, to go to North-West Russia.

But also without stating, in any precise terms, what exactly was meant by 'North-West Russia'.

*　　*　　*

CHAPTER X

PEACE TALKS

WITH the exception of the relics of the North-West Corps which were absorbed unwillingly, into the Estonian Army, the Yudenitch Forces quickly melted away. By early December, therefore, the path lay clear for Peace talks between Soviet Russia (as the Bolsheviks preferred to be called) and Estonia. For their part, the Estonians, now that the threat of *Balticum* was removed, had no desire other than to settle down peacefully to cultivate their farms as of old, provided it was by themselves, and completely independent of overlords.

'Independence' therefore was their watchword, and if they could obtain this with reasonable security of their sea and land frontiers, the Estonians were willing to live at peace with their Russian neighbours, and let bygones be bygones.

The same process of reasoning applied to Finland, perhaps in a greater degree, because the Russo-Finnish frontier lines had always been a bone of contention, even in the days of Tsardom when Finland, no longer a vassal State, had reached a stage of almost 'near Independence'. Thus, while the first overtures for Peace Talks were made by the Bolsheviks to Estonia, these were quickly followed by unofficial discussions with Finnish representatives, and later extended to those of Latvia and Lithuania.

It was obvious to the Bolshevik leaders, that although this last attempt by the White Russians to recapture Petrograd and Moscow had failed and their forces were now dispersed, other attempts might be made (and indeed would have been made). The alternative was to try and break down Allied policy of the *cordon sanitaire*, initiated by the French after the Armistice, since this policy gave impetus and encouragement to every White Russian counter-revolutionary movement.

Peaceful methods, therefore, were the only course open, and especially peaceful frontiers, and relations were necessary with their nearest neighbours Finland and Estonia. An immediate start being essential, a beginning was made by sending military Commissars to discuss and arrange Armistice terms with the Estonians on the spot. This was followed by the arrival in Dorpat, a town near the Estonian frontier, of a top-ranking Soviet delegation from Moscow, headed by Professor Yoffe, Bolshevik Commissar for Foreign Affairs jointly with Tchercherin.

The Soviet delegation arrived on 5th December to find a ready response from Estonia's President Poska, who in the past had been a 'fellow traveller' in 1917 when the Revolution first started. Fortunately, however, Estonia's delegation was led by her Foreign Minister, Professor Piip, a great patriot and man of international reputation. He had recently returned from a visit to London and spoke excellent English. No detail or point escaped his agile mind, nor could any Estonian have negotiated better or with a firmer purpose for his country's independence, for which he obtained proper recognition *de jure* from the Soviet Russians in the subsequent Peace Treaty.

A knotty problem in the negotiations was the security of Estonia's northern coast, and the presence of British warships at Biorko and Revel, from which bases Admiral Cowan on the advice of Piip, refused to budge. The Russian attitude was interesting. Smarting from the Kronstadt attack and recent loss of their two destroyers on the C.M.B. minefield, the Commissars at first refused to recognize the British Navy. They would recognize, they declared, "no foreigners" at the negotiations, neither British nor White Russian. The negotiations were to be solely a Russian-Estonian affair.

For Estonia, it was important to obtain security for her short coastline which was vulnerable to attack by Russian warships. Piip pointed out that if the British warships left Revel, he was sure that if asked to defend Estonia again

they would return; but Estonia would prefer instead a satis-
factory guarantee from the Russians and remain at peace.
He made the somewhat unusual suggestion that the
Commissars should interview an officer from the British
Fleet. The Russians agreed, but they emphasized it must
be absolutely *unofficial* since they refused to recognize
any British interest whatsoever in the eastern part of the
Gulf of Finland.

I had met and talked with Professor Piip before. We had
a mutual friend in Helsingfors, Professor Goode, an
Englishman, who had come out from England on a news-
paper mission for the *Daily Herald* and *Manchester Guardian*
with L'Estrange Malone of my early aviation days, now a
Member of Parliament. Both had just been granted special
permission by the Bolsheviks to visit Moscow to interview
top-ranking Commissars. Through them I was offered what
amounted to a safe conduct pass, which would give me
unofficial contact with the Russian and Estonian delegations
at Dorpat.

Armed with this promise, I put it to the Admiral that
without compromising in any way my previous connection
with the British Secret Service, I should make contact,
under the guidance of Professor Piip, with the Commissars
at Dorpat. My role would be that of a naval officer coming
from the Fleet, who was anxious to obtain their views and
report back unofficially to the British Admiral.

Walter Cowan always favoured initiative and originality.
His career had been spent that way by seeing and doing
things himself; at the same time he was a stickler for
discipline and etiquette with foreigners. I sensed at once
that his first reaction was unfavourable. To him the Bolsheviks were traitors for having signed at Brest-Litovsk a
peace treaty with the Germans when we, as their allies, were
still at war. At the same time, he recognized the predicament
of Estonia after the Fleet left the Gulf, which must inevitably be soon.

It was now December, with at the most a month or

six weeks left before the freeze up. We had as yet no Foreign Office representative in Estonia except an acting Vice-Consul at Revel. The Admiral I knew was anxious about Estonia and would have preferred if possible something settled before the Fleet left Biorko, so I tried another tack. It might be possible, I suggested, to speed up the release of our C.M.B. prisoners if I got direct contact with the Commissar delegates. I put this to him, because I knew he was also most anxious about them and the chances of their early release.

I won my point at once. He agreed to release me for a fortnight. I could go unofficially in plain clothes and not disclose my name, except in confidence to Professor Piip and his colleages; also I must make my own arrangements. I had no official authority to speak for him, but if the Russians asked me what the Fleet was going to do, I could tell them that the British Admiral intended to stay where he was until the ice froze the Gulf, and if any Bolshevik ships approached within twelve miles of the Estonian coast, he would treat them as hostile, unless a guarantee of security was signed to the satisfaction of the Estonian delegates.

Walter Cowan was always forthright. He never beat about the bush and hated arguments, but had an instinctive gift of sorting things out mentally the right way before fixing on the point, and once there, he seldom shifted his ground. The Admiralty had given him a free hand which made it easier for him in his dealings with the Finns and Estonians, whom he knew would support every action he took since he was there to work for their national Independence. As for the White Russians and their leaders, he left that part of the Baltic business to General Gough's Mission.

As for myself, the Admiral knew well enough by now that I was unorthodox, but he trusted me completely. He said that if I found myself in difficulties he was sure his friend Pitka would get me out of them, and anyway I was of such junior rank (I was a Lieutenant R.N.) he didn't suppose the Russian delegates would pay much attention

PEACE TALKS 241

to me or what I said, but he thought my journey might prove worth while if, with the assistance of the Estonians (and especially Professor Piip) I succeeded in expediting the release of our C.M.B. prisoners.

"It was a chance," he said, adding characteristically, "and one I wouldn't hesitate to take myself. You must also decide yourself, of course, if you want to go. Don't get tied up with them in argument," he said. "Tell them the plain truth, and if they won't listen or see you, come straight back." Such was Walter Cowan's advice, succinctly given and typical of the man. He talked in jerks while he took his morning exercise, walking up and down the small space on the boat deck above his day cabin in the flagship H.M.S. *Delhi*, striding out as fast as his small legs could carry him, and wearing black hunting boots and a red hunting waistcoat under his uniform reefer coat against the bitterly cold weather. I remember well the details of this final talk with him before leaving for Helsingfors in a destroyer.

At Helsingfors, I donned once again my plain clothes and made for the Hotel where Professor Goode was staying. He gave me two personal letters of introduction which, he said, would smooth my way to Dorpat. The first I had to give to an Estonian in Revel who he said would arrange my journey, adding, "*It might be in discomfort.*" The second was to an Estonian colonel on Professor Piip's delegation, who would look after me, and would arrange for me to meet unofficially the Bolshevik Commissars. He also advised me to go to an address in Dorpat, where I might perhaps meet another Englishman who might prove interesting and useful.

I thought to myself how strangely in reverse this procedure was, when compared with the almost insuperable difficulties of my original mission earlier in the year to contact Paul Dukes in Petrograd. This assignment seemed so easy. Just two pieces of paper were all that one needed and the trick was done, unbeknown to our own Legation in Helsingfors because Goode insisted and obtained from me a promise to keep my journey secret from them.

Q

There was some delay in Revel before I could contact the Professor's Estonian friend, and eventually together we boarded what was supposed to be an ordinary local train. Never can I forget the discomfort of that journey. It was freezing hard with temperature down to zero and no form of heating. The carriages were fitted with plain wooden benches in two, sometimes three tiers; one sat huddled up, knees to chin just like an animal. For hours on end we crawled along at six miles an hour, with endless stops to replenish the engine with fuel from stocks of wood piled up in heaps at intervals at the side of the track. To relieve nature one had to leave the train, and afterwards fight one's way back into a carriage as people jumped on the coaches— even on to the top—at every stopping place. Thus we travelled for the best part of a day and a night until we reached Dorpat.

Our fellow travellers were an extraordinary collection of peasants, soldiers and refugees, many of whom were ex-officers from the ill-fated North-West Corps apparently on their way back to look for relations in Pskov. All had one main purpose—to reach some place where they could obtain food before the hard winter months made travel impossible.

The cold was intense as we progressed farther inland, but luckily while waiting in Revel I managed to obtain for a few British pounds a good Russian overcoat lined with fur which proved a godsend throughout my journey. We eventually reached Dorpat where, true to his promise, my companion handed me over to the care of an Estonian colonel who spoke excellent English. He was a friend of Professor Piip, and my relief after that hideous journey may well be imagined.

It seems I was not unexpected, for the Colonel immediately took me to a *datcha* where I was conducted to a room on the top floor, and informed me that I must stay there unknown to the other occupants, because this was the villa housing Poska, the Estonian President, who was unaware of my presence. Meals would be brought to me,

and here I must wait under restraint until I saw Professor
Piip who knew the reasons why I had come to Dorpat.

Meanwhile, I was comfortable and well looked after,
although immobile. It appeared the Russian delegation
were housed in another *datcha* near by and the Estonian
negotiators in two adjacent *datchas*, though why I should
have been honoured with a room in the President's *datcha*
I never discovered. I was later taken to Professor Piip who
was extremely courteous and kind. He apologized for my
loneliness, as he called it, but said it was best for my
presence not to be known to anyone, otherwise the Bolsheviks might get suspicious. He had promised the Bolshevik Commissars that there would be no White Russians
on their delegation, but had warned them that a British
officer was coming from the Fleet who would be willing to
talk to them unofficially if they wished, and was still
awaiting a reply.

The whole business seemed wrapt in mystery and I never
could make out why Poska and Piip seemed to act different
roles but learned afterwards there were good reasons. There
was nothing to do but wait until the Russians were willing
to see me, and this Piip promised he would arrange as soon
as he could, but it would not be for a few days yet.

From the windows of my room I could see much coming
and going through the gates where sentries were posted, but
the Colonel asked me not to be seen too much. He knew
all about the other Englishman mentioned by Professor
Goode. It was no less a person than Arthur Ransome, the
well-known writer, and it would be arranged for me to visit
him in the evenings after dark.

No one could possibly have been kinder to me then than
Arthur Ransome. I spent my evenings with this talented
man playing chess and talking, with the inevitable samovar
close at hand, from which we drank innumerable cups of
weak tea sweetened, for want of sugar in this land of
poverty, by acid drops out of a tin he had brought with him.
We had in common a love of boats and sailing, in which he

excelled, and I learned much from him in Dorpat of all places, about Russia and the life of the peasants.

After days of delay and promises, the Commissars decided to see me. Professor Piip told me that on the whole the peace negotiations had gone well, and at last Estonia would be certain of 'Independence'; but the coastal question was not yet resolved, nor would the Bolsheviks recognize the presence of the British Fleet and were anxious only for its departure. At the same time they were inquisitive to see me and learn, if possible, more about the Fleet.

I was granted two sessions of a couple of hours each which were held in a room in their villa. Yoffe, afterwards Soviet Ambassador to Germany and Japan, was the Chief Russian delegate assisted by Commissars Krilenko and Kreichler. In addition to Piip, my Estonian colonel friend acted as interpreter. On the table was an old-fashioned electrical relay instrument which tapped in Morse code any questions they wished to put to Tchicherin (Foreign Commissar) who was at the other end in Moscow, while they waited for the answers. The arrangement seemed ridiculously primitive, but it worked quite well all the same.

Professor Yoffe, who wore spectacles, struck me as a benign old gentleman and the last person one would connect with strong revolutionary ideas. The other two, as I expected, looked and played the part of real firebrands. They opened up at once with a tirade about the British Fleet and the aggressive attack on their ships in Kronstadt for which they said they would demand satisfaction. Professor Piip at once reminded them of the Bolshevik Fleet's bombardments of the Estonian coast earlier in the year when the British cruisers came to their aid and drove the Russian ships back into Kronstadt. "Surely," he said, "we have an equal right to complain." The point was a good one and snubbed Krilenko, who was the most loud-voiced of the trio. With the Admiral's advice firmly in my mind, I sat and listened, while Piip did the talking.

At another point they again became angry and abusive,

with an occasional spit on the carpet from Kreichler, when Counter-Revolutionary activities were mentioned. "And no doubt," he declared, "the British officer must know of the activities in Petrograd and Moscow of the Englishman Paul Dukes?" I began to feel a trifle uncomfortable, wondering where this would lead. Piip, professing complete ignorance, listened in pained silence, which gave me my cue. He let them storm on without interrupting until they came to a full stop, at the end of which the old gentleman, Yoffe, took a hand.

Blandly, he asked what the British Fleet was doing. How long were we staying in the Gulf? What interest was it of ours since both sides were bordered by Finnish and Estonian territory? Lastly, what were the intentions of the British Admiral? I turned to Piip asking him to reply. "The British Admiral," Piip said, "has sent me a message to say that he intends to remain with his ships in the Gulf at Biorko and Revel until the winter ice forces him to return to Copenhagen. He has every intention of returning in the late spring, when the ice clears, but we hope sincerely that by that time it will be a visit of courtesy only."

Turning to me he said, "Perhaps the British Officer can explain what the Admiral's ships have done?"

To this opening which had previously been arranged with Piip, I emphasized with some elaboration how we had cleared of mines long channels in the Baltic Sea, so that food could be brought to the Baltic States and the ports restarted for commerce with Scandinavia. This, I explained, was our peace-time duty and no act of war. To do so we had lost not only some of our warships, but the lives of British sailors.

I could see that this explanation at once struck home with Yoffe, who immediately asked if food ships could be sent into the Gulf of Petrograd. To this I replied they could be brought into the Gulf of Finland, but the rest was up to his own government. The atmosphere was now definitely more cordial and here my share in the talks ended; but not before

I put a direct question to Yoffe about the British prisoners captured at Kronstadt, and extracted a promise that he would ask Moscow about them via the teleprinter.

The Russian Revolution brought new ideas on the status of prisoners captured in operations of war. All alike were regarded as 'Counter-Revolutionaries' and therefore 'criminals'. The White Russian being treated with the greatest severity—usually ending with a pistol-shot in the back. As 'criminals', British and other prisoners were herded together in the common jail, mixed up with political prisoners who had been arrested by the dreaded Cheka (Secret Police) and whose fate depended on the whim of a Commissar.

Different treatment was handed out to men who had been 'conscripted'. These were regarded as having committed no crime, and were therefore offered their immediate release. At the same time they were also offered employment in the Soviet State. Alternatively they could return to their 'volunteer' comrades who were languishing in a filthy Russian jail awaiting exchange. Officers were given the most severe treatment, on the principle that the higher the rank the harder must be their lot.

In my second interview the next day, Yoffe told me that the British sailors captured at Kronstadt were housed in a monastery near Moscow (the Androniev) together with other Counter-Revolutionary prisoners from Archangel and the Black Sea. He gave me their names and said they were all well, except one who had been wounded and was in hospital (Bremner). He asked if they were 'conscripts' or 'volunteers', to which I replied that as all were under naval discipline they had to obey orders and could be regarded as 'conscripts'. He then explained to Piip that 'conscripted' men were allowed free into Moscow, but not the officers. At the same time he said their attitude to us foreigners was to treat us all well, even if we had been 'Counter-Revolutionaries' in the past, and that Litvinov (another Deputy Foreign Commissar) was now in Denmark arranging for their exchange.

This was the first direct news we had received of them other than through the Moscow Radio, and I thanked Yoffe on behalf of the Admiral. He agreed to send them a message to say that their exchange would not long be delayed. In actual practice, however, with the usual procrastination of the Bolsheviks, it was several months before they set foot in England, after experiencing the most horrible privations in their monastery prison.

My interview was at an end and Yoffe actually thanked me for coming. He asked that in return for sending a message to our prisoners, I would take one to the British Admiral with a special request to hasten the entry of food ships into Petrograd. I am sure this was uppermost in his mind, with visions of a starving city in a bitterly cold winter.

In the meantime, arguments went back and forth concerning the coastal sea-limit and whether it should be twelve or twenty miles, but in spite of them it was obvious that agreement between the two sides would soon be reached and Piip was jubilant about getting at long last full Russian agreement to Estonian 'Independence' and as the outcome of the negotiations was so successful, I returned to Biorko. Since I was one of the first Englishmen to meet in person the leaders of the future Soviet Russia, my impressions at that time (December, 1919) were of much interest when we returned home six weeks later (January, 1920). What struck me most was the extraordinary contrast between Yoffe, who led the delegation, and the young firebrands of my own age who were his colleagues. I asked myself how it was possible for the two disparate types to mix and work together in harmony, the one intellectual, elderly and outwardly mild; the others unscrupulous, rough, tough, and seething with Revolutionary zeal. What were the strong bonds which bound this odd assorted trio together? It seemed to me strange, yet subsequent events proved that the ideological links forged by Lenin were so strong that they withstood all personal strains.

As for their views and assessment of the potential threat

of the British Fleet in the Gulf of Finland, Professor Piip was convinced that these high-ranking commissars were much more nervous of the Krondstadt garrison surrendering themselves to the British Fleet than they were of any other threat by land. For Trotsky, who was at the time in charge of all Petrograd defences, the possession of Kotlin Island and the fortress garrisons by the British was just a short step towards its occupation by White Russian Counter-Revolutionaries, when the path would be clear for the recapture of Petrograd and Moscow and the end of the Revolution. And I am sure this estimate was correct.

With Walter Cowan's ships in the Gulf and the main bulk of the Russian Fleet immobilized, there was always the constant fear of a Kronstadt surrender. It was essential then for the Bolshevik commissars to get peace terms settled *as soon as possible* with Finland and Estonia, thereby removing the reason for a British Fleet in the Gulf of Finland other than on a peaceful mission. The Admiral's purpose, therefore, was the simple corollary to stay where he was until the Estonians were satisfied that the terms offered were just and reasonable, which is exactly what Piip had declared and what Walter Cowan intended to do, until the Gulf froze over when his ships would return to England or go into winter quarters at Copenhagen.

In the meantime the pressure exerted by the Fleet served the useful purpose of obtaining for our friends and allies, the Estonians and the Finns, the reasonable peace terms they so ardently desired. My unofficial mission was over, and the Bolshevik delegates under no illusions as to the intentions of the British Admiral.

I made the return journey to Revel in a different style. This time I was accompanied by my Estonian colonel friend in a reserved carriage with two guards posted to keep out intruders and in a quarter of the time. The Admiral was very pleased to see me when I reached the flagship and to hear how the talks had gone, especially the news about our C.M.B. prisoners and told me he was more than ever determined to stay in Biorko until the ice froze hard.

Weather now was our principal anxiety and knowing the Admiral's determination some of us wondered whether he might not overshoot the mark and remain in Biorko a few days too long. Each day the ice crept farther out from the shore towards the Fleet at anchor in the bay. The Admiral sent a cruiser and destroyer daily, working their engines ahead and astern to free the ice that formed overnight in the main channel so as to keep it clear, the Admiral himself taking his turn in the flagship. To add to other difficulties, frequent blizzards and snowstorms swept Biorko making navigation extremely hazardous; nevertheless the Navy's vigil in the Gulf had to be maintained by destroyers on patrol, who had little means of estimating, with floating ice about, what water was free of mines and what was not.

It was during this period that we lost, on a wild and bitter night, H.M.S. *Verulam* and half her company. The Admiral steamed immediately to the patrol area hoping to rescue survivors, and also because of a false report that a Russian cruiser had broken out. Nothing came of either and the loss of men was heavy.

Christmas passed in the Navy's traditional style although the storeship carrying special canteen stores for the Fleet's Christmas dinners was sunk by a mine. It was another blow, but stoically borne by our sailors who will always face these things and unpleasant tasks with a smile when it is their duty. We managed to collect from the Finns a few extras in the way of fresh meat, but turkeys were given a miss. The Admiral promised them their Christmas dinners when they returned home, and ordered a double issue of rum for Christmas Day. By that time the flagship had cleared a space amongst the trees for a football ground, and also made an ice skating rink by the shore where many rough and tumble matches were played with footballs and hockey sticks.

I was sent to Helsingfors in a destroyer (H.M.S. *Wanderer*)*

* Commanded by a very old shipmate Commander Basil Owen, O.B.E., R.N.

to give our Minister, Lord Acton, a resumé of the Dorpat talks, and also a letter informing him of the Admiral's plans. It was not a pleasant interview because the Minister was upset at the thought of our ships leaving the Gulf of Finland and the Fleet being based for the winter in the ice-free waters of Copenhagen under Commodore Duff. The Admiral explained in his letter that as the position in the eastern part of the Baltic Sea had reached stability, the next area of unrest would probably centre around Danzig where our Control Commission would require support. He had decided, therefore, with Admiralty approval, to take half his ships home to England for a well-earned rest, and leave the others at Copenhagen.

The Minister demanded a British cruiser *permanently* at Helsingfors in case of 'emergency', though he did not say how he thought the emergency would arise; but he told me that he considered that this was a personal matter of his own prestige and the safety of the Legation and his family. A few signals were exchanged between the Minister and the Admiral, ending with the Minister having to go without his cruiser, but with an assurance that in case of need one would come at once to his aid from Copenhagen.

There was no destroyer to take me back to Biorko, so I journeyed overland partly by train and partly by sledge. Both were a Government service, comfortable and remarkably quick considering the winter difficulties. I liked the sledge best, with its change of ponies every twenty miles or so, and only wished they had been reindeer as in the north of Finland.

By the New Year Biorko Bay at last was frozen over, and I arrived just in time to board *Delhi* as she weighed anchor, crunching her way through the ice floes, with the band playing *Home again to Merrie England* with freezing fingers.

Walter Cowan had timed his departure almost to the hour, and certainly to the day as far as ice conditions allowed (it was the 28th December). One day more and it might have been extremely difficult to get out without an ice-breaker. As things were, he wisely sent the destroyers on a few days ahead when only thin ice had formed across the bay, but *Delhi* had to back and fill many hours to push a way through before she reached open water, for which great credit was due to her Captain, Geoffrey Mackworth.

Two small Finnish torpedo boats, of rather ancient design and the wooden inshore minesweepers decided to stay on one day longer, and paid for the privilege by being 'nipped' in the ice before they could get out. They were obliged to spend an extremely uncomfortable and cold winter in Koivisto village to the disappointment of our popular Finnish Liaison Officer Lieutenant Foch who was obliged to stay with them. He said that as they escorted the Fleet in they must escort them out. A nice gesture, but it cost them two minesweepers.

Lastly there was the little drifter *Catspaw* who had for the last six months served the flagship faithfully as tender and, like an old servant, never failed at any hour of the day or night to fetch and carry from ship to shore the stores and oddments frequently needed. It was decided to take her with us as far as Revel, and from there sail her under her own steam to England. There was much competition amongst the junior officers as to who should captain and navigate her home, but sad to relate she was lost and only her wreckage found on the Danish coast. She evidently struck a mine and went down with all hands, including her young sub-lieutenant skipper.

There was little point in remaining more than a few hours at Revel, as Pitka told the Admiral on arrival that the terms of the Soviet Russian-Estonian Treaty were definitely agreed, including 'Independence' and safeguards for the coastal area. All that remained was formal signatures which were given on 2nd February, 1920. Taking the *Dragon* and four destroyers with him, the Admiral sailed for England in H.M.S. *Delhi*, to give the crews of his ships a well-earned leave and rest before returning to the Baltic. He arrived in

Plymouth Sound mid-January, a year since he sailed on his Mission and was escorted upstream with full naval honours.

Our naval Baltic story ends here. What our men and ships accomplished in that year can best be described in an official message sent by the Board of Admiralty as follows:

"To Rear Admiral Sir Walter Cowan and to the Officers and men of the Baltic Force.

"The Board desires to convey to Sir Walter Cowan and to the officers and men of the Baltic Force now returning to England, their marked appreciation of the manner in which the work of the Force has been performed. The Baltic Force has, during the past year, cheerfully endured trying conditions and, when occasion offered, has attacked the enemy with the utmost gallantry. It has prevented the destruction of States which have upheld the Allied cause, has supported the Forces of Civilisation when menaced by Anarchy, and has worthily upheld the honour of the British Navy. This record is the more praiseworthy because it comes after the long previous strain of war at a time when other forces of the Crown have, for the most part, been enjoying a relaxation of effort. The Board's gratification is to be made known to all concerned."

For his services, Walter Cowan was created a Baronet with the territorial designation of The Baltic and Bilton, County Warwick.

*   *   *

C.M.B. No. 4
at Terriokki.
June 24th 1919.

Sir,

I have the honour to forward the following report of Naval operations carried out by C.M.B.s Nos. 4 and 7 forming the special service C.M.B. force under my command.

2. On the morning of Friday, June 13th, after completing a special mission in the Bay of Petrograd, I recrossed the Eastern line of forts guarding Kronstadt in C.M.B. No. 7 and proceeded to make a reconnaissance near Tolbouhin Light House. There I saw anchored two Bolshevik Dreadnoughts, the *Petropavlovsk* and the *Andrei Pervozanni*, with a destroyer guard both to the East and West of them. I decided to attack the time being 2.0 a.m. (Finnish Time), but, when only 4 miles away, the engine failed and revolutions dropped below Torpedo firing speed, so I had to turn 16 points and return to my base, arriving there at 3.15 a.m.

3. On the night of Monday, June 16th, I decided to make an attack on the Bolshevik Naval Forces in Kronstadt Roads, with both my boats. I accordingly left harbour at 10.15 p.m. hoping to time the attack for midnight, but when rounding Tolbouhin Light House C.M.B. No. 7 struck some obstruction, or what I think more probable a 'Dud mine', and broke her propeller shaft. I turned 16 points and towed her back to harbour.

4. (i) The next night, Tuesday, June 17th, I again set out in my one remaining boat to make an attack. Left harbour at 10.30 p.m. in C.M.B. No. 4 with the following crew on board besides myself: —

Acting sub-Lieutenant John White Hampsheir, R.N.R.
Chief Motor Mechanic Hugh Beeley, R.N.V.R.,
Official Number M.B.2108.

(ii) Proceeded to round Tolbuhin Light House which I passed three miles to the Westward. When off there the wind got up and there was a considerable sea for our small craft.

(iii) From there I ran due South until within a mile of the Southern shore, in order that, should I be observed, the enemy might think the attack was made either from Krasnaya Gorka, which was then in the hands of the "Whites", or from Biorko Sound.

(iv) From this position I steered East by North and made for Kronstadt Roads.

(v) On entering the Roads and when about four miles South East of Tolbouhin Light House, I observed a large enemy cruiser, which I recognised as the *Oleg*, at anchor. She was guarded by four Destroyers, one Patrol Gunboat or Sloop, and one Torpedo Boat, as indicated in attached diagram. [See illus.]

(vi) Course was shaped to pass between the Destroyers and the Torpedo Boat and I gave Sub-Lieutenant Hampsheir orders to remove all safety pins and prepare for attack. In removing the safety pin of the firing charge, the lanyard broke and the charge fired. Fortunately the side stops were down and the torpedo was in consequence not ejected. I then turned away, eased down to dead slow speed and prepared another firing charge. This was an extremely difficult operation on account of the sea running, and motion on the boat added to which we were very close to the patrol craft and Destroyers (about 700 or 800 yards). In 15 to 20 minutes we had everything ready again and I would like to mention here the coolness with which Sub Lieutenant Hampsheir helped during this trying time.

(vii) I increased speed, passed between the Destroyers and Torpedo Boat, and made for the *Oleg* at full speed. I fired the torpedo when about 800 yards off her Port beam (she was heading due west at the time), and turned 16 points to starboard. Torpedo hit just abaft her foremost funnel throwing up a high column of water and some black smoke.

Either this gave the alarm or else we were observed as fire was directly opened on us from all quarters, though it was difficult under the conditions to see exactly from where.

(viii) I steered West and passed between two Destroyers at full speed, who also opened fire. Most of the firing was wild and very erratic but three shots (fired apparently from the forts and appeared to be of large calibre about 8 inch) were well directed and fell between 15 and 20 yards over, one just by our stern, momentarily throwing it up and straining the engine so I eased down to 800 revolutions and took an observation of the *Oleg*. She appeared then to be settling down by the head and endeavouring to get under way, as large columns of smoke were coming from her funnels.

(ix) The torpedo was fired at 0005 (Finnish Time) and all firing had ceased shortly after we eased down to 800 revolutions at 0030.

(x) I continued on a Westerly course until well clear of Tolbuhin then turned to the Northward and when close to the coast turned down South South East for Terriokki arriving at our base at 1.45 a.m.

5. On board C.M.B. No. 4 there were no casualties but I regret I have since had to send Sub-Lieutenant Hampsheir to Helsingfors on the Doctor's advice for a rest; as he is suffering from nervous breakdown. I would like to call your attention to his conduct together with my motor mechanic Beeley during the action, their devotion to duty and coolness under fire, without which I feel sure the attack would not have been successful.

> I have the honour to be,
>   Sir,
> Your obedient Servant,
>   Augustus Agar.
>   Lieutenant R. N. Commanding
>   Officer, C.M.B. No. 4.

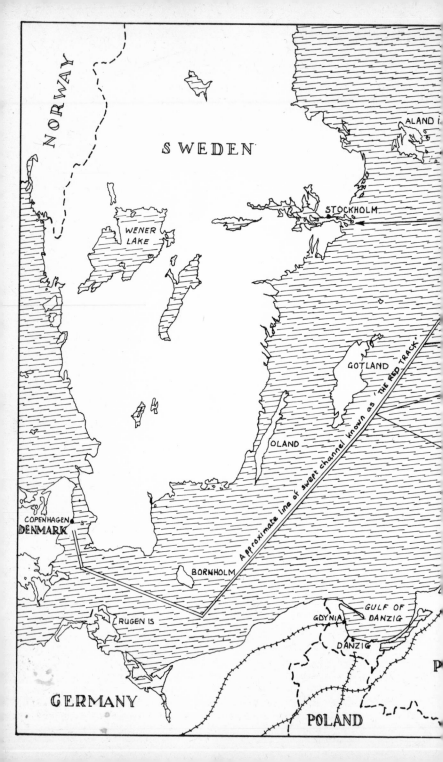